In *This* Economy?

In *This* Economy?

HOW MONEY & MARKETS REALLY WORK

Kyla Scanlon

Ebury Edge, an imprint of Ebury Publishing,
20 Vauxhall Bridge Road,
London SW1V 2SA

Ebury Edge is part of the Penguin Random House group of companies
whose addresses can be found at global.penguinrandomhouse.com

Penguin Random House UK

First published in the United States by Currency, an imprint of the Crown
Publishing Group, a division of Penguin Random House LLC. in 2024
First published in the United Kingdom by Ebury Edge in 2024

www.penguin.co.uk

A CIP catalogue record for this book is available from the British Library

Hardback ISBN 9781529146608
Trade paperback ISBN 9781529146899

Cover design by Christopher Brand
Printed and bound in Australia by Griffin Press

The authorised representative in the EEA is Penguin Random House Ireland,
Morrison Chambers, 32 Nassau Street, Dublin D02 YH68

Penguin Random House is committed to a sustainable future
for our business, our readers and our planet. This book is made
from Forest Stewardship Council® certified paper.

FSC www.fsc.org MIX Paper | Supporting responsible forestry FSC® C018179

To Mom, Dad, Ryan, Moo,
and everyone who has believed in me

Contents

FOREWORD xv
INTRODUCTION xix

PART I
THE VIBE ECONOMY 3

CHAPTER 1 **The Economic Kingdom** 5
The Kingdom 5
Vibes *Are* the Economy 8

CHAPTER 2 **The Vibe Economy** 10
Moods and Markets 10
The Economic Circle of Life 11
Fueling Feelings 12
Vibe-ology and Emotion Economy 13
The Uncertainty Cake 15
Economic Mood Rings 17

PART II
HOW MONEY WORKS 19

CHAPTER 3 **The Weird World of Money** 21
The Weird World of Money 21
Dollars and Sense: What Makes Money, Money? 21

Through the Ages: The Evolution of Money 22
The American Currency Story: Revolution to Recognition 24

CHAPTER 4 **The Mechanics of Modern Money** 28
The Banking Blueprint 29
Fractional Reserve Banking 30
The Art of Lending 31
Decoding Bank Balance Sheets 32
The Invisible Sheriff 33
How Banks Hedge Risk 34
How Banks Can Fail 34
The Dollar's Reign 36
Rethinking the Dollar 40
Final Thoughts 43

PART III
HOW MONEY IS MEASURED 45

CHAPTER 5 **Supply and Demand** 47
Introduction to Supply and Demand 47
The Economics of Banana Bread 48
Supply Chains 50
Semiconductors 52
Used Cars 53
Eggflation: When Eggs Come in Short Supply 54
Beyond Mechanics and into Policy 56
Making Supply Chains Better 56

CHAPTER 6 **GDP and the Economy** 59
Measuring GDP 59
Consumption 60
Investment 61
Government Purchases 61
Net Exports 61
The Gingerbread Yeti Economy 62
Debt-Fueled Growth 63
What Does GDP Really Mean? 64
Growth at Any Cost 66
Looking to the Future 67

Contents

FOREWORD xv
INTRODUCTION xix

PART I
THE VIBE ECONOMY 3

CHAPTER 1 **The Economic Kingdom** 5
The Kingdom 5
Vibes *Are* the Economy 8

CHAPTER 2 **The Vibe Economy** 10
Moods and Markets 10
The Economic Circle of Life 11
Fueling Feelings 12
Vibe-ology and Emotion Economy 13
The Uncertainty Cake 15
Economic Mood Rings 17

PART II
HOW MONEY WORKS 19

CHAPTER 3 **The Weird World of Money** 21
The Weird World of Money 21
Dollars and Sense: What Makes Money, Money? 21

Through the Ages: The Evolution of Money 22
The American Currency Story: Revolution to Recognition 24

CHAPTER 4 **The Mechanics of Modern Money** 28
The Banking Blueprint 29
Fractional Reserve Banking 30
The Art of Lending 31
Decoding Bank Balance Sheets 32
The Invisible Sheriff 33
How Banks Hedge Risk 34
How Banks Can Fail 34
The Dollar's Reign 36
Rethinking the Dollar 40
Final Thoughts 43

PART III
HOW MONEY IS MEASURED 45

CHAPTER 5 **Supply and Demand** 47
Introduction to Supply and Demand 47
The Economics of Banana Bread 48
Supply Chains 50
Semiconductors 52
Used Cars 53
Eggflation: When Eggs Come in Short Supply 54
Beyond Mechanics and into Policy 56
Making Supply Chains Better 56

CHAPTER 6 **GDP and the Economy** 59
Measuring GDP 59
Consumption 60
Investment 61
Government Purchases 61
Net Exports 61
The Gingerbread Yeti Economy 62
Debt-Fueled Growth 63
What Does GDP Really Mean? 64
Growth at Any Cost 66
Looking to the Future 67

CHAPTER 7 **Commodities** 69

Globalization and Commodities 69

External Factors and Commodities 71

Oil 72

Gas Prices 72

Metals 74

The Rise of U.S. Shale Oil Production 75

The Rise of Renewables 75

Artificial Intelligence and Commodities 76

CHAPTER 8 **Inflation** 78

Types of Flation 78

Measuring Inflation 79

The Consumer Price Index: The People's Inflation 79

Personal Consumption Expenditures: The People's Inflation, But for the Fed 82

The Producer Price Index: Inflation for Businesses 84

The Inflation Pizza 84

Inflation Expectations 86

Causes of Inflation 87

#1 Price Hikes 89

A QUICK PROFIT EXPLAINER 90

#2 The State of the Labor Market 93

#3 Globalization 95

#4 Energy Markets 95

Other Types of Flations 96

Deflation 96

Hyperinflation 97

CHAPTER 9 **The Labor Market** 99

What Is the Labor Market? 99

Key Labor Market Metrics 100

The Unemployment Rate 100

The Labor Force Participation Rate 102

Surveys and Measurements 103

Wages 105

The Minimum Wage 107

The Skewed Way We See Wage Growth 109

The International Impact of Low Wages 111

How We Value Work 113

Worker Power 114

How Can the Labor Market Be Improved? 115
Immigration 116
Parental Leave and Disability Policies 116
Rethinking Ownership 116
Building 118

CHAPTER 10 **The Housing Market** 120
The American Dream 120
The Housing Cycle Is the Business Cycle 120
How to Buy a House 121
Mortgage Rates Over the Past Two Years 122
Well, Why Don't We Have Enough Homes? 123
Housing in Other Countries 124
Fixing the Problem 126

CHAPTER 11 **Stock Market** 129
What Are Markets? 129
Risk Types in Markets 130
Stock Market versus Economy 131
Valuation Example 132
Exchange-Traded Funds 135
Is BlackRock Running the World? 135
Index Providers 135
Passive versus Active 136
The Stock Market Is Seven Companies 137
Efficient (and Inefficient) Markets 139
What Happened in 2021? 141
Why Did Markets Become a Meme? 142

CHAPTER 12 **Bond Market** 143
The Bond Market 143
What Are Bonds? 143
Bonds Between Friends 144
Bond Ratings 146
High-Yield Friend 146
Treasury Bills, Notes, and Bonds 147
Treasury Market 148
Markets as Vibe Reflectors 150

CHAPTER 13 **Cryptocurrency** 154
The Cryptocurrency Narrative 154
Nonfungible Tokens 157

Is Dogecoin Alive or Dead? 157
FTX 158
Where Crypto Went Wrong 161

CHAPTER 14 **Recessions** 162
Recessions and Economic Downturns 162
The Semantics of a Recession 163
What Does a Recession Look Like? 166
Historic Recessions 167
2008 Recession 167
2020 Recession 169
Zombie Companies 170
The Vibecession 170
The Benefits of Recessions 172

PART IV
HOW MONEY MOVES 177

CHAPTER 15 **Fiscal Policy** 179
What Is Fiscal Policy? 179
What Does the Government Spend Money On? 181
Taxes 181
Bonds 184
The Debt Ceiling 185
The United Kingdom Shows That Fiscal Policy Is an Art 188
Lessons from the Eurozone 189
Can the Government Survive? 189
Fiscal Policy Is Good, Actually 190

CHAPTER 16 **Monetary Policy** 192
What Does the Fed Do? 192
How Do the Fed's Tools Work? 194
Reserve Requirements 194
Open-Market Operations 194
Repo Agreements 195
TYPES OF REPO AGREEMENTS 196
The Discount Rate 197
The Fed Funds Rate 197
Being a Central Bank Is About Belief 198
Monetary Policy in 2020 199
Fed Cred 202

CHAPTER 17 **The Federal Reserve** 204
Who Started the Fed? 204
How Does the Federal Reserve Work? 205
Board of Governors 206
Federal Open Market Committee (FOMC) 206
Federal Reserve Banks 206
The Chair of the Board 207
The Fed's Narrative 208
Narrative Creation 208
Resistance to the Narrative 209
The Fed's Mountain 209
The 1970s 210
Volcker in 2022 212
2 Percent Target 212
How the Fed Deals with Markets 213
The Fed and the Labor Market 214
Navigating the Fog 216

PART V
THEORIES, PROBLEMS, AND OPPORTUNITIES 219

CHAPTER 18 **Old Guy and New Theories** 221
Classical Economics 222
Keynesian Economics 223
Monetarism 224
New Growth Theory 225
Other Theories 225

CHAPTER 19 **Problems** 230
How to Give Up 230
The State of the American Dream 230
Economy and Mental Health 232
The Shifting Nature of Work 233
Demographics 234
When Systems Fail 235
Your Eyeballs Are Dollar Signs 237
Social Media Makes It Worse 238
Media Literacy Crisis 239
Media, Nostalgia, and Consumerism 241
Things Are All the Same Now 242

What GME Really Meant 243
Economic Inequality and Cooperation 244

CHAPTER 20 **Opportunities** 247
Healthcare 247
Immigration 249
Housing 251
Education 254
Clean Energy 255
The Abundance Mindset 256

ACKNOWLEDGMENTS 261
NOTES 263
INDEX 271

Foreword

By Morgan Housel

There are more than two hundred million businesses in the world.

Five hundred trillion dollars of financial assets.

One hundred trillion dollars of GDP.

There are almost two hundred countries, thousands of cultures and norms.

With eight billion people in the world, a rough calculation shows there are about two tons of pure serotonin careening through the global economy right now.

Economists try in earnest to model all of this in Excel.

The global economy is wildly complex. You can imagine how hard it is for anyone to wrap their head around it.

Keep that in mind and realize that there are two topics that apply to everyone in life, no matter who you are, where you live, or what you do: health and money. It doesn't matter if you aren't interested in those topics; those topics *are interested in you.*

When the global economy is infinitely complex, and it is fundamental to everyone's life, you get some problems.

Which is a good way to describe modern economic history: "We've had some problems."

In the past century we, as a society, have made incredible strides in medicine, engineering, and information technology. Experts in these fields one hundred years ago would not recognize today's world. We have gotten so, so much better.

But finance? Economics? It's hard to see the progress, even if you squint.

Are we better at predicting recessions than we were a century ago?

Are individuals better at managing money than their grandparents were?

It's not at all clear. Actually, I take that back. It's *quite clear* that we are not.

Average household incomes adjusted for inflation have increased by more than a third in the last generation. But a recent survey showed more than 70 percent of American households are stressed about their finances. More than 60 percent live paycheck to paycheck. Some of the most dominant financial stories of the last twenty years have been: How dumb we've been buying tech stocks, how dumb we've been buying real estate, how dumb we've been buying crypto, and how easy it is to steal people's money.

This maze of confusion doesn't just affect individuals. It extends to the broader economy.

The Economist magazine—truly one of the best financial publications in the world—publishes a special edition each January that previews the year ahead.

Its year-ahead preview published in January 2020 does not say a single word about covid-19.

Its year-ahead preview published in January 2022 does not say a single word about Russia invading Ukraine.

Its year-ahead preview published in January 2023 does not say a single word about Hamas attacking Israel.

That's not a criticism, because the editors from *The Economist* could not have known about those events when the editions went to print. The events were anywhere from a few weeks to several months away from coming into our lives. But it highlights how massively difficult it is to wrap your head around how this behemoth called the global economy works, where it's going, and how we can all learn to live with it.

Why is it that we've become so much better at things like engineering and physics, but not economics?

There could be all kinds of answers to that question, but a big one is that economics is one of the few fields that requires equal parts precise technical knowledge and an appreciation for how messy, flawed, emotional, and irrational people can be.

Money—personal finance, investing, and economics—is typically taught as a math-based field, where you take the data and plug it into a formula and out pops an answer. Not just *an* answer, but *the* answer. Iron laws, like in physics.

The problem when thinking like this is that in theory people should do what the economic laws tell them to do, but in reality they are impatient, misinformed, bad at math, hungry, irritable, short-sighted, guided by incentives, and a slew of other unavoidable characteristics that create a mile-wide gap between theory and reality.

And that's why I'm so excited about the book you're holding.

There are quite a few people who understand the technical details of the economy. There are many who understand the human side of how people make decisions with money.

There aren't many who understand both. Kyla Scanlon is one of them.

I came across Kyla years ago, when she made short videos about the economy that were as funny as they were informative. It was instantly apparent that she had not only mastered the technical details of how the economic machine works; she could also explain it in a way that had so much empathy for the human side of this field.

Her work exploded in 2022 when she coined the term "vibecession" to describe a situation in which the economy was technically okay but people still felt glum about it, and their vibes could become a self-fulfilling prophecy. It's a perfect example of understanding the gap between the chalkboard and the real world.

Let me tell you: Roughly 0 percent of economic PhDs understand that gap, and exactly 0 percent can explain it like Kyla can.

Introduction

What do we really need to know about how the economy works?

The answer is pretty simple. Most of it is intuitive, even if it doesn't seem so.

Honestly, it might be for the best if you can't remember a thing your teacher said about monetary policy, since our normal ways of thinking about the economy bake in untested assumptions, "the way we've always done it" models, and a troubling disconnect between theory and the concerns of real people.

I know the last few years of economic news have been . . . disorienting. Reality feels almost like a dream state. That's because the algorithms controlling our news feeds reward alarmism over objectivity, and the Fed—and all other central banks, for that matter—purposefully speaks in vague, wordy language—known as Fedspeak, defined by the economist Alan Blinder as "a turgid dialect of English"—in an attempt to stop the markets from overreacting, and with the unfortunate side effect of confusing everyone.

In other words, the headlines are served to us with a nice topping of whipped cream: fluff and froth exacerbating each and every issue so we become as reactive and worried and *mad* as possible. After all, the key to capturing clicks is convincing people that you have the answers to their questions—that you hold the proverbial key to all the solutions. If you can overcomplicate simple things loudly, people will pay attention.

Economic literacy *for all* has been my mission since high school, when I dabbled in options trading and wrote about it for my first blog, Scanlon on

Stocks. After majoring in finance, economics, and data analytics in college, I worked in asset management at Capital Group, conducting macroeconomic analysis and modeling investment strategies. But I found myself spending more and more time making videos and writing my newsletter, trying to connect the dots between what's happening and why for everyone out there sweating over the hypersensationalized, jargon-filled economic headlines.

This book is for anyone who wants to understand how the economy works and their role in it, anyone trying to make sense of the way monetary policy plays games with their bank account balance, anyone wondering why borrowing money is expensive and how a downturn could impact their home buying opportunities, anyone intimidated by the terrible terminology and dusty theories, and anyone who's ever looked outside their window into the world beyond and said, "Hmm, what really is going on out there?"

You might have scratched your head over questions such as:

- Is our high (and constantly increasing) national debt really a threat?
- Is money just a meme?
- What is a "mild" recession, exactly?
- What are Fed cred, Fed flexing, and Fedspeak?
- If many companies are earning record profits, why are they passing costs on to consumers?
- What are the behavioral pushes and pulls that make economies work?

When you become an informed economic citizen, you become aware not only of how economic problems and concerns affect you but also how you can benefit from those problems and concerns.

At the most basic level, economics is the study of change: how to handle change and how to predict change. Money changes hands. Just think of when you buy something as simple as a coffee. You swipe your card, the money goes from your bank account to the store's bank account and eventually back out into the economy as the store buys more coffee beans or pays their workers or their rent. That's a lot of change, and that's just one transaction.

The economy is also a reflection of volatile human emotions, going up and down, surging and quieting. Things can be quite unstable in the long term, but business cycles trend upward toward growth—but the struggle toward stability can lead to economic events such as recessions and downturns. But just like how most things trend toward okay-ness in life, so does the economy! We often forget that the economy is really a bunch of people peopling around. This book in your hands right now is an economic activity. The car you drive is an economic activity. Going to the coffee shop, buying a new pair of pants, eating an apple—everything has some element of economics threaded into it.

I know that sounds kind of dorky—"You're the economy!"—but it's true. And everyone deserves the opportunity to understand it.

By using analogies, stories, illustrations, and even quotes from poetry, literature, and philosophy, I'll connect seemingly disparate dots into a beautiful economic constellation that you can look at in awe but also deeply understand—because it affects you.

A quick note for international readers—I am a U.S.-based author, writing from a U.S. perspective, and much of this book examines the U.S. economy, monetary and financial policy, and markets—which, for better or worse, set off domino effects around the world in advanced economies and emerging markets. But the lessons in this book on how economies work and affect the citizens within them apply broadly. I'll also explore the delicate interplay of macroeconomic forces around the world, the complexities and quirks of the global financial system.

Economics is for everyone—so if you've felt left behind, or if you're cross-eyed from reading painfully convoluted (or straight-up misguided) financial commentary—this book is for you. Let's go.

In *This* Economy?

PART I

The Vibe Economy

The Economic Kingdom
Inflation
Labor market
Monetary policy
Fiscal policy
Housing market
For Sale
Bond Market
Stock Market
FAST TRACK
US Dollar
Commodities
Private markets
Crypto
Developed markets
Emerging markets

CHAPTER 1

The Economic Kingdom

The person that turns over the most rocks wins the game.
And that's always been my philosophy.
—PETER LYNCH

When I was younger, I loved to play a game called "The Princess and the Kingdom."

My brother and I would build fantastical lands with our toys, complete with castles, moats, and tiny LEGO armies that really hurt if you accidentally stepped on them with your bare feet.

For me, empire building was the best part. How fruitful the land was, how protected the entrances were, what tools the people had access to—that's what really determined how the game would play out.

The same holds for the financial infrastructure that's woven through our lives, our very own Economic Kingdom.

Let's start with the biggest castle: the monetary policy castle.

THE KINGDOM

The monetary policy castle is presided over by the Federal Reserve, which is supposed to be managing the entire kingdom.

We'll get into the inner workings of the Fed soon, but for right now what you need to know is that the monetary policy castle is most directly in charge of two other castles: inflation (defined as a rise in prices that creates a decrease in purchasing power, something we are all familiar with) and the labor market (where we find critically important metrics such as the labor force participation rate, the quits rate, the unemployment rate, and more). As I dive deeper, I'll describe how the Federal Reserve's actions can have far-reaching effects on the economic well-being of the kingdom's citizens, influencing their ability to afford goods and services and to find meaningful employment.

Each castle (such as the housing market, stock market, and bond market) has a moat around it that provides a little insulation. That's why the Fed may fire a cannon (say, raising interest rates), and the cannonball might land without much of a hit—meaning that it really didn't do much. In other cases, it might damage the drawbridge and make day-to-day functioning harder, or it might take out a squadron of an attacking army (such as unwanted inflation). The Federal Reserve is constantly firing cannons near all of those castles in an attempt to exert control over the empire.

Near is an important part of that sentence because the Fed cannon can occasionally make direct hits—but the castles are pretty strong, and it's hard to take them down easily. Sometimes, the Fed simply doesn't have enough (or the right kind of) ammo to directly hit them. Unlike my Princess and the Kingdom game, where castles could be knocked down chessboard style, there are too many variables influencing the Economic Kingdom for "I hit this and there are direct consequences" to work.

More on all this later, but contractionary monetary policy is the Fed's way of putting the brakes on the economy. Hiking interest rates—their major tool for fighting inflation—makes borrowing money more expensive, which cools down demand for goods and services. On the flip side, expansionary monetary policy is the Fed's way of speeding the economy up by cutting rates—no cannon fire, but more an injection of money into neighboring kingdoms.

The U.S. dollar castle is a "secret weapon" of the monetary policy castle because of the impact that the dollar has on the neighboring lands of developed and emerging markets. When the Fed uses its tool kit to strengthen the dollar—meaning that you can exchange it for more money in foreign countries—there are geopolitical consequences! For example, a strong U.S. dollar makes Chinese imports *more* expensive for American consumers and businesses—so Americans buy less stuff from China. As a result, Chinese goods become less competitive in the U.S. market, potentially leading to a decline in Chinese export revenues. Far-reaching impacts from the almighty dollar! Later on, I'll walk through the intricate relationships between global currencies and the ways in which fluctuations in the dollar can influence trade, inflation rates, and especially geopolitical dynamics.

The commodity castle is another core part of the Economic Kingdom. Commodities are basic goods that are used by everyone: agricultural products such as cotton and wheat, energy products such as oil and gas, metals such as gold and silver, and more. They are the common denominator between everything that we interact with on a daily basis—the phones we carry, the clothes we wear, the food we eat, the cars we drive. If the commodity castle did not exist, neither would the Economic Kingdom. While it's easy to downplay their significance in our daily lives, commodities play a vital role in shaping inflation, supply chains, and the overall economic health of the kingdom.

The Economic Kingdom reflects one of the harshest forms of reality, because what's going on there really, really matters and is also really difficult to predict or control. A significant decline in the real value of the dollar could result in soaring prices of everyday necessities, causing financial hardships for families. The unpredictable and drastic fluctuations in the housing market could lead to a housing crisis, leaving many people without a stable place to call home. The turbulent movements of stocks in the market could wipe out people's life savings, affecting their retirement plans and future well-being.

Policymakers typically measure the prosperity of the Economic Kingdom through the gross domestic product, or GDP, the total value of all goods and services produced in an economy. Nations around the world fixate on getting that number to climb. GDP is one of several key metrics that influence the directions in which the monetary policy castle fires its influential cannon (and isn't a great measure because it doesn't really capture anything beyond spending). Later on, I'll explore other metrics that provide a more comprehensive understanding of the kingdom's health and well-being.

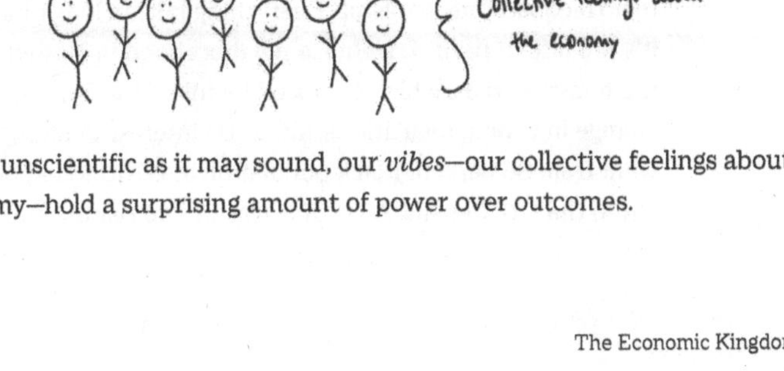

As unscientific as it may sound, our *vibes*—our collective feelings about the economy—hold a surprising amount of power over outcomes.

VIBES *ARE* THE ECONOMY

You might scoff and say, "Vibes? I haven't had an emotion in years," but consumer sentiment—more holistically, our vibes—not only affects how much we borrow, spend, save, and earn but also moves the needle on food prices, gas prices, shelter costs, wages, and more.

Frenzied stock market rallies can stoke irrational optimism, and grim headlines can stoke worry and uncertainty. It's not data alone informing our gut feelings about the state of the economy. If people have an experience (say, living through the 2008 recession) and evidence (home prices skyrocketing), that might shape their interpretation ("Another unprecedented event to live through!"), which shapes their expectations ("Things are starting to suck, and I think they're going to start sucking a lot more"), which shapes their behavior ("I'd better ask for a raise at my next performance review"), which shapes company behavior ("We need to raise prices to keep pace with these increased labor costs"), which shapes Fed policy ("We need to slow down inflation, so we're going to hike interest rates by seventy-five basis points").

Then of course, there are downstream consequences to the Fed hiking and implementing **contractionary** monetary policy—things slow down, people don't spend as much, businesses don't make as much money, some people lose their jobs. That's how rate hikes can put people out of work. But rate cuts (**expansionary** monetary policy) do the opposite—more money flowing around, more hiring activity. Usually. Of course, this is the economy—and no one really knows what will happen. The Fed did one of their largest rate-hike cycles in years during the early 2020s, and the labor market improved!

The big-picture takeaway is that a lot of the policy that influences the Economic Kingdom is based on theory, on the past, on what-has-already-happened-so-it-will-happen-again-ism—including some people advocating that we return to the gold standard even if it isn't suitable in the current economic conditions.

The U.S. government tends to have outdated regulations, inflexible and rigid implementation, limited policymaker engagement with the policies they set, one-size-fits-all solutions, ignorance of technological advancement, and few to no feedback mechanisms. Everything takes a long time to fix, and sometimes it's too late to fix it. Edgehill, a neighborhood in Nashville, is a key example of the housing crisis, which is caused by misaligned local zoning regulations, little change in zoning regulations, and little interest in fixing the situation. Edgehill went from 86 percent Black population in 2000 to 14 percent by 2020, according to the U.S. Census. A lot of it was due to rising home prices and the loss of old, naturally affordable housing units, as well as low-density zoning (which doesn't allow more affordable multifamily homes to be built).

As Ursula K. Le Guin wrote in *Tales from Earthsea: Dragonfly*, "What goes too long unchanged destroys itself. The forest is forever because it dies and dies and so lives."

Though some policy paths definitely rely on historical patterns and the presumption of stability, it is really important to recognize that people are not static entities but dynamic beings with evolving needs and aspirations, and growing economies should reflect that.

The Economic Kingdom is ultimately made up of people—people with dynamic, constantly changing needs—and therefore, the policy that shapes the Economic Kingdom should evolve, too, including a progressive labor market policy regarding working parents and people with disabilities and supporting employees through expanded employee stock option plan (ESOP) possibilities, ideas that I will explore in later chapters as I analyze other castles throughout the book.

Embracing such philosophical considerations can lead us toward a more nuanced and inclusive approach to shaping the Economic Kingdom, ensuring its responsiveness to the needs and aspirations of its inhabitants—which gets us into vibes.

CHAPTER 2

The Vibe Economy

So what is economics?

Economics can be seen as the ultimate tool for decoding our collective decisions. It's about understanding the whys and hows of our resource use—the choices we make in the corridors of legislation and regulation and in our everyday lives.

It isn't just a dry collection of figures and theories; it's a dynamic map of human behavior, a guide to navigating the complex networks of supply, demand, and market forces, and a primer on the policy and perspectives that guide our societal wants and needs.

MOODS AND MARKETS

Living in an uncertain world is challenging. We have animal brains, and our animal brains like to know what is happening. Our brains are built to process the negative first because it helps us plan for future survival.

It's tempting for talking heads to point to economic data and say, "Look at these industrial production metrics; you should feel optimistic right now." But let's be honest—that doesn't reflect many people's everyday experiences. In this chapter, I will focus on how expectations, theory, and reality create the vibes of our economy.

THE ECONOMIC CIRCLE OF LIFE

The circular flow diagram helps to chart the flow of resources and money. It's a blueprint that illustrates the interactions between two key players: households and businesses. Households provide labor to businesses and, in return, get compensated with wages and salaries.

They then use this income to purchase goods and services from businesses. Businesses depend on households not only as a source of labor but also as consumers who buy their products.

The government is there, too, of course, collecting taxes and redistributing income, which has a ripple effect in impacting how much households can spend and how businesses plan their investments. The financial sector manages the flow of savings and investments and conducts external trade with other countries.

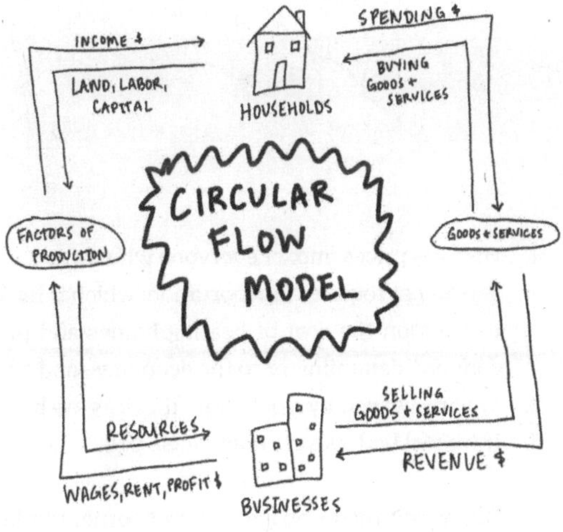

The diagram is just one model of the economy, but it shows how many moving parts there are. There's a lot of complexity in the way the economy works, and this is why there's such a gap between the data and lived reality sometimes.

Navigating the economy's twists and turns can feel like decoding a secret language of acronyms and figures. While these metrics—think GDP, CPI, PCE, and PPI (terms that will all get explained later on)—are pivotal in measuring economic health, they often miss the mark in reflecting people's day-to-day realities.

The pinch of escalating food costs, the sting of rising rent, and the stress of mortgage payments don't always sync up with the so-called success stories these numbers narrate. This discord between hard data and the lived experience is the core of the "vibes economy."

FUELING FEELINGS

When gasoline prices increase in the United States, consumer sentiment tends to decrease, and this can shape how the economy works. High gas prices make us feel bad—and it's not hard to see why.

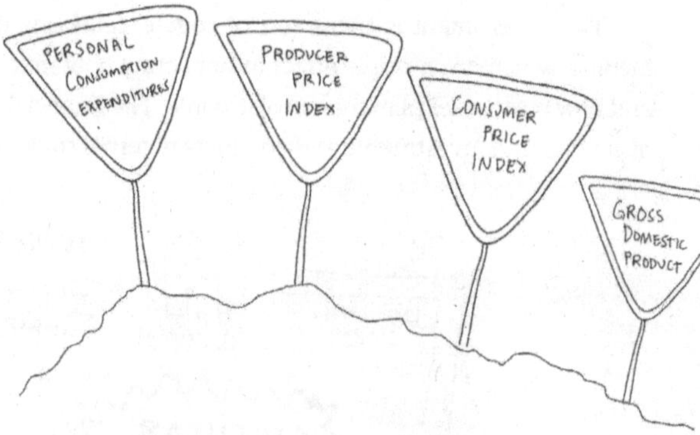

1. High gas prices impact everyone who owns a car, and also affect the prices of goods that require transportation, which is basically everything we buy—not to mention the cost of heating homes and producing electricity. Oil is the common denominator to the economy—and everything is swayed by its cost.
2. We are swayed by prices, and if prices are high, we feel bad.
3. If we feel bad, the economy feels bad.

Bright neon signs on every street corner remind us of how expensive it is to be alive. High gas prices do not a recession make. But they sure can feel like one.

WHAT IS OPEC?

Understanding OPEC helps us see why oil prices change and why it's such a big deal in the world. Short for Organization of the Petroleum Exporting Countries, OPEC is a group of thirteen of the world's largest oil-exporting countries. Together they decide how much oil they should produce, which affects the price of oil worldwide.

The OPEC countries produce a lot of the world's oil, which is why their decisions are so important. When they produce more oil, the price may go down, and when they produce less, the price may go up. OPEC's actions can impact how much we pay for things such as gasoline, which comes from oil. So when you hear about OPEC in the news, it is about how much oil these countries are drawing out of the ground and how it affects all of us.

The oil market is influenced by how much oil is being produced by the Organization of the Petroleum Exporting Countries, or OPEC (as well as other producers, including the United States) and how many people are consuming that oil—supply and demand! It balances international relations, is affected by domestic politics and policies, and manages the extensive network of supply chains that gets oil from the ground into basically everything. Oil prices are just one example of how our feelings can shape the economy—and how important it is to manage sentiment.

VIBE-OLOGY AND EMOTION ECONOMY

There is nothing new or unique about the concept of sentiment driving the economy. John Maynard Keynes coined the term *animal spirits* to describe how emotions can influence people's decisions and market behavior. Concepts like irrational exuberance, herd mentality, and risk appetite all fall under this sentiment-driven economic umbrella.

ECONOMIC THEORY	THE ROLE OF EMOTIONS
Prospect Theory	The theory that our emotions, such as loss aversion, impact our risk choices
Framing Effect	The theory that emotions can be influenced by how information is presented
Anchoring and Adjustment	The theory that emotions may affect how individuals anchor on initial information and adjust from there
Endowment Effect	The theory that our emotional attachment to possessions influences their valuations
Regret Theory	The theory that our emotions of regret impact our decision-making and risk aversion

ECONOMIC THEORY	THE ROLE OF EMOTIONS
Intertemporal Choice Theory	The theory that impatience can influence our choices between present and future outcomes
Affective Forecasting	The theory that predictions of future emotions impact our decision-making
Social Identity Theory	The theory that our emotions tied to social identity influence economic behavior
Consumer Emotional Engagement	The theory that our emotional connections impact our preferences and brand loyalty

One theory worth studying more closely is *reflexivity*, the legendary trader George Soros's theory that there's a feedback loop between what people think and what actually ends up happening, which in turn changes the way people think. The internet bubble is a key example of this—

1. **Initial Perception/Belief:** In the late 1990s, there was widespread belief that the internet would revolutionize businesses (which it did!) and that traditional valuation metrics didn't apply to internet-based companies (which they ... did). This belief led to increasing valuations for tech startups, many of which were making no money.
2. **Market Action Based on Belief:** Investors began pouring money into technology stocks and internet startups, driving their prices up. This was partly based on the notion that the internet's potential was so vast that even high valuations were justified.
3. **Reflexive Feedback Loop:** As more money flowed into the tech sector and share prices rose, it reinforced the belief that the internet was fundamentally transformative! And that these high valuations were justified. The rising stock prices attracted even more investors, further driving up prices.
4. **Bubble Bursts:** Eventually, when the realization set in that many of these companies wouldn't be profitable for years (if at all), the bubble burst. Stock prices plummeted, leading to the dot-com crash in the early 2000s.

Soros argues that highly valued companies that have attracted significant investments based on the *expectation* of their future profitability—often due more to narrative than to objective analysis—gain a critical edge in hiring and get the best talent in the field. Who doesn't want to work for the new hot startup, which could be the next Google or Apple or Microsoft? Then their valuation (based on expectations) brings in more investors, more money, more growth, and even better talent. This example highlights the blurred line between perception and reality: Is the stock price high because the company is growing, or is the company growing because the stock price is high? Perhaps worst of all, is the company stagnant with a high stock price—overvalued, a bubble, not reflective of reality?

This passage from the economist Fischer Black's 1986 paper "Noise" also discusses the same concept.

> *I think that the price level and rate of inflation are indeterminate.* They are whatever people think they will be. *They are determined by expectations, but expectations follow no rational rules. If people believe that certain changes in the money stock will cause changes in the rate of inflation, that may well happen, because their expectations will be built into their long-term contracts. (Author's emphasis.)*

Of course, our expectations influence our reality. What we think will happen ends up happening, which influences what happens later. Emotions (vibes) are the key driver of a lot of the decisions that we make.

All of this, coupled with our personal experiences in the world, influences our perception and interpretation of the world and our subsequent discourse about it. This is how we feel. This is vibes.

THE UNCERTAINTY CAKE

When we're worried about the economy, we are usually worried about our own money. This creates the perfect recipe for a cake of uncertainty, composed of expectations, theory, and reality, based on:

- **Expectations:** How we expect things to be
- **Theory:** How things are supposed to be
- **Reality:** How things are

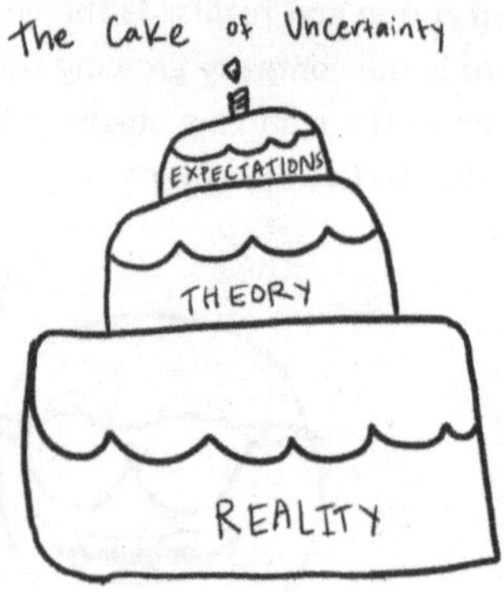

Our vibes are multiplied across the economy. Your vibes compound with everyone else's vibes, and that, at a very basic level, creates consumer sentiment. As I talk about in the GDP chapter, consumer sentiment is everything because it drives consumer spending, the central driver of GDP growth.

When expectations, theory, and reality diverge, that's when the vibes get really weird. Economic theory is the perfect example of this. There is a gap between what textbooks say is going to happen and what companies actually end up doing. Economics is known as the dismal science, but it really should be known as the dismal art. Most stock valuation models are an educated guess about the future; most economic theory is measurable, but on the basis of loose facts. As the English author Hilary Mantel wrote in a 2017 *Guardian* piece on facts, history, and truth, "Evidence is always partial. Facts are not truth, though they are part of it—information is not knowledge. And history is not the past—it is the method we have evolved of organising our ignorance of the past. It's the record of what's left on the record."

Random facts may not always tell the whole truth! This creates cognitive dissonance as it makes us hold conflicting beliefs, because like, hello! What do you mean nothing ever really makes sense and no one really knows what is going on?

ECONOMIC MOOD RINGS

We can look at certain metrics to gauge this element of cognitive dissonance. The Consumer Confidence Survey, for example, is a measure produced by the Conference Board that provides key insights into consumer confidence. Other measures of global consumer confidence, including the Conference Board Global Consumer Confidence Index, and survey firms such as Nielsen, Ipsos, and GfK, give us insight into consumer attitudes, economic expectations, and labor market perception, providing a general sense of how people feel about the present situation and their expectations. When there is a gap between the present situation and people's expectations, that's not good, because that means people are like, "Wow, things are really bad and they are about to get a whole lot worse."

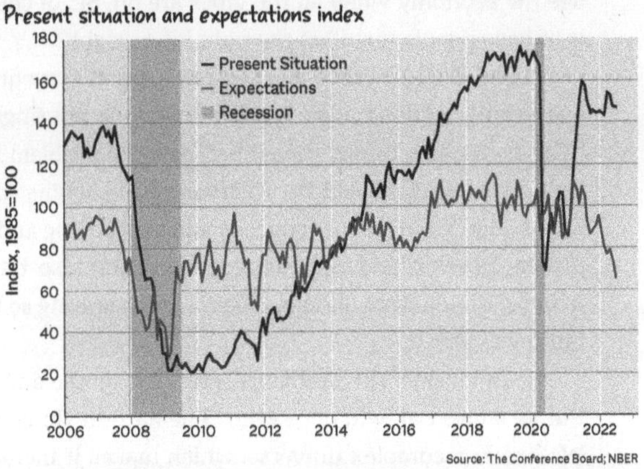

Of course, the feeling of things being bad compounds. There is a gap between confidence measures, so we aren't even that confident in our confidence! But when there is a divergence between reality and expected reality, that is not good.

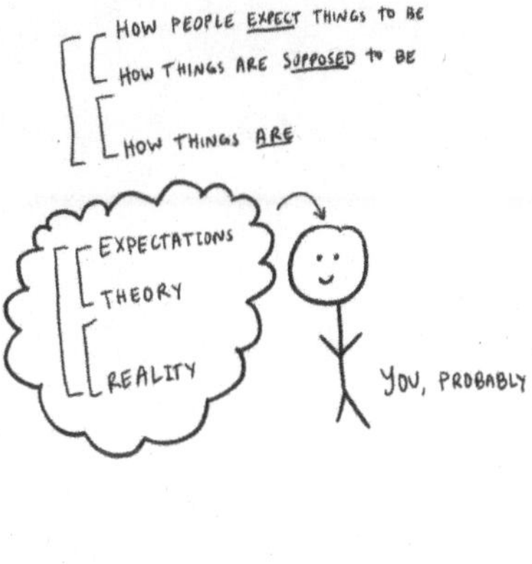

We can apply the vibes-based model to our world pretty easily. When people are feeling bad, they often run their actions through this vibes-based model subconsciously. If people are feeling uncertain, they might stop spending money, which impacts the entire economy. That's the power that people—including you—have in shaping our economic reality. This applies to all sorts of economic data points, too. As Josh Zumbrun in *The Wall Street Journal* put it, "Expected inflation is, in some sense, a self-fulfilling prophecy. If people expect it to continue, they might raise prices for their business or ask for raises at their jobs, fueling continuing price increases."

Think about how vibes based that is: Inflation is entirely dependent on what people expect to happen! Experience, evidence, expectations, perception, and interpretation are all key economic variables—and it can be tough to manage the economy when all the vibes are off. So, of course, the obvious solution is to have people manifest the right vibes, right?

Ha-ha, I wish. Vibes are just one part of the equation. When it feels like everything is falling apart, people want to point fingers, place blame, and say, "This is not how things should be!" And the problem is that they are right; this isn't how things should be. Everyone is searching for broader freedoms in a world dominated by corporations and advertising and also if you have a feeling just medicate it and also student loans and also the housing crisis and also hyper-individualism and also the Earth is burning so there is nothing left to do but try to save it.

In an ideal world, problems would be simple and solutions would be easy. But as James Baldwin once said, "The hardest thing in the world is simplicity." We live in a complex universe, which makes it incredibly difficult to point at any one thing as the Number One Problem.

PART II

How Money Works

CHAPTER 3

The Weird World of Money

Money has always been a meme from Day 1. What seems wacky and modern is a return to the traditions of the ancients.

—SID VERMA, GLOBAL EDITOR AT *BLOOMBERG MARKETS*

THE WEIRD WORLD OF MONEY

Money is an ever-present aspect of our daily lives, serving a crucial and complex purpose. Despite its significance, it's difficult to talk about it. In a room full of people, you might have an easier time talking about bowel movements than feelings about money.

But what is money, really?

Mostly, it is a social construct that relies on people's trust. Money is a commodified product, a promise. It's the glue that holds society together because it facilitates transactions, enables growth, and expresses convictions.

DOLLARS AND SENSE: WHAT MAKES MONEY, MONEY?

Money has three core attributes, and we can talk about them through the analogy of bananas and trucks. It is:

- **A store of value.** It holds value over time (however, inflation does complicate this). One dollar today will buy the same number of bananas or trucks tomorrow.
- **A unit of account.** It can be used to compare the values of goods and services, so one dollar can buy one banana, whereas many dollars can buy a truck.

- **A medium of exchange.** You can go to the grocery store or truck dealership with your dollars, and both will accept your dollars as valid payment for whatever you are trying to buy.

The concept of money is broad and can be pretty much anything that people believe in.

THROUGH THE AGES: THE EVOLUTION OF MONEY

To understand how money functions in our day-to-day world, we need to look back—way back.

A long time ago, people used things like seashells or mineral chunks as means of exchange. Really, anything that can meet the three pillars—medium of exchange, store of value, and unit of account—can *technically* be money. For example, if our ancestors had collectively agreed and trusted that toenail clippings had value and could be used reliably for transactions, savings, and accounting, then technically, toenail clippings would have been money in their society (though not a formal currency, which is money that is printed and minted by a government).

A lot of the ancient systems depended on bartering, the exchange of goods and services without the use of money. But as society kept evolving, it became more complicated to carry around a herd of cows in an attempt to trade them for some grain.

Anthropologists like David Graeber, author of *Debt: The First 5000 Years*, suggest that early societies operated on the principles of communal sharing rather than strict bartering. However, as societies grew and contact with other civilizations happened, there was a need for a standardized medium of exchange.

Some people thought a certain amount of grain was worth only fifteen cows, some thought it was worth maybe nineteen cows, and that was frustrating for both sellers and buyers to deal with.

Around 3500 B.C.E., Mesopotamia was the first region to establish a monetary system, using clay tokens that represented goods and services. These tokens were one of the first forms of currency, and merchants recorded transactions on clay tablets, a process developed around 3200 B.C.E. As Edward Chancellor wrote in *The Price of Time*, "We do know that the Mesopotamians charged interest on loans before they discovered how to put wheels on carts."

Around 600 B.C.E, coins were developed in Lydia, an ancient kingdom in Asia Minor. The coins were made from electrum, a natural alloy of gold and silver, and were much easier to carry around than cows. The coins were a significant advancement, providing a stable, standardized medium of exchange and unit of account.

The coin-based monetary system financed empires for thousands of years, and helped to develop trust in the underlying economic system. Markets were formed, society advanced, and economies continued to grow.

In modern times, most societies have now transitioned to fiat currency, which is money that derives its value not from physical commodities, but from government regulation and public trust. Unlike gold- or silver-backed currencies, fiat money, such as the U.S. dollar, is valued based on the government declaring that it is valuable rather than on its material worth—it's just made of linen and cotton.

THE AMERICAN CURRENCY STORY: REVOLUTION TO RECOGNITION

The story of how money evolved in the United States can tell us a *lot* about the function of money and the monetary system it exists in. In the early 1700s, the American colonies relied mostly on European currencies such as the Spanish piece of eight—though those were in short supply—and barter (want to trade some dried fish for pewter dishes?) as a way to maintain a functioning economy. To help finance the Revolutionary War, the Continental Congress issued a currency called continentals that was backed by the anticipation of future tax revenues, which was a pretty ballsy bet on the projected new country.

Funnily enough, this is actually pretty similar to the way the U.S. currency works now. The U.S. dollar is backed by "the full faith and credit of the U.S. government," which essentially equates to the value of all the drones, tankers, and military bases that are waiting to pulverize anyone who dares question its status.

Sure, the U.S. government has come a long way in the past 250 years. We're still using the same foundational document, the Constitution, in an era where technology like an iPhone would have melted a Founding Father. But the method of currency in the 1700s was unstable and inefficient. The fledgling United States required something different if it wanted to grow. The continental was the first currency, but it was plagued by excessive inflation during the Revolutionary War and lack of trust because of that. So in 1785, the Continental Congress dropped the continental, adopting the dollar as the national currency, and five years later the Constitution was ratified.

Alexander Hamilton came along with a plan for banks. There weren't any banks making loans, so there wasn't really any way to start a company. The ultrawealthy personally controlled most lending, which isn't really the best way to distribute scarce resources. Hamilton wanted a federal bank that would provide credit to the government and businesses, issue a national currency, and be a place for people to safely store money. But soon, Thomas Jefferson rolled up, saying that the bank was a bit too central and that the newly created Constitution didn't give the government power to have anything to do with a national bank or a currency.

The two went to battle, Hamilton won, and the First Bank of the United States was created in 1791. However, it failed to be rechartered twenty years later, for a variety of reasons including the worry that a national bank was an encroachment on states' rights (and state-chartered banks) and served only commercial and industrial interests. States took matters into their own hands and issued their own currencies, which was an absolute nightmare.

We can make a comparison to the modern-day eurozone, a monetary union of twenty of the twenty seven European Union countries. These nations have adopted the euro as their shared currency and legal tender, facilitating easier trade and financial transactions across borders. However, this union has faced its challenges, notably during the eurozone crisis that began in 2009. The crisis was primarily fueled by high sovereign debt levels in countries like Greece and Spain, economic imbalances within the zone, and vulnerabilities in the banking sector, all exacerbated by the constraints of a shared monetary policy without a corresponding fiscal union and the spillover effects of the 2008 global financial crisis. The union is a tricky thing to balance with so many countries and the volatile financial climate! But just imagine how difficult it would become if, all of a sudden, some of the member countries stopped accepting the euro and each of them tried to do business and buy things across borders with twenty different currencies. It would be a nightmare! It would be confusing, scattered, and a breeding ground for conflict—which, sure, can be functional, but not really great for long-term growth, stability, and EU unity.

In 1816, when people's eyeballs were melting out of their skulls from exasperation with the monetary system, Congress chartered the Second Bank of

the United States. That lasted twenty years, until Andrew Jackson said, "Absolutely not."

The Free Banking Era began—when, again, each state made its own rules and created an absolute mess with little to no regulation from the government. It was called the "wildcat" era and for good reason: There were eight thousand state banks, each of which issued its own notes that were denominated in dollars but represented claims on the bank's assets. Because they were issued by state-chartered banks, the value and stability of the banknotes were variable, depending on which bank had issued the note; some banks were reliable, and others were not. That made it very difficult for customers to do what they needed to do at the banks: banking. The banks essentially became useless.

The government was ripping their hair out of their heads in frustration. So in 1863, the National Banking Act was passed, which created a uniform national currency and allowed only *nationally* chartered banks to issue notes.

For a long time, money in the United States was tied to the value of gold. For a myriad of reasons, the country went off the gold standard in 1971. Each dollar had a specific value in terms of gold and could be converted into gold at that rate. It's pretty tough to maintain fixed exchange rates when economies are waffling as they did in the 1970s, so the fixed exchange rate system had to end. After the gold standard fell apart, money became an abstract way to keep score (the shift from money being a physical representation of value through gold, to it being a symbolic representation of value based on trust and shared agreement) and maintain a stable economy. Our money today is fiat money. It doesn't have an intrinsic value, but it does have "the government says this is valuable and therefore it is" value.

Despite what some might say, it's actually good that we aren't on the gold standard anymore. The gold standard was restrictive, and switching to fiat has allowed greater flexibility in monetary policy, which is crucial for enabling governments to respond more effectively to financial crises, regulate inflation, and stimulate economic growth. To this day, the Federal Reserve helps enforce the promise and collective trust that we all have in money.

All central banks, including the Fed, are economic vibe setters, the guardians of the money. Central banks gained a significant amount of power in the nineteenth and twentieth centuries, such as the Bank of Japan being established in 1882 and Germany's Bundesbank (a significant inspiration for the European Central Bank) in 1957, something we will discuss in a later chapter.

Money functions to get us onto the roller coaster of life: to stand in that long line, get buckled into the seat, and go for a ride over all the ups and downs.

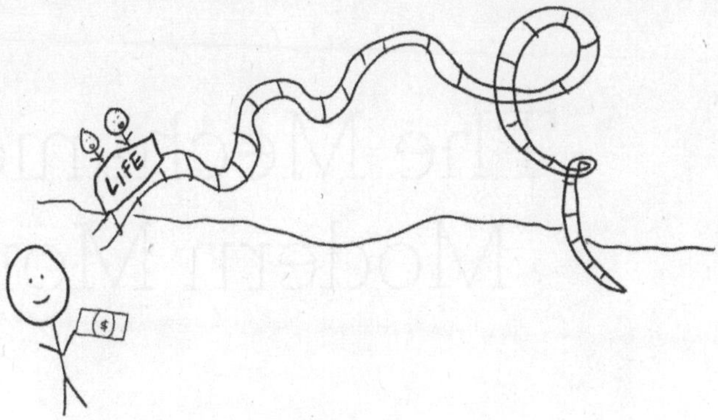

But how does money work in the modern economy?

CHAPTER 4

The Mechanics of Modern Money

Today, money mostly takes the form of 0s and 1s in a computer program as opposed to physical cash or coins. So what happens behind the scenes when you swipe your debit card for a coffee?

1. You have a bank account, which holds your bank deposit.
2. Your money on deposit at the bank is actually an "Oh, man, I owe you money" note from the bank. It's a promise that you will be paid from your account when you go to the bank and ask for money.
3. You swipe your card for coffee.
4. The bank processes the payment by taking money out of your bank account, thereby reducing your deposit (or, if you use a credit card, adding the amount to what you owe your credit card company).
5. The bank transfers the money to the seller, thereby increasing the seller's bank deposit.

Banks are the gatekeepers of money. They are the money business model. The U.S. government is the creator of the money, the ultimate facilitator of what the banks are able to do. The government "creates" money in two ways:

1. **By issuing coins and notes.** The U.S. Treasury (specifically the U.S. Mint and Bureau of Engraving) creates currency notes, whereas the Federal Reserve issues them. The money goes into the bank system right away—so banks still are running the ring of money, facilitated by the government.

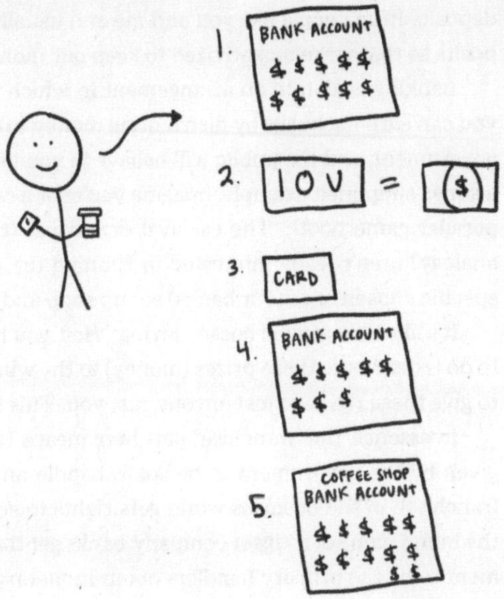

2. **Through credit markets.** The government issues bonds, promises to pay money back at some point in the future. The markets (made up of foreign governments, asset managers, and the Federal Reserve at present) say, "Ah, yes, we will buy those from you," and with the money gained, the government is able to execute on public infrastructure, social spending, insider trading, and other activities. Corporations do the same thing: They issue bonds, which serve the same functionality but have a different interface (which I will talk about later).

The government doesn't really control the money supply; it can nudge it around via all sorts of mechanisms that I will get into later, but it's really the Big Boi Banks that are in charge. If all of this seems abstract and convoluted, that's because it is. You're not crazy! And there are times when collective trust can go *poof,* and money is no longer money.

THE BANKING BLUEPRINT

The banking business model is built on trust, but it's also built on their ability to borrow short (mostly through customer deposits) to lend long (through longer-term loans such as mortgages); that is their business model. They collect deposits from people like you and me and usually pay us interest on those deposits so that we're incentivized to keep our money with them.

Banking is akin to an arrangement in which the government says, "Banks, you can earn big bucks by distributing money to the public on behalf of us, the government, and the public will believe in you because we believe in you." For a super-simplified example: Imagine you're at a carnival, and there's this mega-popular game booth. The carnival organizers (that's our government in this analogy) aren't really interested in running the game themselves, so they let specific chosen ones (our banks) set up shop and run that game.

It's like the carnival bosses saying, "Hey, you banks. You won. All you've got to do is distribute these prizes (money) to the winners (public). We're not going to give these rights to just anyone, just you. This is trust."

In essence, the "franchise" part here means the exclusive right or privilege given by the government to banks to handle and distribute money. Just as a franchisee in the business world gets rights to sell a product or service under the brand name of a bigger company, banks get the "franchise" from the government to be the primary handlers of our monetary system. And because of this official stamp of approval, people trust banks with their hard-earned cash. The banking business model's success relies heavily on a key concept known as fractional reserve banking. This concept plays a pivotal role in how banks operate and contribute to the broader economy.

FRACTIONAL RESERVE BANKING

Of course, as a bank, you're getting money from deposits and interest payments, so you can loan out more than you have—the fundamental concept of fractional reserve banking! Banks are allowed to loan out the majority of the deposits on their books, the theory being that not all their depositors will want to withdraw their money at the same time. If you deposit $100, the bank doesn't have to keep the whole amount in the bank. It can loan that money out! That is how it makes money! If it does not lend out deposits, it is going to have trouble making money and continuing to operate as a bank.

But it also has its own money, called its reserves—all the cash it holds plus any money it is holding at the Federal Reserve. It must keep a fraction of those reserves on hand, but the rest can roam wild and free.

Where did this business model of borrowing come from?

For a long time, gold was the primary medium of exchange. But no one wanted to carry around large quantities of gold, so they started leaving their gold with a goldsmith. The goldsmith was like, "Sure, I will hold on to these for you. Here's a piece of paper representing your gold." Then people started trading their gold receipts and the goldsmiths started lending out gold with interest.

This is fractional reserve banking: lending out more than technically exists, making it so that not every dollar can be given back all at once.

So the banks take the money, invest it in securities that earn maybe 2% to 3%, and keep the spread between the interest they're being paid and the interest they're paying to their customers, or the net interest margin. Understanding the principles of fractional reserve banking sets the stage for exploring the next crucial aspect of banking: the process of making loans.

THE ART OF LENDING

Banks take a variety of factors into account when making decisions about loans and investments, including the movements interest rates are expected to make. This is a function of expected loan demand and risk assessment: If rates are expected to rise, banks will charge higher rates on the loans they issue and prioritize shorter-term loans to reduce any potential losses of long-term assets due to those higher expected borrowing costs.

Once the loans are made, money is created because the banks are essentially creating new money through loaning out deposits.

To understand this better, we can take a look at a bank's balance sheet.

A balance sheet is composed of assets and liabilities—what a bank owns and what it owes.

- The bank's assets: what it owns, including loans extended to customers, government securities held, deposits maintained at the Federal Reserve, and other holdings.

- The bank's liabilities: things that it owes, which are the checking and savings accounts that people have with it, certificates of deposit issued by the bank, and loans taken by the bank.
- There is also net worth, which is owner's equity, or how much would be left after the bank pays off all its liabilities.

This ties in to something known as the accounting equation: Any company's total assets—everything it owns or controls—must be equal to its liabilities—its financial obligations and debts, shareholders' equity, the initial investment made by shareholders, and retained earnings generated over time. This is what makes the balance sheet balance. So the bank has to ensure that its assets match its equity and liabilities.

DECODING BANK BALANCE SHEETS

Let's say you go to ABC Bank and deposit $100 into your checking account. That money now becomes part of the bank's reserves as an asset, whereas the deposit in your checking account becomes a liability. When you deposit money, the bank makes a promise to you that it will pay you back. The dual nature of bank deposits is a fundamental principle of banking. When you deposit money, the bank makes a promise to you that it will pay you back. Deposits come with costs to the bank: the bank branches that seem to haunt every corner of cities, the apps we use to access our accounts, and the interest you are paid on the deposit are all things that the bank has to pay for.

Depending on the current macroeconomic environment, banks' reserve requirements can vary widely. During 2020, it was dropped to 0 percent because everyone was like, "Banks, please lend all your money right now and save the economy." Before then, it was 10 percent for a long time and should eventually tick back up as the Federal Reserve imposes a tighter monetary policy.

Returning to ABC Bank, it would be required to hold reserves of $10 on your deposit ($100 times 10 percent) to be kept on hand just in case the bank implodes, and it takes the $90 in excess reserves, the amount it's allowed to lend out, and does exactly that. To the bank, the $90 loan is an asset and the checking account of whoever borrowed it is a liability. The books are still balanced!

THE INVISIBLE SHERIFF

Excess reserves are like the secret sauce in the banking world, particularly when it comes to lending, snapping up government securities, and ensuring that the folks who've stashed their cash in banks can get it back when they want. These reserves are what banks have tucked away above and beyond what the rulebook says they need to keep on hand. They're super important because they give us a sneak peek into how banks might influence the whole money game through something called the money multiplier effect.

Now, when it comes to the money banks can lend out, the rule of thumb is usually tied to how plump their reserve cushion is—assuming there's some kind of minimum reserve requirement. But let's say this requirement is zero, like it was in 2020.

In theory, banks could go wild, lending out as much money as they've got in deposits. But here's the catch: If they get too loan-happy, they could end up with severe liquidity issues (translation: not enough quick cash to meet immediate demands). So even if we're thinking, "Yeehaw, let's go full Wild West with banking," there's still this invisible sheriff in town—the unspoken rule that going overboard with loans could cause a major freak-out. Banks need to keep enough in reserves to keep their depositors from panicking.

In the past decade, things went pretty well for banks. Interest rates were basically zero, so they didn't really need to pay much of anything to their depositors—around 0.01% on average. That was good for the banks! They were earning 2% to 3% on all the money people put into them. But if the Fed raises interest rates, the banks are going to need to pay more on deposits, meaning that they aren't going to be making as much money as they used to. That's well and good, but if banks are caught way off guard—say, they need to start paying 4% on deposits but are earning only 3%—they are going to be in trouble.

HOW BANKS HEDGE RISK

This is why banks employ strategies such as hedging, a risk management strategy that can protect against unexpected fluctuations in interest rates. Hedging is similar to planning a beautiful party in the park, complete with non-weatherproof snacks and drinks, and having a backup plan in case it rains. Banks use similar backup plans to protect themselves against sudden changes in the financial weather. A common practice is using interest rate swaps, which involve swapping interest rates. Let's say Institution A has a variable-rate loan (the rate moves when the financial market moves) and Institution B has a fixed-rate loan (the rate stays the same regardless of financial market movement).

- The two institutions can enter into an interest rate swap agreement, in which they agree to pay each other's interest rate obligations.
- In this scenario, if rates rise, Institution A might face steeper loan payments. But here's where Institution B steps in, saying, "No sweat, we'll cover the fixed interest rate to balance out your increased payments."
- Conversely, if rates fall, Institution A will pay less on the loan and will say, "Okay, Institution B, I'll pay you the lower variable interest rate."
- This way, both are hedged against fluctuations that may occur either way as they have the other institution there to bail them out.

When banks don't have such protective measures in place, things can get messy. While hedging strategies are crucial for managing risks, it's important to recognize that even with these measures, banks can still face significant challenges—like complete failure.

HOW BANKS CAN FAIL

A bank can fail for a number of reasons, such as insolvency, in which it runs out of money due to making risky loans. They can also fail due to illiquidity. If all of a bank's customers panic and line up (or click a button) to try to get their money back at the same time, the bank will not be able to give every dollar deposited back to every person who wants it, leading to a bank run—like with what happened with the Silicon Valley Bank (SVB) failure in 2023.

SVB had constructed its banking business model perfectly well, borrowing short to lend long. That would have been fine, except that it had no hedges on to protect against downside risk, so when the Fed started raising rates and defining a new normal, its soft underbelly was exposed to the vicious elements of the cruel, cruel world.

Imagine this: The bank's in hot water, losing money left and right. Then the drama unfolds on social media, sparking a digital-age bank run. Ultimately the Federal Deposit Insurance Corporation, or FDIC (which insures consumers' bank deposits), and the Treasury went in to save the bank via coverage with three tools:

- The FDIC's Deposit Insurance Fund
- The new Federal Reserve Bank Term Funding Program, which provides loans to banks and other financial institutions
- A $25 billion backstop from the Treasury's Exchange Stabilization Fund

In 2008, the 10 percent reserve requirement was in place. Banks needed to hold on to money. But they were offering subprime mortgages to high-risk borrowers (people who do not have strong creditworthiness and who will likely be unable to pay back the loan) and then bundling the mortgages together into mortgage-backed securities, or MBSs (a pool of mortgages with similar characteristics that represents fractional ownership of the entire pool and pays the MBS holders money through the principal and interest rate payments the borrowers make), and selling those time bombs to investors.

The banks found a way around the reserve requirement by using something called a collateralized debt obligation, or CDO, a complex financial instrument that packages all types of debts, such as bonds, loans, and mortgages, into a single security that is sold to investors. Similar to the MBS, the cash flows from the debt payments are what make these things juicy to hold on to. They are divided into senior tranches, which hold the least risky debt, and junior tranches, which hold the more risky debt. It's all about redistributing risk. But during 2008, CDOs held some of those subprime mortgages. Their issuers took the risky mortgages and other risky loans and piled them into CDOs to sell even more time bombs to investors. But because they were backed by a pool of all sorts of assets, they achieved an AAA rating, meaning that everyone was like, "No problems here, fellas, this is safe and good."

There were *definitely* problems here, fellas.

The housing bubble burst. Mortgage payment defaults began to rise. The time bomb blew up. And because the banks had been sneaky and had gotten around the reserve requirement via CDOs, they needed help. They began to fail. Then the Fed had to step in, and the economy has never really recovered, resulting in the decline in economic growth, the high unemployment rate world that Millennials graduated into, the slowdown in investment in housing (leading to the housing crisis that we have right now), the sovereign debt crisis that echoed across other nations, and the complete erosion of trust and confidence that people had in our systems—and of course the decade-long zero-interest-rate policy, or ZIRP, world that we lived in up until mid-2022.

The central banks and physical cash provided by the government help support the banks, but the banks are really the P. T. Barnums running the circus.

Banks influence markets and people and the economy across the board, but what they influence most directly is credit availability for consumers, the money supply, interest rates (they are de facto members of the Federal Reserve!), and payment systems, which gets into the cross currents of the economic kingdom—the U.S. dollar!

THE DOLLAR'S REIGN

Think of the U.S. dollar as more than just paper and coins; it's a powerhouse of economic strength. The U.S. GDP (Gross Domestic Product, which is the total economic value that a country is producing during a specific time period) is giant, making up over a quarter of the global economic pie. This dominance lends immense power and stability to the dollar, making it the world's principal reserve currency. Countries worldwide hold the dollar in their reserve, use it for international trade, and rely on its value to stabilize their own economies.

That's why when the world gets weird, the dollar usually becomes stronger. During periods of global economic uncertainty, more people demand the dollar because of its perceived stability, which (usually) results in its value increasing relative to that of other currencies—more demand, more value. When we say that the dollar increases in value, it means that the exchange rate of the U.S. dollar has increased against other currencies and each dollar can be exchanged for more units of another currency. Let's say that $1 used to equal 0.85 euro but now equals 0.95 euro. If you want to take a trip to Paris, $1,000 used to be equal to €850, but now it's equal to €950.

	STRONGER U.S. DOLLAR	WEAKER U.S. DOLLAR
U.S. multinational company or a U.S. investor abroad	NOT HAPPY: Costs more for other countries to buy U.S. goods because foreign currency now buys less with the same amount of currency. Profits are worth less when brought back to the U.S.	HAPPY: Cheaper for other countries to buy U.S. goods because the foreign currency now buys more with the same amount of currency. Profits are worth more when brought back to the U.S.
Foreign company exporting to the U.S. or a foreign investor in the United States	HAPPY: U.S. people can buy more of their goods because you can buy more with the same amount of dollars and investments are worth more	NOT HAPPY: U.S. people buy less of their goods because you can buy less with the same amount of dollars and investments are worth less

If you're a U.S. tourist abroad you love the stronger dollar. You can buy more things in other countries because the dollar is worth more. But if you're an international corporation, it's a bit of a different story.

Netflix ran into the problem of a stronger dollar back in 2022. As Jack Farley, a macro researcher at Blockworks, explained, "Netflix says the rising dollar will cost them about $1 billion in revenue for the year." The situation arose because Netflix conducts business overseas. Its subscribers pay in local currencies, and when those local currencies are converted to U.S. dollars—and the dollar is strong—it diminishes how many dollars those local currencies turn into. So Netflix was walloped by the strong dollar in 2022.

A stronger dollar is a wrecking ball in a lot of ways—but funnily enough, the dollar is the only real hedge against inflation. Xiang Fang, Yang Liu, and Nikolai Roussanov published a 2022 paper titled "Getting to the Core: Inflation Risks Within and Across Asset Classes" that explored this. As they explained:

> *The only "real" hedge appears to be the U.S. dollar which is contrary to much conventional wisdom, but entirely consistent with our historical evidence! Why does USD strengthen when US Core inflation is up? One obvious reason is the expected tightening by the Fed, which makes dollar interest-bearing assets more attractive. A more subtle reason that we point to in the paper is the real exchange rate appreciation—core goods, which are inherently less tradable than energy, become more valuable, driving up consumers' "marginal utility" of consumption.*

The dollar is an inflation hedge, backed by nuclear bombs, F-22 fighter jets, aircraft carriers, and millions of American military personnel. All the talk about the United States being a really stable place is essentially a big red arrow pointing to the power of the U.S. military and its allies. European Union countries, Japan, Korea, Mexico, Australia, and other countries all say, "Yes, the U.S. dollar is the way to go."

As Karthik Sankaran once tweeted, "The most important aspect of USD centrality is not its role as the dominant international reserve asset, but rather its role as the dominant denomination of cross-border liabilities. Here I stand, I can do no other."

Recently, there has been a lot of worry over the dollar maintaining its status as the reserve currency because of the potential reallocation of economic interest and influence, mostly due to the rise of countries such as China and the issues in the U.S. political system (a bipartisan issue!). There is speculation that often sounds like "We are going to have hyperinflation [implying an infinite number of dollars being printed] and the purchasing power of the dollar will go to zero [be worthless]."

All countries' debts to other countries are denominated in dollars, so the currency won't blow up anytime soon. When people—whether they be policymakers or posters on social media—talk about the dollar being printed into oblivion, it's really important to talk about the fact that the dollar is a symbol and a transactional tool. It's the means by which we buy goods and services, but

U.S. Dollar Index: YTD 2022

The U.S. dollar has strengthened against most other currencies at a historic rate this year. Based on our YTD actuals and Q4 guidance, we estimate that this appreciation since January 1, 2022, will negatively impact our full-year 2022 revenue and operating income by ~$1 billion and $0.8 billion, respectively.

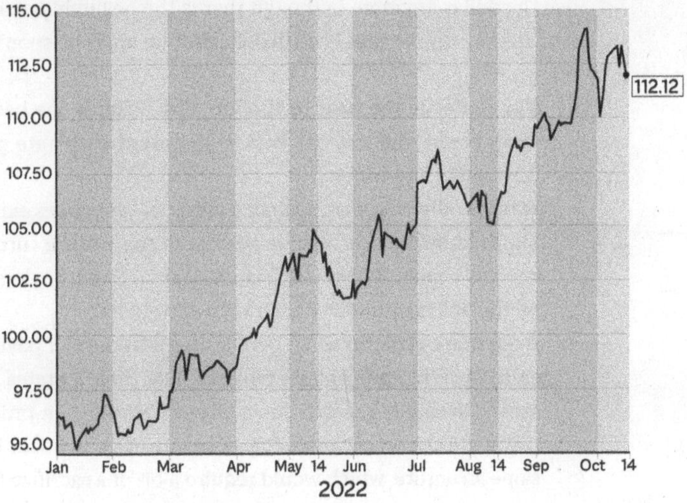

Source: Netflix Q3 2022 Earnings Report

it's also used to conduct trade deals and international negotiations. As such, the U.S. foreign policy establishment is always working to defend the value of the U.S. dollar.

The most notable trend in recent decades has been the rise of nontraditional reserve currencies—the currencies of countries without the economic scale and volume of cross-border transactions that distinguish traditional reserve currency issuers.

If the dollar dominance comes to an end (a scenario, not a prediction), the greenback could be felled not by the dollar's main rivals but by a broad group of alternative currencies. So it's sort of as though the dollar will remain the dollar until money fragments into many other currencies—but there probably isn't another currency that is going to take its place for a while.

RETHINKING THE DOLLAR

Michael Pettis, an expert on the Chinese economy, has written extensively on how hard it would be for us to dedollarize—it's not just countries deciding to not use the dollar anymore (although that is the beginning of a worrying pattern). And here's why we won't see dedollarization anytime soon (probably):

- **The dollar is the best of the lot.** The dollar is the best thing out there—clear, liquid financial markets, transparent corporate governance. It's the least nasty alternative.
- **Structurally.** Surplus and deficit national economies exist. What the United States is doing right now is absorbing the world's surplus from countries such as China, Russia, and Saudi Arabia. Export-oriented economies rely on the dollar to stabilize their own currencies!
- **Even more structurally.** There is also a balance of payments to be considered! Current and capital accounts! The United States has a surplus in its capital account, a deficit in its current account. In order for another currency to take on the role of reserve currency, it would have to take on the same structure, which would require a bit of a sacrifice from China (assuming it would go along with that!).

Structure is hard to erode quickly. The IMF sees the shift out of dollars as a shift into currencies of smaller economies—not a shift to one main currency—and one that's happening slowly, not quickly. That makes sense, right? This ties into the broader themes of domestic protectionism, onshoring, and deglobalization; everyone is going to try to protect their own space.

People have all sorts of incentives for dollar doomerism, such as making money off a newsletter or an investing subscription service to promote the narrative of the dollar losing its status as the reserve currency. And that circles back to detachment, accepting everything at face value, taking media as capital-*T* Truth.

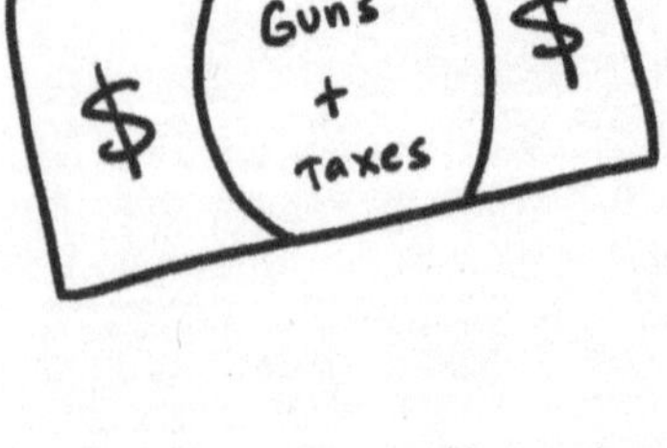

We spend a lot of time worrying about dedollarization, when we really should be worried about other economic woes. As the economist Brad Setser at the Council on Foreign Relations put it, "Waiting for the day when the tax avoidance strategies of US multinationals generate as much sustained attention as 'de-dollarization'!" Setser did a presentation on tax avoidance by big pharmaceutical companies, and yep, most of their profits are offshore. That's probably a bigger deal than the very low chance of the dollar losing its reserve currency status.

United States v. foreign profit and revenue, 2022

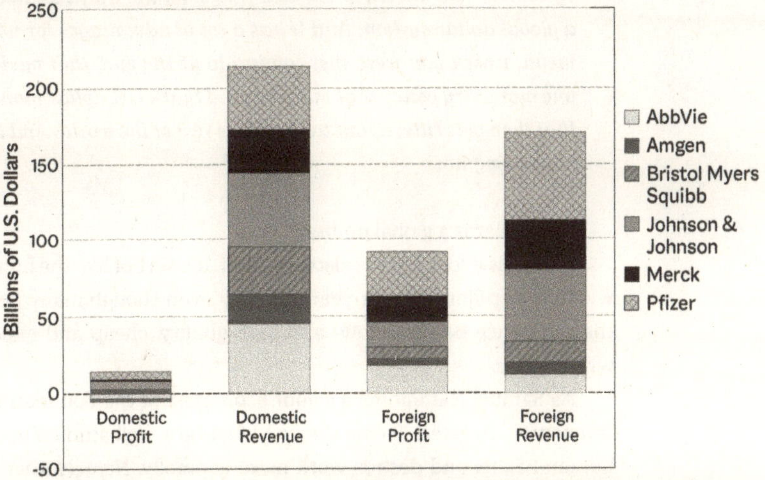

Source: Companies' Annual Reports on Form 10-K Data; Brad Setser

A lot of people feel that the dollar is not going to be able to maintain its reserve currency status in an increasingly polarized world. But because the dollar is the common denominator of the global economy, it makes everything complicated. If any country pivots away from the United States, the U.S. government can remove it from trade agreements, issue tariffs against it, decline military assistance to it, and basically hang it out to dry—as it did in 2022 after Russia invaded Ukraine.

People want to spend and they want the dollar, and it's the only real inflation hedge we have, which is definitely counterintuitive. So when we ask, "Can the dollar be replaced?" the answer is, of course, "Maybe."

There is no real yes or no answer. As we know, anything can happen. But as

Perry Mehrling, a professor of economics at Boston University, said on an episode of Bloomberg's *Odd Lots* podcast:

> *The logic of why it's a good thing to have one currency for the whole country and par clearing for the whole country, the logic is just the same for why it might be a good idea to have one currency for the whole world. And that's what people get out of it, is that it makes it easier to do trade, to do calculations, to unite the globe into a unified economy.... This notion of separate nation states with separate currencies. This is something that was inherited in our minds from World War II, when that system had all broken down. But that's not the world we live in now. It's a global dollar system. And it has a lot of advantages for now that does mean, which you were just coming to at the end, that basically there's one monetary policy that matters. And that's U.S. dollar monetary policy that then gets filtered out to the whole rest of the world. And that's what's happening now.*

The dollar is a global unifier.

Money is a tool, but it's also a symbol. It's sort of like the luxury wine sector, which is a trillion-dollar-a-year industry even though many people can't taste the difference between low- and high-quality, cheap and expensive, red and white wines.

As Samuel Hammond, a senior economist at the Foundation for American Innovation, tweeted, "Wine seems to just be a well-studied microcosm of how human beliefs and desires work more generally. Namely, that they're socially mediated, easily falsified, unconsciously influenced by cues of status and distinction, and relatively impervious to rational self-reflection."

How we interact with the world around us is all social! It's almost unconscious, and it's all a little silly.

Hammond continued, "If a bottle of aged grape piss can sell for thousands of dollars, what other trillion dollar industries and worldviews are constructed on a foundation of mass preference falsification and status driven self-deception? Almost all of them?"

Money, though seemingly as arbitrary as expensive wine, serves as the universally accepted tool that keeps our global economic engine running. It gets its value from a combination of economic, financial, and political factors, as well as collective trust. The only reason it works, like many things in the economy, is because we believe that it does—it's all about the people's faith.

FINAL THOUGHTS

It's a symbol, a tool, and a reflection of our collective beliefs and desires. We've seen how money, in all its forms, from seashells to digital entries, shapes economies and influences global dynamics.

The next section is a deep dive into the world of how we measure, track, and analyze money. Money, after all, is not just about what it is, but also about how much of it there is and the stories of growth, challenge, and change that accompany it.

PART III

How Money Is Measured

CHAPTER 5

Supply and Demand

Mankind must acquire two things which are at present increasingly disappearing: loving kindness and scientific impartiality.

—BERTRAND RUSSELL

INTRODUCTION TO SUPPLY AND DEMAND

Ever wonder why your favorite coffee brand gets pricier or airline tickets fluctuate in price? It all comes down to the seesaw of supply and demand—balancing what we have versus what we want.

Supply and demand is a pretty intuitive theory that we use almost every day without knowing it! There are a lot of complicated graphs that explain it in granular detail, but the general idea is that the price we pay for things is determined by how many people want it (demand) and how much is being produced and sold (supply).

When demand is low (no one wants a thing) and supply is high (there is a lot of a thing being produced), that will push prices down. Conversely, when demand is high (a lot of people want a thing) and supply is low (not a lot of the thing is being produced), that will push prices up.

In 2021, the Pokémon Company printed 9 billion Pokémon cards to stop speculators from making a bunch of money selling rare cards. It was able to stop people from making a bunch of money on the demand for rare cards by simply managing supply and producing more cards. Turn on the supply faucet, and prices usually tend to go down.

Think about Taylor Swift concert tickets in 2023. A lot of people wanted tickets! However, there was not enough space in most of the arenas to hold all the people who wanted to attend the concerts. So, the ticket prices were pushed up to test how much people really wanted tickets—a reflection of the high demand for tickets and the limited supply.

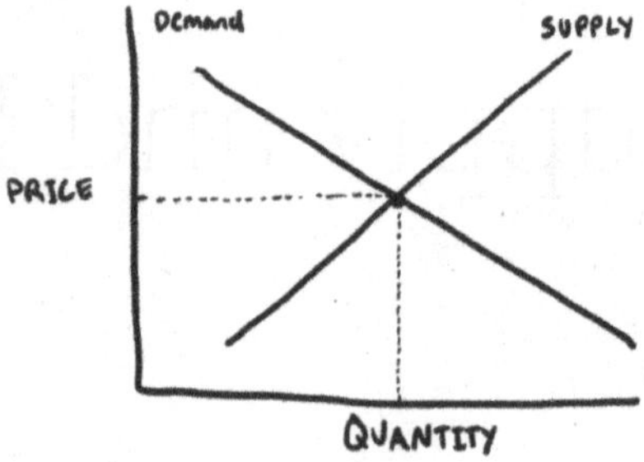

Taylor Swift tickets show the influence of corporations and how sometimes price fluctuations are not just about supply and demand. There was a huge controversy about Ticketmaster price gouging and using weird selling mechanics that kept the prices from being determined by the market. Sometimes corporations, especially those that have a monopoly over what they sell, can set prices regardless of the level of supply and demand.

Supply and demand—it's everywhere and everything.

THE ECONOMICS OF BANANA BREAD

In every marketplace, whether it's global commodities or a local bake sale, the principles of supply and demand are at play. Anyone familiar with planet Earth knows that sellers try to sell their goods and services at the highest price pos-

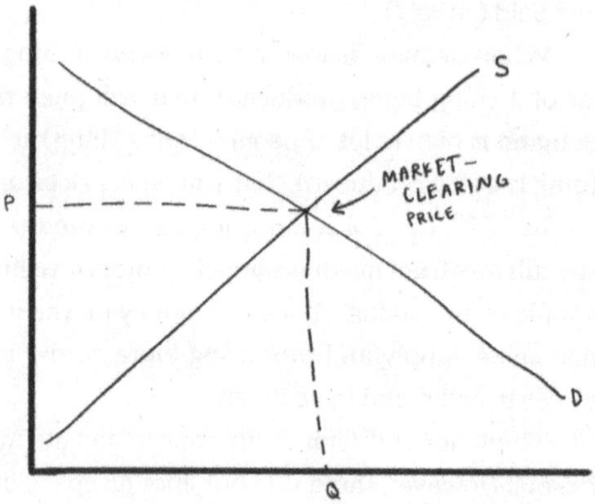

sible, whereas buyers try to buy things at the lowest price possible. The market price is where supply and demand meet: the lowest price a seller will accept and the highest price a buyer will pay.

When supply and demand are balanced, there is a state of equilibrium in which they meet. That is when the market price is reached!

- A price above equilibrium is a price at which people want more things than are available.
- A price below equilibrium is a price at which there are more things available than people want.

Let's visit my grandma's kitchen to see this in action. She's been baking banana bread for the past thirty years, and it's a perfect example to illustrate these concepts.

The demand for Grandma's banana bread is the quantity of bread that customers would buy at all possible prices and is represented by a downward-sloping curve, as shown in the graph on page 48. If Grandma decides to hike up the price of her banana bread, people aren't going to buy as much. But if she lowers the price, they are likely to buy more.

A change in demand might also occur if, for example, a new study comes out that says eating banana bread is healthy for you. Suddenly, more people will want to buy Grandma's banana bread, because they have more incentive to eat it, and the demand curve will shift upward.

On the other hand, the supply of Grandma's banana bread is the quantity that Grandma is willing to produce and sell at all possible prices and is represented by an upward-sloping supply curve.

If the price of the ingredients goes up, it will become more expensive for her to make the bread, so she may produce less. Grandma is willing to sell at each price point along the curve. If prices go up, the quantity supplied of banana bread will increase, and if prices go down, the quantity supplied of banana bread will decrease.

However, if the price of flour goes up—an input to her good—Grandma may have to raise the price of her banana bread or produce less bread to maintain her profit margin. This would result in an upward shift of the supply curve.

The market price of my grandma's banana bread is determined by the intersection of the supply and demand curves—the equilibrium. These are not just abstract economic theories; they're everyday realities impacting how goods (like banana bread) are priced and sold. Supply and demand plays out on a global scale in a more complex and far-reaching system through the intricate and expansive world of supply chains.

SUPPLY CHAINS

While the principles of supply and demand in Grandma's kitchen might seem a world away from global trade, they are indeed connected. The history of supply chains can be traced back to ancient civilizations, where horse-drawn carts moved silks and other wares along newly established trade routes. The early trade networks such as the Silk Road made it possible for global trade to be conducted. The Industrial Revolution was when modern supply chains truly came into existence, with steam-powered ships moving across oceans and railroads crisscrossing nations. Ever since then, supply chains have become increasingly complex—and delicate.

Suppliers use ships, planes, trains, and trucks to rapidly move goods around the world, winding through farms, manufacturing sites, warehouses, distribution centers, retail shelves, and more. However, due to the numerous links in these networks, they are easier to break than to improve, as seen during the covid-19 pandemic, when the global supply chain was disrupted. Planes were grounded. Shipments were delayed or halted, causing a buildup of container ships outside major ports such as Los Angeles. As a result, shipping rates soared, reaching levels not seen in twenty-five years. The already overwhelmed supply chain struggled to cope with the influx of goods and the limited number of available transportation routes, as well as a shortage of personnel and equipment to move the goods.

There are various metrics used to measure the performance of supply chains, such as the Global Supply Chain Pressure Index and the Manheim Used

Vehicle Value Index. This 2022 chart from Apollo shows the decline in container freight rates across the board. It became very expensive to ship things during the pandemic—but then it wasn't expensive as supply chains began to normalize.

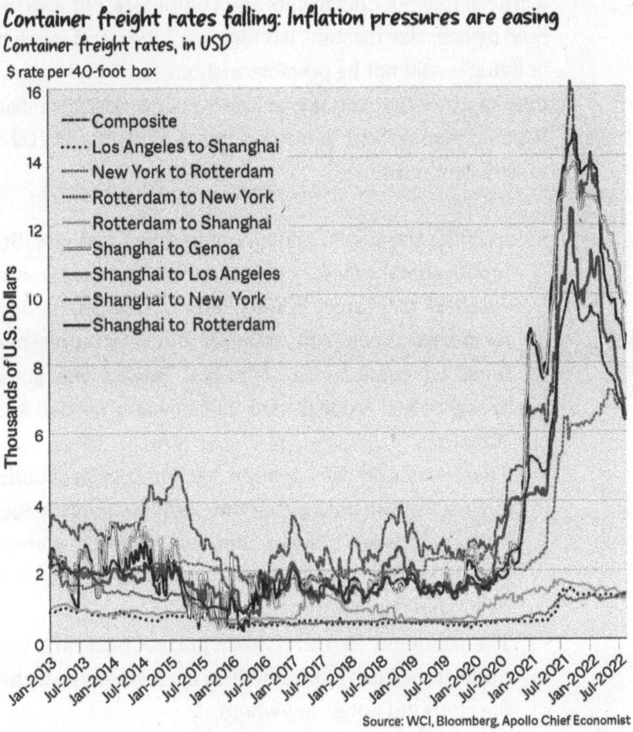

In 2020, the global supply chain fell apart because so many companies had shut down. But the world still had to function, despite the disruptions and challenges that were occurring on an unprecedented scale. The main lesson learned during that time was that supply is not infinite. The early 2020s were when things stopped "thinging." They exposed our fragile reliance on something that powers almost everything in our daily lives and is constantly exposed to natural disasters, geopolitical tensions, and the rickety nature of the physical world. The backbone of our global economy became a question mark rather than a foundation.

SEMICONDUCTORS

Remember those teeny chips that had supply and demand going bonkers? Semiconductors are an electrically conductive material that are the building blocks of modern technology. They're basically the brain of electronics, playing a crucial role not only in cars and computers, but also in a wide array of household devices like toasters, laundry machines, and much more. Most of our ways of living would not be possible without semiconductors. For example, the two-minute timer that you use to brush your teeth? It's reliant on a semiconductor. What happened with semiconductors in 2021 and 2022 was a perfect supply-versus-demand storm.

- In 2020, the covid pandemic shut down factories. Semiconductors can't be produced if the factory isn't running! Factories were also plagued by natural disasters that forced some plants to stop production. In Texas, there were ice storms (a complete anomaly and very representative of the anomalous times we seem to be living in). Taiwan was going through a series of droughts that made it hard for the water needed for chip production to be supplied.
- There was also the constant backdrop of geopolitical tension. China was circling Taiwan during that time, which was stressing everyone out because if China invaded Taiwan, that would greatly increase the probability of a global conflict. Taiwan is the world's leading semiconductor producer, so that created a pressure-cooker situation.
- The pandemic also shut down ports. Chips can't be delivered to manufacturers if they can't be landed! So even when the factories did produce chips, the chips did not go anywhere.
- Later on, demand came into play. The supply chain went into chaos because people were emerging from lockdown and wanted more things, and all those things contained semiconductors.

Various supply issues and outsized demand, coupled with breakdowns in semiconductor production and delivery, produced a perfect storm of not-enoughness. Car companies were reducing production over chip worries, Apple warned that the shortage would impact iPhone production, and there were doubts that the semiconductor supply would *ever* recover.

Ultimately, the issue was solved mostly through policy and technology (although supply chains are never completely perfect). Apple began to make its own chips in-house, switching from Intel to M1; Tesla announced the Dojo supercomputer; and the Taiwanese company TSMC, the world's first and largest semiconductor foundry, announced plans to build factories in the United States. The semiconductor crisis, which rattled the core of global technology and manufacturing industries, extended into the auto market, which was its own peculiar supply-and-demand situation.

USED CARS

Used cars are an essential part of the automotive market, usually providing a very affordable option for those who don't want to buy a new vehicle. But during the pandemic, used cars were more expensive than new cars, which is bonkers! The problem was, of course, caused by supply and demand. Supply chain disruptions, a semiconductor shortage, and a raw materials gap led to issues in producing new cars, and, therefore, car buyers had to buy used cars. Just to make things extra spicy, there was a shortage of used cars, too. There just weren't enough cars anywhere!

That of course led to a wild spike in car prices. January 2021 was the beginning, with the average used-car price reaching a peak of $25,000 in February 2022. In comparison, the median price of used vehicles had been $17,500 in July 2019—a 40 percent jump!

Manheim Used Vehicle Value Index

January 1997–January 2023

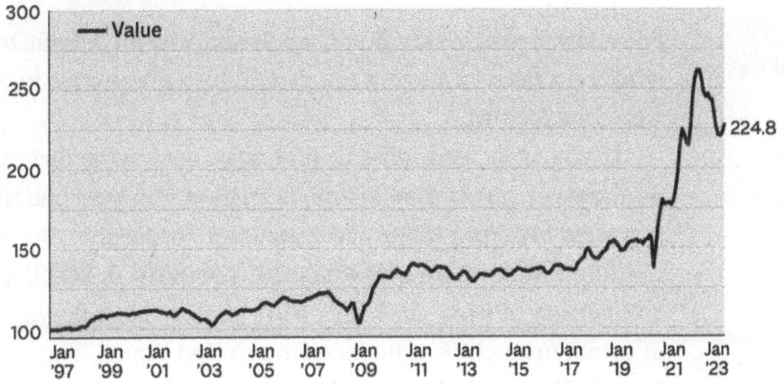

Source: COX Automotive, Manheim

Cars with hundreds of thousands of miles on them were selling for well north of $10,000. This is opposite to how we think the used-car market should work! A new car depreciates by almost 20 percent as soon as you drive it off the lot. A vehicle that has been driven to near nonusability should be inexpensive! Not cost $10,000!

It gets even weirder. Older cars were actually more expensive than younger cars, completely throwing aside any rational market model of pricing. A 2009 Camry went for roughly $8,000 in 2019. The price skyrocketed to $16,000 in 2022. A 2016 Camry going for $22,000 in 2019 sold for $33,000 in 2022. Both cars got more expensive. The price of the 2016 Camry went up 50% but the price of the 2009 Camry doubled—something that doesn't really make a lot of economic sense.

That showed the power of supply and demand. There weren't enough new cars to satisfy the demand, so people turned to used cars. They wanted sedans because they were (theoretically) cheaper. It also showed the pricing power that companies have. Manufacturers' profits surged, as reported by Axios, despite less car production and fewer cars being sold. The whole thing was a mess. It flipped what we understood about markets and pricing dynamics and gave it all a big middle finger.

Used-car prices were a clear example not only of pricing mechanics but also of the importance of supply and demand. In most cases, a supply chain breakdown is the result of policy failure. And policy will be required to repair it.

So let's talk eggs.

EGGFLATION: WHEN EGGS COME IN SHORT SUPPLY

For a few weeks in late 2022, eggflation was a big topic of discussion. People who were used to buying ten dozen eggs a week for bodybuilding purposes were in shambles.

If you were even able to find eggs, they were likely going to cost $3 to $4 more per carton than before. Eggflation was an economic phenomenon that impacted breakfast tables and restaurant chains alike. But how did it happen?

There were quite a few culprits. February 8, 2023, marked the one-year anniversary of when the highly pathogenic avian influenza, or HPAI, was found in commercial chicken flocks in the United States. The infection had begun in Dubois County, Indiana, and spread quickly across the country, decimating chickens and thus the egg supply. In 2022, almost 60 million birds were lost to HPAI. There were roughly 300 million egg-laying hens left at the end of the year, far fewer than normal.

Supply chains also played a role. Chickens eat a *lot* of corn and a *lot* of soybeans. Not only did the cost of chicken feed spike, but breaches in the supply chain made it much more difficult to get the feed to the chickens. (There are still breaches in the supply chain, with millions of chickens starving in California because corn wasn't delivered on time due to delays on the part of the Union Pacific railroad.) Egg suppliers are very reliant on railroads, which means that the supply of eggs can get very volatile very fast—and add to egg price concerns. Compound that with a very cold, wet winter, and the feed supply chain was in shambles.

Then there's demand. We eat way more eggs than we used to! Per capita annual consumption is forty eggs more now than it was in 2012. A greater demand for eggs and not enough egg production due to a lack of laying hens was a recipe for distress.

The egg crisis was bad. Prices shot up quickly and aggressively. But the outrage we saw was largely a function of the media and the story behind *why* eggs were going up in price. When news reporters started complaining about the price of eggs, there actually wasn't much of a markup! Stores were selling eggs for roughly the price at which they were buying them from producers. But once people get freaked out, just as they did about toilet paper during the pandemic, it can lead to an insane price spiral, which was partially what we saw with eggs because the news was like "*there are no eggs go panic mode everyone.*" So of course, people went into panic mode. That put even more pressure on the supply chain because people tried to buy extra eggs and hoard them, which exacerbated the shortage, and so on and so forth.

Hand-wringing headlines created a loop of people freaking out about prices, prices rising, and people freaking out more. As Mike Gauntner, a reporter for 21-WFMJ, wrote, "High consumer prices for shell eggs has [*sic*] caught the attention of the national media, raising consumer awareness and fueling a rising resistance." That's why Jerome Powell, the chair of the Federal Reserve, prefers rational inattention to inflation; if people are watching what is going on, they are more likely to respond to it, which can exacerbate the issue at hand.

What got less coverage was that, adjusted for inflation, egg prices were actually lower in 2022 than they had been in 2015. Prices peaked in December 2022, with a dozen eggs selling for around $5 on average. Egg supply and prices were already recovering in early 2023. Producer prices, the prices farmers charge grocery stores, began to fall. The retail price, the price consumers pay in the grocery store, fell sharply (by $1 in one week in early January!) and continued to fall into 2023.

The moral of the story is: We need more egg-laying chickens.

The eggflation story is emblematic of what could happen to the rest of the economy. We are dependent on fragile systems that can break when stressed.

BEYOND MECHANICS AND INTO POLICY

The basic idea is this: When there is more demand for a thing than there is supply, the number of people wanting it is greater than how much is available and the price will rise to sift out the people who don't truly want the thing. If there is a greater supply than demand, more people are selling the thing than buying it and the price will drop. But we've seen one price distortion after another in recent years, thanks to the screams of the media, reflexivity, shortages of raw goods, supply chain disruption, and good old-fashioned price gouging. How can this be fixed? By fixing the bad policy that creates misdirected incentives.

MAKING SUPPLY CHAINS BETTER

After what happened to supply chains in the first two years of the 2020s, businesses and local government bodies *should* be funneling money into capital investment: repairing or upgrading old equipment (such as installing air-conditioning units inside delivery trucks), buying new equipment (including new cranes and larger container ships), investing in new technology (such as a software system that doesn't have employees tearing their hair out or logistics services that improve tracking and inventory management), building bigger warehouses and fulfillment centers (which are needed especially in the ecommerce industry), and more. All of this is done with the goal of helping goods, services, and information flow more efficiently and making workers less miserable.

Of course, putting money toward rebuilding supply chains isn't as exciting as investing in the hot new thing, whether it be deepfakes, artificial intelligence, or cryptocurrency. One of the most crucial links in the supply chain was built on the premise that workers would provide labor for free. As Bloomberg journalists wrote:

> *Port truckers are typically independent contractors, without the benefits and protections of unionized transport sectors or even major com-*

panies with shipping divisions, such as Amazon. Their jobs require them to line up for hours to pick up cargo, and they're paid only when they move it. "The port truck driver, for decades now, has basically been the slack adjuster in the whole system," said Steve Viscelli, an economic sociologist with the University of Pennsylvania who studies labor markets and supply chains. The entire system, he said, is built around free labor from truck drivers as they wait for containers.

Essentially, companies tell their truck drivers and crane operators, "Hey, listen, we are going to underpay you, we are going to expect you to do more work than you should and thus create a completely misaligned incentive structure."

In 2020, all the small details of our supply chains were highlighted: railroads, ports, and cranes; how long ships spend at the dock and the touch points for the RTG/RMG container crane operators, truck drivers, and clerks; how long containers sit without drivers available to drive them away; maintenance of yard equipment; package unloading. Each of these factors has a cascading, knock-on effect.

Policymakers aren't directing dollars to where they need to go. When the 2020 financial crisis occurred, the government was able to solve the problem by providing monetary support—a *lot* of monetary support. But when ports shut down, they can't be reopened the same way. Real-world solutions are called for. Anthony Lee Zhang, a professor at the University of Chicago, once tweeted, "As resources get cheaper, we find progressively dumber uses of them."

Things like artificial intelligence, autonomous vehicles, 3D printing, virtual reality, and potential innovations like quantum computing will of course change how we interact with the world. But we have gotten very good at taking raw materials out of the earth and making things out of them. However, the cost of repairing things (labor) has skyrocketed, hence the "I'll buy cheap things because they're cheap rather than repairing those I already have" mindset.

That's the thing about presumed infinity. Because we live in a time of abundance in most developed nations, it can feel as though we are always going to have everything, forever. But the reality is that we aren't always going to have everything, forever.

CHAPTER 6

GDP and the Economy

GDP is the total market value of all finished goods and services produced *within* a country's borders. It serves as a comprehensive scorecard of a country's economic health, measuring both (1) the total income in the economy and (2) the total expenditure on what an economy produces (goods and services).

MEASURING GDP

GDP is usually expressed in an equation:

GDP = C + G + I + NX
Where

C = consumption
G = government purchases
I = investment
NX = net exports

Most economists explain GDP via a pie chart, but I think it makes more sense to explain it with a diagram, where we can zoom in on consumer spending, the most critical component of GDP.

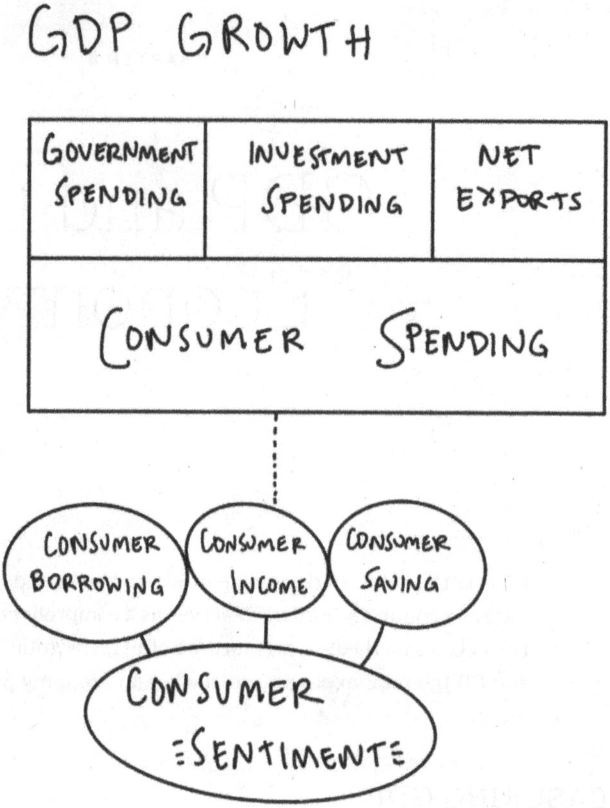

CONSUMPTION

This is what people buy. It is normally divided into three main categories: non-durable goods (things that don't last long, such as food and gasoline), durable goods (things that last a long time, such as cars and furniture), and services (getting things done, such as getting a haircut and going to the doctor). Consumer sentiment serves as a baseline input for all of this, as how people feel about the general economic situation ultimately impacts what they do and buy. Consumer spending is fueled by:

1. **Income:** How much money people are making in their jobs
2. **Borrowing:** How much people are borrowing and how often they are using their credit cards to finance purchases

3. **Savings:** How much people are saving from their income and how much they are spending relative to how much they make

INVESTMENT

This is people and businesses spending money on things that will generate economic benefits over a long period. It could be the auto parts factory getting a new machine to produce components faster (this is known as business fixed investment), someone buying a newly constructed house—rather than an old house—(residential investment), or clothing stores stocking up on sweaters for the holiday season (inventory investment).

GOVERNMENT PURCHASES

Government purchases can range from desks for government offices to tankers for the military. This is money spent directly on goods and services that the government buys, and it excludes government transfers such as stimulus checks, because the money from those goes back into the economy when people spend them.

NET EXPORTS

This is the dollar value of the products that we buy from other countries (imports) minus the dollar value of products that other countries buy from us (exports). Put simply, it refers to all the things that U.S. companies make that are shipped overseas (exports) and all the things that people in the United States buy from overseas (imports). This is used to measure what share of the things consumed or invested in within the United States are produced domestically.

Finally, the difference between nominal and real GDP is pretty important.

- **Nominal GDP:** This measures the value of goods and services at current prices, thus including the effects of inflation. It doesn't provide an accurate picture of economic growth, as price increases can inflate GDP figures without reflecting real output.
- **Real GDP:** Adjusted for inflation, it reflects the actual growth in goods and services, offering a more accurate depiction of economic progress.

THE GINGERBREAD YETI ECONOMY

Let's say there is a country called Gingerbread Yeti, a booming nation populated by giant gingerbread people who have a strong and growing economy. Its nominal GDP is calculated as follows:

- Consumption = $17 trillion. The Gingerbread Yeti people are consuming roughly $17 trillion in goods every year! We could further break this down into nondurable goods, durable goods, and services, but the main thing is that the people are spending!
- Government purchases = $6 trillion. The Gingerbread Yeti government has bought a bunch of military tankers, which contributed to GDP growth.
- Investment = $5 trillion. Gingerbread Yeti businesses are spending money on new machinery and buying up newly constructed gingerbread houses.
- Net exports = ($1 trillion). Gingerbread Yeti businesses also sold a lot of goods abroad! However, the country imported more goods than it exported, leading to the negative number.

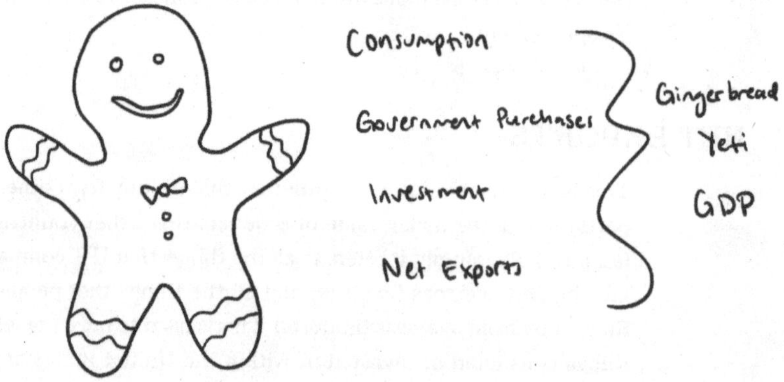

So the nominal GDP of the Gingerbread Yeti economy is roughly $27 trillion. Not bad! Assuming an inflation rate of 2 percent, the Gingerbread Yeti economy has a Real GDP of:

Nominal GDP = $27 trillion
Deflator (1 + the inflation rate) = 1 + 0.02 = 1.02
Real Nominal GDP = Nominal GDP / Deflator Rate = $26.47 Trillion

But *how* economies grow, including the Gingerbread Yeti Economy, matters. Contrary to popular belief, government debt isn't always a bad thing. But too much of anything, from Sour Patch Kids watermelon candy to government debt, is harmful.

DEBT-FUELED GROWTH

Fiscal growth, or economic expansion influenced by government policies on spending and taxation, can sometimes lead to short-term increases in nominal GDP. This happens when a government either boosts its spending or cuts taxes, stimulating the economy.

However, this type of growth can often be fueled by increased borrowing, leading to higher national debt. While such debt-fueled growth can initially uplift economic indicators like nominal GDP, it may threaten the economy's long-term health.

- When is it okay? Debt-fueled growth is considered healthy when it involves investment in productive assets, when interest rates are low, and when the debt-to-GDP ratio is stable or decreasing. This indicates that the economy is growing in proportion to its debt.
- When is it not okay? Debt-fueled growth is concerning when debt is already at unsustainable levels with no clear repayment plan. It's also concerning when creditors lose confidence—meaning that no one trusts that the debt will be used efficiently.

Rating agencies such as Fitch, Moody's, and S&P play a significant role in determining the path of debt-fueled growth. In August 2023, Fitch Ratings, one of the rating agencies that evaluates government creditworthiness, downgraded the United States due to worries over the national debt and fiscal deterioration. S&P had already downgraded the United States back in 2011 because of the government shutdown fiasco over the debt ceiling.

Fitch pointed out that legislators seemingly did not care that there was no safety net for Social Security and Medicare costs despite the rapidly aging population, as well as the lack of a medium-term fiscal framework, complex budgeting, and the continued fights over the debt ceiling. It also cited concerns over rising interest expenses. The Fed was raising rates to battle inflation, but that had created a substantial burden for the U.S. government to make the payments on government debt. Interest expenses surged in 2023, growing by about 50 percent to $1 trillion.

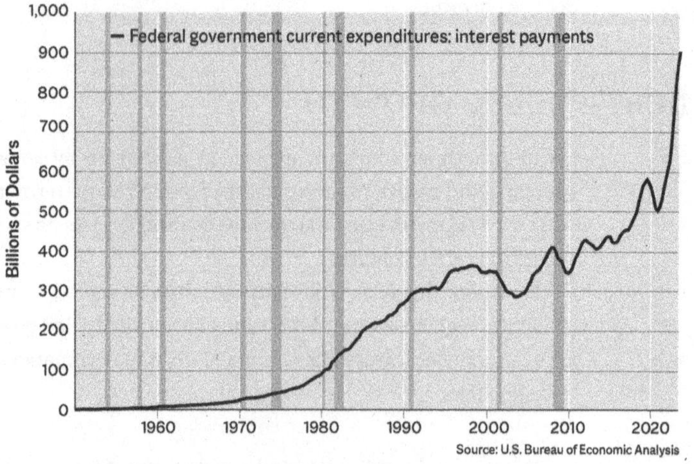

Basically, Fitch was saying, "The U.S. debt situation kind of sucks, and it's only getting worse." But GDP is growing, so everything is okay, right?

Right?

WHAT DOES GDP REALLY MEAN?

There's a point to be made that GDP is not a reliable measure of our economy in a social-media, hyper-online, tech-driven world. That seems like a big thing to write about in an economics-oriented book, but the big thing that's important for you to take away is that our economy has changed, but our measurement methodology hasn't.

What does it mean to have a "strong" GDP? Does it mean that people are healthy and happy (what even is happiness?), or does it just mean that they are spending money? And if they are spending money, does that somehow mean that they are happy and healthy?

There are a few different ways to slice and dice the data.

Real GDP per capita (remember, we want to control for inflation, which is why we are using real and not nominal GDP) is a preferred measure of calculating consumer well-being. This is a country's total GDP divided by its population. It tells us how much an average person can buy in a year. It measures the economic output per person.

Productivity is another possible measure. This is a driving force of economic growth that is equal to the ratio between output volume and input volume and therefore shows how efficiently labor and capital—such as factories and equipment—are used to produce something.

THE PRODUCTIVITY PARADOX

In 1987, the economist Robert Solow said, "You can see the computer age everywhere but in the productivity statistics," referencing the dramatic slowdown in productivity in the United States despite outsized investments in technology. In the 1990s, the world caught up to tech, with huge amounts of innovation in semiconductors, manufacturing, supply chains, and more. The computer age had arrived, culminating in the 1999 tech bubble. But productivity stagnation happened again from the 2000s to the 2020s, even with cloud computing, AI, and the Internet of Things; all those resources were available, but productivity was flat. Presumably, productivity will improve as it did after the 1980s, but there are many questions as to when and how and if. With the advent of AI and quantum computing and all those big technical advances, it certainly seems like we will get some sort of productivity. The big question is, will it look like people getting more efficient, or will it look like computers taking over?

GDP might not be an accurate reflection of the economy. Many people have written about how GDP kind of sucks, but a more important consideration is how the suck manifests in our lives. When we use metrics that kind of suck and those metrics say that things suck, we get a double dose of suck. This margin of suck is essential: If the metric can't even measure how much things suck but then loudly underscores that yes indeed, things suck, it is a very bad combination for consumer sentiment!

We live in a consumption-on-demand world, with our lives designed around the presumption that we can and should be constantly consuming—fast fashion, shopping malls, and advertising being the main revenue models of many of our big tech and retail companies. Everything can be bought quickly—and discarded quickly, too.

This is another trade-off of economic growth. It's really nice to have a big, booming economy, as the Gingerbread Yeti people do, but there are costs to unconstrained bigness and boomness. One of the biggest prices we pay lies in our tendency to focus on short-term gains at the expense of long-term stability. Currently, we are seeing this play out in the form of severe harm to our climate and workers' mental health, and the phenomenon of "planned obsolescence."

This is the hyper-consumptionist concept of intentionally designing products to have a limited life span—a strategy that so many companies have implemented to increase their profits.

Think about how silly it is that we "need" to buy a new cell phone every few years because the phone simply stops working. Reflect on the alarming reality that global temperatures keep rising and have reached 2.5°C above preindustrial averages, putting 30 percent of the earth's species at risk in areas surpassing their thermal adaptation thresholds. Think about the countless workers experiencing severe burnout who don't have enough sick days to take time off work to recover.

GROWTH AT ANY COST

Growth at any cost isn't humane. When we put the economy ahead of human lives, it creates perverse incentives that benefit only a few (usually the very wealthy). A few schools of thought—including degrowth, ecological economics, postgrowth, and more—challenge the idea of GDP as the main measure of progress.

- **Degrowth:** This philosophy asserts that in order to address environmental issues and social inequalities, advanced economies need to reduce their scale of production and consumption. Instead of focusing on "growing" the economy, it emphasizes creating an economy that meets human needs within ecological limits.
- **Ecological Economics:** This school of thought focuses on sustainability. It posits that economies are bound by environmental limits and that we should aim for an equilibrium rather than perpetual growth.
- **Postgrowth:** This theory suggests that societies can achieve prosperity and well-being without perpetual economic expansion. It emphasizes the importance of developing new indicators of progress, ones that better reflect societal well-being and ecological health.

They propose that progress should be evaluated based on the quality of life, equal access to resources, and the environmental impacts of human activity. Going back to the point about spending money versus being happy, we constantly focus on the idea of the Capital-*C* Consumer as a tool for economic growth, which has worked in the past, but at a cost. It's no secret that consumerism, the focus on material possessions and the endless pursuit of economic growth, isn't really that great for either us or the planet. There is a passage from Matt Haig's *Notes on a Nervous Planet* that's always stuck with me:

> *If everyone is spending hour after hour on their phones, scrolling through texts and timelines, that becomes normal behavior.... If everyone is maxing out their credit cards to pay for things they don't really need, then it can't be a problem. If the whole planet is having a kind of collective breakdown, then unhealthy behavior fits right in. When normality becomes madness, the only way to find sanity is by daring to be different. Or daring to be the you that exists beyond all the physical clutter and mind debris of modern existence.*

In a world that sees us merely as vectors for economic growth, how can we truly be ourselves?

LOOKING TO THE FUTURE

The way that we think about the economy is going to have to evolve. It probably can't be based on Big Growth forever. As economists at the Federal Reserve Bank of Dallas wrote in 2022, "As trend GDP growth slows due to aging demographics and slower productivity gains, *there may be more frequent periods of negative GDP growth without an increase in unemployment*, making the distinction between increasing slack and declining activity more relevant than in the past." (Author's emphasis.)

A rising GDP often signifies economic growth, and nations worldwide have long pursued policies to boost this number. However, as we grapple with global challenges such as climate change, income inequality, and diminishing natural resources, there is a growing awareness that we need a rethinking of success that goes beyond our current economic metrics—a global consensus for change. It's becoming increasingly clear that GDP alone may not be a holistic measure of well-being or societal progress.

So when we talk about "growth," and GDP, we must consider all of these other policies—safety nets, fiscal frameworks, budgeting, and more. Growth doesn't matter if there is nothing to support people. Of course, as I've discussed extensively, data shape our reality—but a large portion of the data are influenced by vibes. And if the vibes get worse, so will the economic reality. As Terry Pratchett wrote in *Night Watch:*

Tomorrow the sun will come up again, and I'm pretty sure that whatever happens we won't have found Freedom, and there won't be a whole lot of Justice, and I'm damn *sure we won't have found Truth. But it's just possible that I might get a hard-boiled egg.*

We seek many things. The simplest ones, such as hard-boiled eggs, are usually the most reliable, especially compared to more complicated ones such as Freedom, Truth, and GDP.

CHAPTER 7

Commodities

The reasonable man adapts himself to the world: the unreasonable one persists in trying to adapt the world to himself. Therefore all progress depends on the unreasonable man.

—GEORGE BERNARD SHAW

When it comes to the economy, it's important to remember that (at least right now) we are humans here on Earth. Despite all our computers and cool AI tools, we still need to eat food. Get electricity. Have running water. And because of that we need commodities.

Commodities are the raw materials that create the building blocks of our economy. They are the common denominator of everything we interact with. On the surface, they may seem incredibly simple—of course, it seems like oil will always come out of the ground and copper will always be mined (until it runs out). These are commodities! They are the foundations of life.

GLOBALIZATION AND COMMODITIES

Globalization is a core component of how our world works, and it has arguably helped create the standard of living we have today. A lot of countries rely on imports for the majority of their consumption, and that isn't a bad thing! Comparative advantage allows countries that are theoretically "better" at producing certain goods and commodities to produce them and, theoretically, the utilization of resources should be more effective across the board. For instance, warm and humid Mexico is much better at growing oranges than cold Canada is—so Mexico, based on its climate, should have a comparative advantage in orange production.

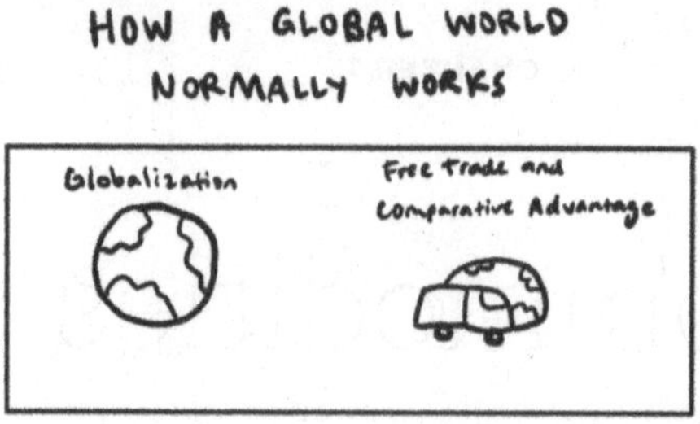

However, wars, pandemics, and natural disasters such as floods and wildfires can massively disrupt global supply chains, destabilizing industries and even entire economies. Recently, the supply of wheat, fertilizer, oils, and other products from major producers such as Russia and Ukraine basically disappeared due to the war, reverberating down the entire supply chain.

COMMON COMMODITIES

AGRICULTURAL PRODUCTS

- Corn: A grain crop used for animal feed, ethanol products, and food products
- Sugar: A sweetener made from sugarcane
- Soybeans: Legumes used in animal feed, cooking oil, and food products
- Cotton: A soft, fluffy fiber used to make clothing, bedding, and other textiles
- Live and feeder cattle: Live cattle are cows that are raised for meat; feeder cattle are young cattle that are raised for a period of time before being sold to feedlots.
- Wheat: A cereal grain used in flour production, animal feed, and food products

ENERGY

- Natural gas: A fossil fuel used primarily for heating and electricity generation
- Ethanol: A biofuel made from corn or other plant materials and used as a gasoline additive to reduce emissions
- Heating oil: A fuel oil used for heating homes and buildings
- Gasoline: A fuel made from crude oil that is used for transportation
- West Texas Intermediate (WTI) crude oil: A benchmark grade of crude oil that is used to price other types of crude oil
- Brent crude oil: Another benchmark grade of crude oil that is used to price other types of crude oil
- Coal: A fossil fuel used primarily in electricity generation and steel production

INDICES

- Baltic Dry Index: A measure of the cost of shipping dry bulk commodities such as iron ore, coal, and grain by sea

Other downsides of globalization are well established: Greater benefits are reaped by multinational corporations and the extremely wealthy than the general population; the environmental impact from the emissions generated by the planes, trains, and trucks transporting goods around the world; and increased interdependency among countries that have begun to rely more and more on one another in an era of increasing geopolitical instability.

EXTERNAL FACTORS AND COMMODITIES

These effects are compounded by the fact that most products we buy require inputs from other products—that are often imported—to manufacture them. Natural gas and potash go into fertilizer, fertilizer goes into crops, and so on. Grain represents the number one cost of feeding cattle, so when grain prices increase, the cost of cattle and therefore meat is going to increase, too. If one of the commodity dominoes tips, the entire line begins to topple.

- Commodity Research Bureau (CRB) Index: A commodity price index that tracks the prices of nineteen commodities, including energy, metals, and agricultural products
- London Metal Exchange (LME) Index: An index that tracks the prices of a variety of metals, including aluminum, copper, zinc, lead, nickel, and tin
- S&P GSCI Index: Formerly the Goldman Sachs Commodity Index; a commodity price index that tracks the prices of twenty-four commodities, including energy, metals, and agricultural products

METALS

- Gold: A precious metal used in making jewelry, as an investment vehicle, and as a reserve asset by central banks
- Steel: A metal alloy made primarily from iron and used in construction, infrastructure projects, and manufacturing
- Aluminum: A lightweight metal used for a wide range of products, including packaging, construction materials, and transportation equipment
- Silver: A precious metal used in making jewelry, as an investment vehicle, and as an industrial metal in manufacturing electronics, medical equipment, and solar panels
- Copper: A metal used in electrical wiring, plumbing, and a wide range of other products
- Lithium: A key component of lithium-ion batteries, a big part of electric vehicles and energy storage
- Spodumene: A lithium-containing ore that is plentiful in the United States and can be stored safely and economically
- Cobalt: An element of lithium-ion batteries that adds stability to various processes; there are a lot of concerns over ethical sourcing of cobalt
- Nickel: A key component of batteries; helps with battery performance, energy density, and stability

A good example of this was what happened to Pakistan during the start of the European energy crisis in 2022. As Bloomberg reported, Pakistan State Oil Company wasn't able to buy diesel fuel from Kuwait Petroleum Corporation because at that time "product [was] moving toward the west." Pakistan wanted to buy, but the European countries captured the available supply because they could pay a premium over what Pakistan was willing to pay. This kind of situation has a lot of ramifications—specifically, exacerbating inequality between the developed and developing worlds and making it so those who can pay more might be the only ones who can stay alive. It's a "those who pay can play" situation.

Commodity crises are a great reminder to pay attention. This stuff feels so simple, so easy, but when it's gone, a process that will only be accelerated by climate change, the fallout is calamitous.

OIL

For better or worse, oil is a crucial commodity, and its markets are some of the most closely watched in the world. The price of crude oil is a broad indicator of the entire economy's health, impacting everything from the cost of transportation to what we pay for the petroleum-based plastic food containers at the grocery store.

Oil prices are volatile because of geopolitical realities. Recently, Saudi Arabia and Russia have drawn closer together, which could elevate oil prices more in coming years as the two countries work in cahoots. The two countries set oil production levels together—as the top two oil exporting countries in 2023—and this decided supply of oil is what determines the price of oil. However, oil supply is tenuous. Shale oil producers and OPEC underinvested in production for many years, making it more difficult to produce oil, thereby making it more expensive.

GAS PRICES

Gasoline prices are a direct way that consumers feel the impact of changing oil prices, particularly in the United States. While one might expect that oil and gasoline prices have a linear relationship, they do not! When oil prices increase, gasoline prices increase, too; but when oil prices *decrease*, gasoline prices... don't. Which is cute!

A research paper titled "Do Gasoline Prices Respond Asymmetrically to Crude Oil Price Changes?" made a key observation:

- When crude oil prices increase by a certain amount, the corresponding increase in gasoline prices at the pump tends to be *even greater*, costing consumers more than the increase in crude oil prices.
- On the other hand, when crude oil prices decrease, the corresponding decrease in gasoline prices at the pump tends to be *smaller*, saving consumers less than the decrease in crude oil prices!

In other words, the relationship between crude oil price changes and gasoline price changes is not equal in both directions. This phenomenon is known as *asymmetric price transmission* or "rocket and feathers."

- When oil prices increase, gas prices go up, too—like a rocket shooting into outer space!
- But when oil prices fall, gasoline prices also fall—but at a slower rate. Like a gracefully falling feather, weaving its way across the sky.

This is why gas prices can stay high, even as oil prices drop.

This asymmetry in price changes is annoying and means that regardless of the volatility and variability of oil prices, they will have a negative impact on people's wallets. Even though consumers might benefit when crude oil prices decline, they do not fully reap the savings that might be expected based on the magnitude of the drop in crude oil costs.

Variability is bad! And that's what we have had a lot of as a world during the past few years.

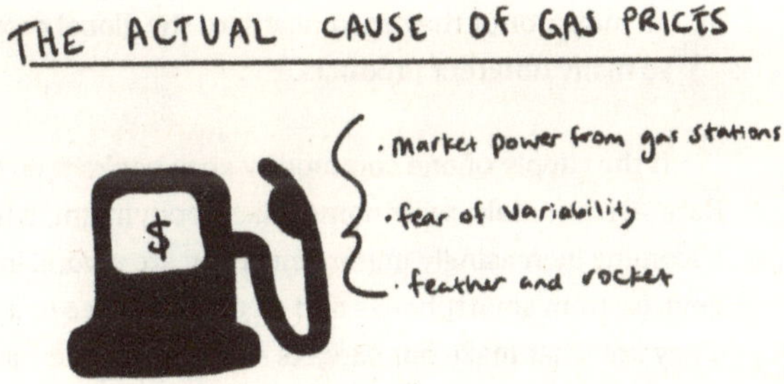

The rocket-and-feather world of gas prices is determined by a combination of:

- **The market power of gas stations.** Gasoline is what's called an inelastic good; most of us have to buy it even if the price goes up. Refiners acquire crude oil and turn it into fuel, and then it's sent to service stations and distribution facilities, which all costs money.

- **Fear of price variability.** If oil prices go up again, gas stations don't want to be caught on the wrong foot. It's much easier to keep gasoline prices high to hedge against that.

The problem is that gasoline prices are a political hot potato in the United States. If they are high, people are not happy with their politicians. Thus, a lot of "friendships" (trade partnerships) are forged by the price of gas. The energy trade is sort of the world's balancing act. We know that we all have to get along, because if we don't, there goes the functionality of everything we interact with.

METALS

Metals play a crucial role in our daily lives and in the global economy. Steel, copper, aluminum, and other metals are the foundations of the objects we interact with every day.

- Steel is used in construction, infrastructure, cars, appliances, and many other products.
- Aluminum is a lightweight metal used in airplanes, bikes, tech products like phones, and cans and is tightly tied to transportation and packaging.
- Copper is used in electrical wiring, electronics, plumbing, and coins and is an indicator of the broad health of the global economy because it's used in so many different products.

If the supply of one commodity goes bonkers, so does that of all the others. Rare earth metals, with names like neodymium, lanthanum, and cerium, are becoming increasingly important. They are pivotal in manufacturing high-tech devices, from smartphones and electric vehicles to advanced military systems. They are what make our gadgets smaller, batteries last longer, and electric motors more efficient.

But, of course, it's a geopolitical hot potato. Most of these metals are mined and processed in a handful of countries, with China being the dominant player. Supply-chain concentration and environmental costs are headwinds, as we increasingly grapple with the idea that our current path of technological advancement hinges on us having the real world figured out.

THE RISE OF U.S. SHALE OIL PRODUCTION

The rise of U.S. shale oil production is an excellent illustration of the dysfunctional dynamics of the commodities markets. In the late 2000s and into the 2010s, cheap ways to get hydrocarbons from shale rock formations were discovered, and shale oil extraction technology improved so much that U.S. shale producers were able to produce more oil than the traditional producers such as Saudi Arabia and Iran.

When the United States began producing shale oil, all of a sudden the proverbial geopolitical table turned; there was a new oil king in town. It also changed U.S. employment patterns, increasing jobs in the oil industry and creating a reduced reliance on oil imports. OPEC and other producers had to adjust their output (and economic growth projections) to maintain prices.

However, shale oil producers got a little too excited and produced too much shale oil. That caused a glut of oil and gas, putting downward pressure on prices and making everyone pretty mad. Especially the investors in the shale industry! The shale oil industry burned through enough cash during that time to make those people very upset—to the point where "capital preservation" became a key part of the energy industry.

After Russia invaded Ukraine, there was an energy crisis in Europe, because both Russia and Ukraine are suppliers of oil to the European energy market. Ideally, U.S. shale oil production should have been increased during that time to make up for the lost supply, but investors in the industry were still not happy. The industry had lit its investors' money on fire a few times during the past several years (to the tune of $600 billion), and now investors are being very conservative. They say, "Shale, please focus on giving us money! Thanks! No more expansion, no more rapid growth, just free cash flow and dividend yields, and that's all."

So the shale people are like, "Ah, okay, no problem, sugar dad—I mean *shale daddy.*" They remained focused on providing returns to investors instead of meeting the European demand for oil that Russia and Ukraine can't supply because of the war and OPEC can't supply because of misaligned incentives. This created value for shareholders at the expense of the global energy market as demands were not met with supply, even though the market demanded it!

THE RISE OF RENEWABLES

Many might be asking, "What about renewables? Surely we have made great progress there?" We have! But unfortunately, green energy policy cannot be carried out without green energy investment. We have to deal with the "oil spill" before we can make a full transition to more sustainable resources. But everyone is like, "What if we just drive electric vehicles? That will show Big Oil!" Electric vehicles (EVs) are great, but the raw materials and metals needed to produce EVs and their batteries are all increasing in cost due to their increased demand—and there is not enough manufacturing capacity. For instance, lithium, crucial for battery production, has gone exponential in price. And it just gets back to the idea that we can't have green energy without dirty energy. We need oil to build out the infrastructure to make EVs, solar panels, and nuclear reactors.

The shift to renewable energy isn't just about technological advancements—it hinges crucially on global cooperation. Climate change, after all, doesn't care about borders. To effectively transition to renewables, countries must transcend their individual interests and work together. This means wealthy nations aiding less developed ones through technology transfers and financial support. It's about more than just signing international agreements like the Paris Climate Accord. It's about actual, tangible actions.

We're talking about easing trade barriers to allow the free flow of renewable tech, sharing breakthroughs in energy storage and efficiency, and truly committing to a collective approach. However, the challenge lies in aligning disparate economic interests and political agendas. It's a delicate dance of diplomacy and mutual understanding as the world tries to balance national priorities with the pressing need for a sustainable future.

The green energy transition isn't a clean break; it's a complex, winding road toward progress. It involves balancing our current energy needs with the goal of a more sustainable future. As we navigate this path, both at the domestic and global level, we must be mindful of the economic, environmental, and logistical challenges that come with such a monumental shift in how we power our world in a more sustainable way.

ARTIFICIAL INTELLIGENCE AND COMMODITIES

There is a world in which AI helps us manage our crops, sow them in the perfect temperature, and provide them with the perfect amount of water, but it is dependent on an electrical grid! Similarly, in the mining industry, AI can significantly enhance the extraction of the key commodities like steel and copper that I mentioned. By using machine-learning algorithms, mining operations can predict and locate resource deposits more accurately, improving efficiency and reducing environmental impact. But it all required a foundation. AI requires massive computational power and servers that run constantly. That is a risk!

We need food. We need copper and steel and wheat and corn and lumber. The maintenance of the real world outside the vast and deep void of the internet is important! Commodity shortages remind us that, as the evolutionary biologist Lynn Margulis put it, "We abide in a symbiotic world." She wrote about lichen, a partnership of algae and fungi, as a metaphor for the interdependence of all living things, surviving through collaboration rather than competition:

> *Like a farmer tending her apple trees and her field of corn, a lichen is a melding of lives. Once individuality dissolves, the scorecard of victors and victims makes little sense. Is corn oppressed? Does the farmer's dependence on corn make her a victim? These questions are premised on a separation that does not exist. The heartbeat of humans and the flowering of domesticated plants are one life. "Alone" is not an option.*

The brilliance of AI's computational power is linked to the raw, tangible materials it helps to produce and manage. It's a symbiotic relationship where each domain—the digital and the material—enhances and enables the other, illustrating that our digital-driven world and journey toward a more AI-integrated future is as much about the resources we extract from the earth as it is about the data we extract from our algorithms.

Nature is part of us, and so are commodities—because they are part of nature. We need to respect that fact in our pursuit of survival.

CHAPTER 8

Inflation

Panics do not destroy capital; they merely reveal the extent to which it has been previously destroyed by its betrayal into hopelessly unproductive works.

—JOHN STUART MILL

Inflation is a decline in purchasing power over time: Your dollar buys less than it used to, and your paycheck doesn't go as far as you need it to. As Ryan Sweet at Moody's calculated in 2022, inflation running at a 7.5 percent yearly rate costs the average consumer approximately $276 per month.

Inflation began to decelerate into late 2023, falling from a peak of 9.1 percent in June 2022 to 3 percent by June 2023. This is disinflation, a slower rate of price increases over time. This means that prices are still rising but at a more moderate pace compared to the previous period.

Just because the inflation rate is falling doesn't mean that *prices* are falling. The inflation rate is a percentage change, not a change in price level. So when news headlines say, "Inflation Rate Falls to 3 Percent," that doesn't mean that prices fell three percent; it just means that the rate of change of price increases fell three percent.

TYPES OF FLATION

There are a lot of "other-flations" that we have to deal with, too.

Deflation is when the inflation rate falls below zero, indicating a decrease in the general price level of goods and services. Hyperinflation, on the other hand, is an extreme form of inflation where prices skyrocket at an extraordinarily rapid rate, often leading to a loss of confidence in the currency as it becomes worth a lot less. Stagflation is another complex economic condition, characterized by slow economic growth, high unemployment, and high inflation. It leads to an economic downturn while simultaneously causing the cost of living to rise basically exponentially—a combination for disaster.

I remember buying a carton of strawberries sometime in 2022, looking at the $3 price tag, and thinking, "I remember when these were $2—like a year ago!" Things got really expensive really fast in the early 2020s due to these outsize inflationary pressures.

In order to better understand inflation, there are some key metrics to look at.

MEASURING INFLATION

- **Consumer Price Index (CPI):** Tracks changes in the prices of a basket of goods and services consumed by households, covering food, housing, transportation, healthcare, education, and more.
- **Personal Consumption Expenditures (PCE):** Based on expenditure data, it tracks changes in the prices of goods and services consumed by individuals or households.
- **Wholesale Price Index (WPI):** Tracks changes in the prices of goods at the wholesale level, focusing on the prices paid by businesses for goods they purchase for further processing or resale.
- **Producer Price Index (PPI):** Tracks changes in prices received by domestic producers for their output.
- **GDP Deflator:** Tracks changes in prices across the economy, measured by comparing nominal GDP with real GDP. (This is what we used with the Gingerbread Yeti Economy.)

THE CONSUMER PRICE INDEX: THE PEOPLE'S INFLATION

Understanding the Consumer Price Index (CPI) is crucial, as it measures the average change in prices of goods and services paid by urban consumers. It is used to adjust Social Security payments and is also the reference rate for financial instruments, like Treasury Inflation-Protected Securities (TIPS), that help safeguard your money *against* inflation. The basket of goods and services includes such things as food, housing, transportation, and medical care.

It's a way to track how much more or less things cost for the average person. To calculate the CPI:

- The Bureau of Labor Statistics (BLS) is responsible for calculating the CPI. They survey thousands of households across the country to gather data on what they buy and how much they pay for it.
- The BLS then uses this information to create a "market basket" of goods and services representing what the average household buys. The market basket tracks a lot of things: foods and beverages, housing, transportation, medical care, education, recreation, apparel, and other goods and services, such as haircuts and household cleaning supplies.
- Then the BLS compares the price of this year's basket to the basket price of previous years, enabling the BLS to determine the inflation rate. This method of measuring inflation is followed by other countries as well, and each country has its own entity that measures its own inflation basket, which can vary from country to country.

Here are some examples of how baskets vary across different countries:

1. United Kingdom (Office for National Statistics):
   • Food: fish, tea
   • Clothing & footwear: women's leggings, men's athletic shoes
   • Recreation & culture: streaming music subscriptions, ebooks
   • Restaurants & hotels: takeaway coffee, pub snacks
2. Japan (Statistics Bureau of Japan):
   • Food: fresh fish, rice, mochi
   • Clothing: women's suits
   • Culture and recreation: karaoke box fees
3. India (Ministry of Statistics and Programme Implementation):
   • Food: rice, milk, onions, tea leaf
   • Clothing: saris (traditional wear), footwear
   • Fuel and light: cooking gas, electricity
   • Miscellaneous: tuition fees, gold ornaments

The basket is applied broadly across the economy to get a general measure of inflation, but you have your own market basket as well! For example, my market basket would be what I eat every day, my apartment rent, the cost of maintaining my bike (my primary mode of transportation), my healthcare costs, my cell phone and internet bill, dog food costs (my dog, Moo, eats a well-balanced diet!), and clothes.

Here's an example of how the market basket is put into action.

- Let's say that in a base period (2020), the price of a pineapple was $3 and the price of a cowboy hat was $20. Pineapples went up to $4 in 2021, and cowboy hats went up to $22 (howdy, inflation!). In the current year (let's say 2022), the price of a pineapple is now $5 and a cowboy hat is $24.

- To calculate the price of the pineapple and cowboy hat basket for each year, we add the prices of the two items. In this case, the basket prices for the three years would be $23, $26, and $29, respectively.
- To calculate the CPI for each of those years, we would take the price of the basket in the current period ($29 in 2022) and divide it by the price of the basket in the base period ($23), then multiply by 100 to get a percentage increase. In this case, the CPI for the basket for each year would be:
  - 2020: ($23/$23) × 100 = 100
  - 2021: ($26/$23) × 100 = 113
  - 2022: ($29/$23) × 100 = 126
- We then can calculate inflation, which is the percentage change in CPI between the two years. So from 2020 to 2022, the percentage change in the CPI basket was 26 percent—quite a pricey pineapple-cowboy hat combo!

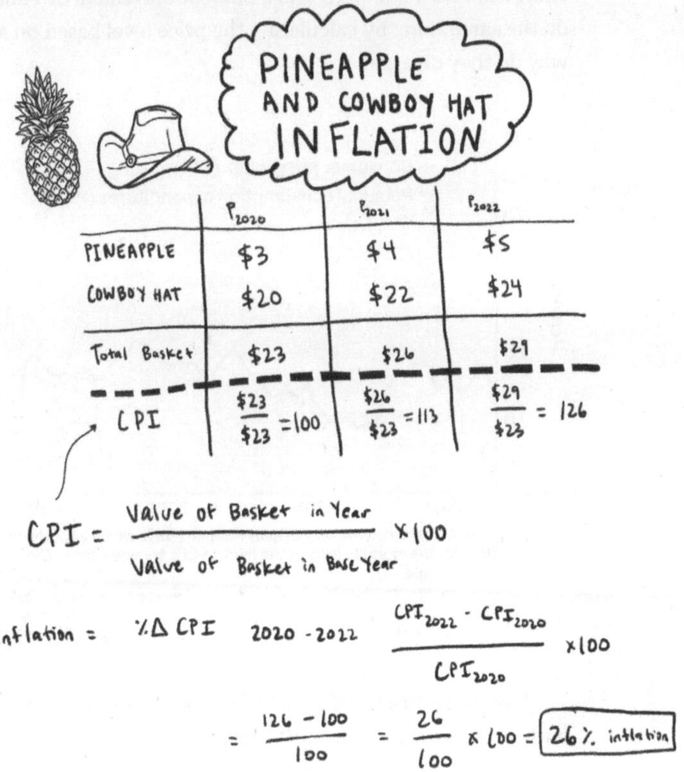

The Bureau of Labor Statistics and other agencies in different countries calculate CPIs for all the items in the market basket by using the same method. They then combine the CPIs to determine an overall CPI for the market basket.

PERSONAL CONSUMPTION EXPENDITURES: THE PEOPLE'S INFLATION, BUT FOR THE FED

Then there is Personal Consumption Expenditures (PCE), which is what the Federal Reserve and other policymakers like to look at to gauge household spending. In contrast, many European countries use a metric called Household Consumption Expenditure (HCE) to measure spending. Most countries have an inflation measure such as PCE or HCE that they use to make policy decisions.

The PCE is based on the data of what these households, businesses, and governments are selling, capturing consumer spending from the transactional side of businesses and governmental bodies. As you can see in the following chart from the Federal Reserve Bank of Cleveland, CPI and PCE diverge. They do the same thing by calculating the price level based on a basket of goods. So why do they diverge?

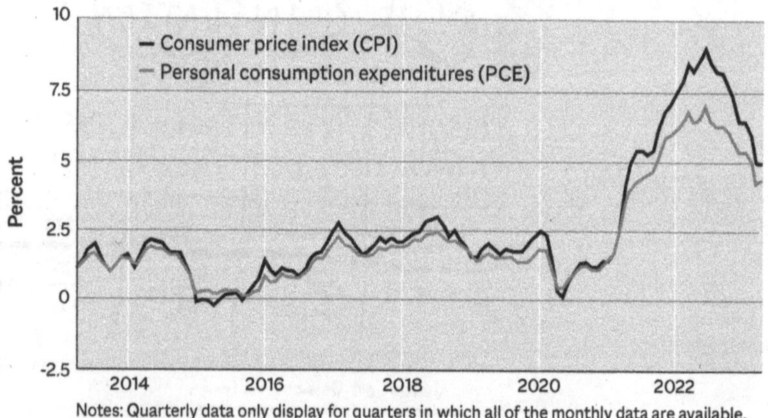

Notes: Quarterly data only display for quarters in which all of the monthly data are available. Data for the monthly level of the median CPI, trimmed-mean CPI, and trimmed mean PCE are not available.

Source: Federal Reserve Bank of Cleveland calculations based on data from the BLS, BEA, Federal Bank of Cleveland, Federal Reserve Bank of Dallas, and Haver Analytics

Joseph Haubrich and Sara Millington, two economists at the Cleveland Fed, outlined three reasons in a 2014 paper:

1. **The scope effect.** The CPI doesn't include things that people don't pay for directly, such as medical care via employer-provided insurance. However, the PCE includes them as personal spending.
2. **The weight effect.** The two indices weight basket items (like gasoline or limes) differently, which impacts how they measure inflation.
3. **The formula effect.** PCE uses a chain-weighted index, which allows the weights to change more frequently (annually or even monthly) with consumers' spending patterns. This means the PCE can more accurately capture shifts in consumer behavior as they substitute away from goods and services that have become relatively more expensive, whereas CPI is a fixed basket that updates less frequently.

The PCE and CPI measure things differently—the weight effect—which includes airline fares. The PCE index for airline fares is based on airlines' passenger revenues and the total number of miles traveled by passengers, which equates to average revenue per passenger. The Bureau of Economic Analysis (BEA) collects data from airlines on these two data points and uses this data to calculate the PCE index for airline fares. The CPI is based on airfares on a few sample routes.

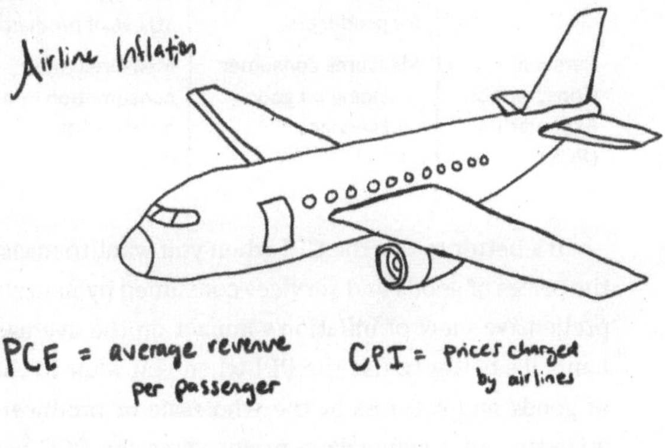

Sound confusing? Yeah. That's why sometimes the two numbers can diverge. In fact, due to a variety of factors, the gap between PCE and CPI has widened substantially a couple of times.

Direction and magnitude are the most important things to glean from these two metrics. If the PCE and CPI are going up quickly, that isn't great. If they are going down quickly, that also isn't great, because consumer demand is falling. What's important is the rate of change, not simply the actual price level.

THE PRODUCER PRICE INDEX: INFLATION FOR BUSINESSES

The Producer Price Index (PPI), used in the United States, and the Industrial Producer Price Index (IPPI), used in the European Union, are important metrics that measure the average change in prices received by producers for goods and services. These indices track the prices of goods and services at various stages of production, including raw materials, intermediate goods, and finished goods.

While the CPI and PCE look at how much consumers are paying, the PPI focuses on the prices of goods and services received by domestic businesses. Changes in the PPI can impact how much businesses are willing to invest and how much they charge their customers. If a business's costs go up due to higher PPI, it may need to raise its prices to stay profitable, which can in turn impact inflation at the consumer level—a never-ending, vicious feedback loop.

METRIC	PURPOSE	METHOD	FOCUS
Consumer Price Index (CPI)	Measures inflation and changes in the cost of living for consumers	Measures consumer spending	Tracks price changes at the consumer level
Producer Price Index (PPI)	Measures inflationary pressures in economy for producers	Measures goods and services at various stages of production	Tracks price changes at the producer level
Personal Consumption Expenditures (PCE)	Measures consumer spending on goods and services	Measures total consumption by and on behalf of households	Reflects consumer behavior across a broader range of expenditures

It's better to use the CPI when you want to measure the overall changes in the prices of goods and services consumed by households, as it provides a comprehensive view of inflation's impact on the average consumer. On the other hand, it's better to use the PPI when you want to check out the price changes of goods and services at the wholesale or producer level. Additionally, some analysts and policymakers prefer using the PCE because it covers a broader swath of consumption (especially stuff like healthcare) and captures more nuance within its methodology as compared to CPI.

THE INFLATION PIZZA

We can calculate inflation (and the broad impact it has) through the inflation pizza, inspired by Politico's "inflation cheeseburger." Everything that goes into a pizza is exposed to inflation: the salt, the tomato, the peppers, the dough! Although this is a pretty simple example, it will illustrate how expensive ingredients can get and how important food prices are in maintaining an economy.

- Dough: The cost to make a pizza begins with the dough. The price of flour went up by 12.1 percent from June 2022 to June 2023 (the price of all bakery products climbed by 8.8 percent). It skyrocketed due to terrible weather—wheat being grown in drought conditions—as well as the geopolitical pressures caused by the Ukraine war.
- Cheese: Cheese prices increased by 1.1 percent in the same time period. This was driven by labor shortages, heightened costs of water supply due to drought, and the escalating cost of cattle.
- Salt: Salt prices increased by 4.3 percent, driven by supply shortages and higher salt processing costs.
- Various Meats: Meats, including beef, pork, and ham, increased by 0.6 percent, but lunch meats (pepperoni!) increased by 4.9 percent as meat processors focused on producing other products.
- Vegetables: Vegetables increased by 2.1 percent due to labor shortages and climate change.

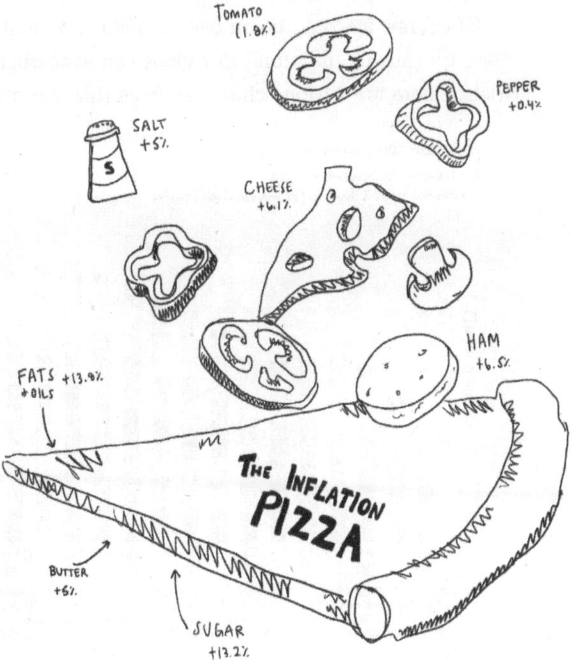

- Fats and Oils: Fats and oils increased by 8.7 percent in price, driven by geopolitical conflict and rising fuel prices for transport.

A lot of the price pressure came from labor market disruptions, as Politico reported: "The limited availability of work visas continues to be an issue for many employers—over 50 percent of agriculture and 90 percent of dairy workers are estimated to be foreign born or undocumented." This was also compounded by higher transportation costs and supply chain delays.

This is just one example of the sweeping impact that inflation can have.

INFLATION EXPECTATIONS

Inflation expectations can significantly impact economic behavior, influencing spending, saving, and investing. If you think that the price of bread is going to increase by $2 tomorrow, you're going to go buy bread today.

The underlying concept of inflation is sort of intertwined with the idea of vibes. A lot of the Federal Reserve's role involves managing these vibes through monetary policy, trying to make sure that people's expectations are aligned with true economic reality.

Of course, it would be an oversimplification and very untrue to say, "Bad vibes are causing inflation!" But vibes can exacerbate a problem that already exists. There are various charts, such as this one from JPMorgan Chase, that

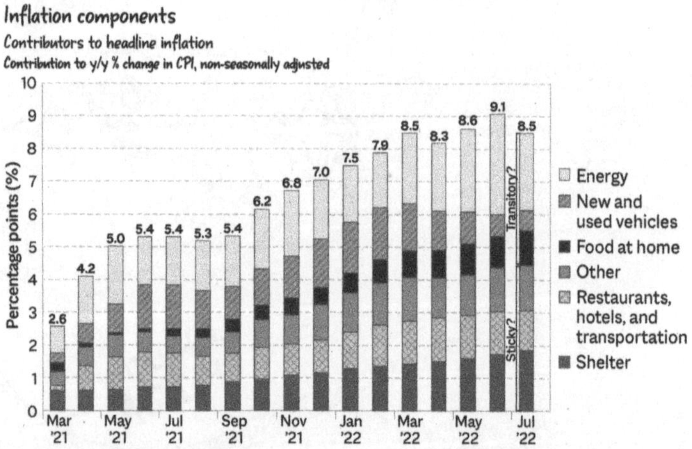

Source: BLS, J.P. Morgan Asset Management. Contributions mirror the BLS methodology on Table 7 of the CPI report. Values may not sum to headline CPI figures due to rounding and underlying calculations. "Shelter" includes owners' equivalent rent and rent of primary residence. "Other" primarily reflects household furnishings, apparel, education and communication services, medical care services, and other personal services. Guide to the Markets - U.S. Data are as of August 26, 2022.

demonstrate what contributes to inflation—energy, new and used vehicles, food prices, restaurant costs, shelter costs—but the *causes* of inflation are different.

CAUSES OF INFLATION

Inflation has a mix of many complicated causes. Supply and demand is the root of most of it, but other significant factors include pressure from firms raising prices, fiscal and monetary support, and international trade fissures.

The supply and demand imbalance was calculated by the New York Federal Reserve, with supply chain bottlenecks driving 3 percent of the total inflation number. As Julian di Giovanni, an economist at the NY Fed, wrote:

> *Our work shows that inflation in the U.S. would have been 6 percent instead of 9 percent at the end of 2021 without supply bottlenecks.... Put differently, fiscal stimulus and other aggregate demand factors would not have driven inflation this high without the pandemic-related supply constraints. In the absence of any new energy or other shock, it is therefore possible that the ongoing easing of supply bottlenecks will cause a substantial drop in inflation in the near term.*

Broken supply chains created a lot of problems. The San Francisco Fed found something similar, estimating that supply chain disruptions accounted for approximately 60% of the "above trend run-up of headline inflation in 2021 and 2022."

Combine that with government spending and Fed policy, and you get a perfect storm. Fiscal policy took a huge step forward at the same time that supply collapsed, pushing support such as the 2020 $2.2 trillion Coronavirus Aid, Relief, and Economic Security (CARES) Act. As the economist Glenn Hubbard wrote in the *Financial Times:*

> *To consider excessive government spending as a culprit along with the Fed's loose monetary policy, it is useful to draw a contrast with policy in the global financial crisis of 2008 and the subsequent economic recovery. As in the pandemic, the Fed kept short-term nominal rates at zero for a long time and expanded its balance sheet more than fourfold. Both inflation and inflationary expectations remained anchored at around 2 per cent—with actual inflation sometimes lower—during the decade after the onset of the financial crisis. A key difference, though,*

was that fiscal policy expansion was comparatively weak relative to that of the pandemic recovery.

Supply- and demand-driven contributions to year-over-year core PCE inflation

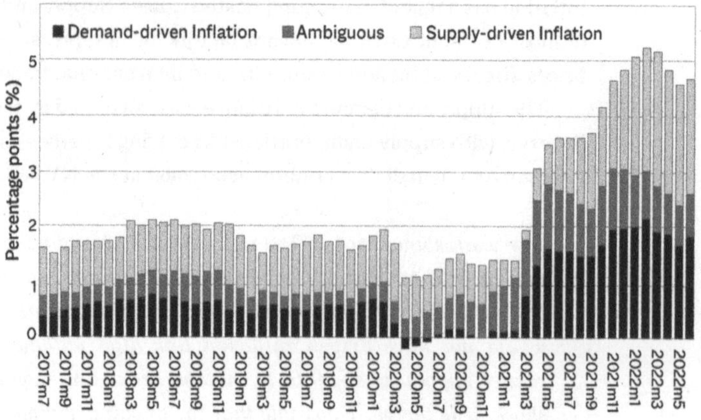

Inflation arises from the combination of fiscal policy, monetary policy, supply chains breaking, expensive energy, and so much more. But the shock hampered the supply of goods through "sticky prices, input-output linkages, and labor reallocation costs"—the costs of making more things to meet the higher demand and not enough people working to make more things.

The imbalances bleed into the economy, leading to the four main amplifiers of inflation over the past few years:

1. Price hikes
2. The state of the labor market
3. Globalization
4. Energy markets

Inflation is a multiheaded hydra, with several complex causes and not that many solutions.

#1 PRICE HIKES

Many people tend to attribute inflation to rising profits, but the reality is more complex. In 2023, Isabella Weber and Evan Wasner published a paper titled "Sellers' Inflation, Profits and Conflict: Why Can Large Firms Hike Prices in an Emergency?," which explored corporate concentration and pricing power.

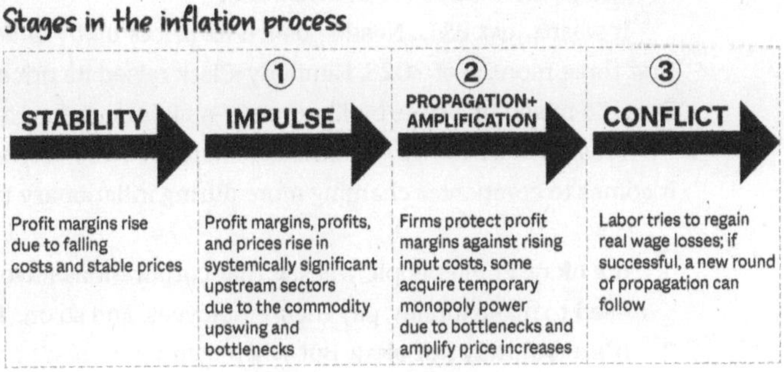

They found that, for the most part, companies increase prices whenever they can; after all, their goal is to generate a profit. In 2022, Tracy Alloway, a journalist at Bloomberg, reported on the "excuseflation" phenomena, where companies take advantage of uncertain times as a pretext to raise prices.

Unfortunately, the Weber-Wasner paper was often confused with the concept of "greedflation," which suggests that companies operate solely out of spite. In reality, sellers' inflation is a result of companies simply being companies—they raise prices to protect their profit margins, cover their costs, and so on, although greed may sometimes play a role.

But this isn't due to companies being directly greedy (although, let's be real, there is some of that). The problem is that they want to maximize their profits—the amount of money left over after they deduct all expenses such as operating costs, taxes, and interest. In order to maintain their profits, they need to (1) sell more product or (2) raise their prices.

A Quick Profit Explainer

We can look at the "United States of Apple" to get an idea of what it means to be a profitable company. Apple's gross profit margin, or how efficiently it produced goods and services, increased by about 5 percent from 2020 to 2022. To increase its profit margin further, it could either sell more products and services (more MacBooks and iPhones) or reduce the internal company cost of selling those products and services.

Raising prices is much easier to do than *selling more things* to turn a profit.

Procter & Gamble's Q1 2023 earnings report shows the ease of increasing prices versus selling more products; price increases were a huge net sales driver, whereas sales volume was negative. The company was selling less but charging more, which enabled it to maintain its margins (and therefore have its stock remain golden in the eyes of investors).

It wasn't just P&G. Nestlé pushed its prices up by almost 10 percent in the first three months of 2023, Kimberly-Clark raised its prices by 10 percent, and PepsiCo raised its prices by 13 percent—a nightmare for consumers.

This is where things get difficult. There are two main lines of thought when it comes to companies charging more during inflationary times:

1. **It's okay.** Some people will say that corporations have to raise prices; they need to make money, pay their employees, and so on. This makes sense.
2. **It's absolutely not okay.** But when companies don't pass those gains off to their employees (and raise prices just to appease the stock market gods), things get dicey. The massive UPS strike in 2023 is a good example of what can happen: Employees get fed up, so they strike for higher wages and better working conditions.

Apple Inc.

CONSOLIDATED STATEMENTS OF OPERATIONS
(In millions, except number of shares, which are reflected in thousands and per share amount)

	Years Ended		
	September 24, 2022	September 25, 2021	September 26, 2020
Net sales			
Products	$ 316,199	$ 297,392	$ 220,747
Services	78,129	68,425	53,768
Total net sales	394,328	365,817	274,515
Cost of sales			
Products	201, 471	192,266	151, 286
Services	22,075	20,715	18,273
Total cost of sales	223,546	212,981	169,559
Gross margin	170,782	152,836	104,956
GROSS PROFIT MARGIN	43.3%	41.8%	38.2%
Operating Expenses			
Research and development	26,251	21,914	18,752
Selling, general and administrative	25,094	21,973	19,916
Total operating expenses	51,345	43,887	38,668
Operating income	119, 437	108,949	66,288
Other income (expense), net	(334)	258	803
Income before provision for income taxes	119,103	109,207	67,091
Provision for income taxes	19,300	14,527	9,680
Net income	$ 99,803	94,680	57,411
Shares used in computing earnings per share:			
Basic	16,215,963	16,701,272	17,352,119
Diluted	16,325,819	16,864,919	17,528,214

2022

GROSS PROFIT MARGIN = $\frac{\text{GROSS PROFIT}}{\text{REVENUE}} = \frac{170,782}{394,328} = 43.3\%$ } HOW EFFICIENTLY A COMPANY PRODUCES GOODS + SERVICES

July–September Quarter Discussion

Net sales in the first quarter of fiscal year 2023 were $20.6 billion, a 1 percent increase versus the prior year. Unfavorable foreign exchange had a 6 percent impact on net sales. Organic sales, which exclude the impacts of foreign exchange and acquisitions and divestitures, increased 7 percent. The organic sales increase was driven by a 9 percent increase from higher pricing and a 1 percent increase from positive product mix, partially offset by a 3 percent decrease in shipment volumes.

July–September 2022

New Sales Drivers	Volume	Foreign Exchange	Price	Mix	Other	Net Sales	Organic Volume	Organic Sales
Beauty	(1)%	(6)%	7%	(2)%	2%	–%	(1)%	4%
Grooming	–%	(8)%	8%	(4)%	–%	(4)%	1%	5%
Healthcare	(2)%	(5)%	6%	4%	–%	3%	(2)%	8%
Fabric and Home Care	(4)%	(6)%	11%	1%	(1)%	1%	(4)%	8%
Baby, Feminine & Family Care	(3)%	(5)%	8%	1%	–%	1%	(3)%	6%
Total P&G	(3)%	(6)%	9%	1%	–%	1%	(3)%	7%

(1) Net sales percentage changes are approximations based on quantitative formulas that are consistently applied.
(2) Other includes the sales mix impact from acquisitions and divestitures and rounding impacts necessary to reconcile volume to net sales.

All in all, companies are companies and they are going to do what they do best, which is to charge people more for the goods and services they make. As Paul Donovan, the chief economist at UBS Global Wealth Management, explained about corporate price hikes in 2022:

Two forces have combined. Despite negative real wages, consumers have carried on consuming. Strong postpandemic household balance sheets have allowed lower savings and increased borrowing to offset the sorry state of real wages. The resulting resilience in demand has given companies the confidence to raise prices faster than costs.

In addition, the power of storytelling has conditioned consumers to accept price rises. Imagine a story about a farmer who takes wheat to the windmill, where it is ground into flour, and then baked into bread. In that fantasy world, a rise in the cost of wheat of say 22 per cent might be used to justify a 15 per cent rise in the price of bread.

A lot of the price hikes are storytelling—conditioning people to understand that prices have increased for a reason, and there is no other option than to accept them. People also need to buy things. Going back to Procter & Gamble, they "raised prices across all of its main divisions, leaving them 7 per cent higher overall from a year earlier. Customer demand remained resilient with only a 1 per cent sales volume decline." Net sales are up 6 percent from a year earlier, driven by higher prices, not by Procter & Gamble selling more things.

Companies usually raise prices when they can, which has a lot of consequences. Nestlé, Coca-Cola, and other companies raised their prices by more than 10 percent in the first quarter (first three months) of 2023. And it's very easy for them, since power is so consolidated. After all:

- Four companies control 85 percent of the U.S. beef market.
- Four companies control 80 percent of the U.S. soy market.
- Three companies control 78 percent of the U.S. pasta market.
- Three companies control 72 percent of the U.S. cereal market.

This concentration of power makes it more expensive for people to live and can definitely contribute to inflation. In a capitalistic society, it's normally taboo to advocate for price caps, or restricting how much the prices can increase on things (and they come with their own issues, including market distortions, reduced investment, discouragement of competition, and the emergence of a black market). And, of course, companies do have to absorb rising input costs and pay their employees.

#2 THE STATE OF THE LABOR MARKET

This is the second cause of inflation. I previously talked about wage-price spirals, the idea that workers are the ones who are causing inflation by asking for raises. Just to reiterate: People *are* the economy. The people doing the hard work in fields and construction sites and along waterways are the underlying force of our economy. They should be paid for the work they do, especially if companies are benefiting from rising prices.

However, this is not always possible since most workers are not in a position to demand higher wages. In 2022, the Bank for International Settlements published a paper exploring the possibility of a wage-price spiral, finding that "institutional changes also hint at an environment less conducive to wage-price spirals than in the past. In recent decades, workers' collective bargaining power has declined alongside falling trade union membership.... Relatedly, the indexation and COLA clauses that fuelled past wage-price spirals are less prevalent."

Due to the decline in union membership over the years, it's more challenging for workers to demand higher wages. As a result, the traditional approach of employees seeking raises has become less common. Most people can't just march into their boss's office and ask for a raise.

Tactics such as "quiet quitting" (doing the job you were hired to do, no more and no less), demanding raises, and switching jobs all indicate a shift toward valuing workers. That said, when people demand higher wages, companies are "forced" to raise their prices to pay workers more, so goods and services become more expensive, resulting in people asking for even higher wages. This creates an endless loop of higher wages and higher prices, leading to a *wage-price spiral* in which:

1. Workers say, "Wow! Prices are super high! Please pay us more."
2. The company says, "Okay, we get that, sure."
3. The company raises its prices to offset the cost of higher wages for its employees.
4. Rinse and repeat.

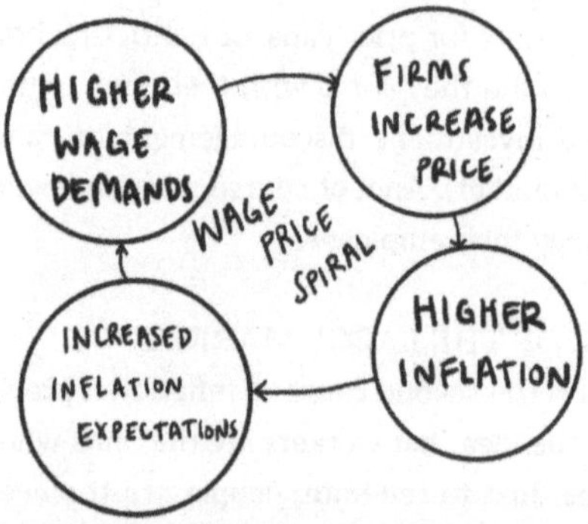

But Lael Brainard, a former vice chair of the Federal Reserve, pointed out that this could be more of a price-price spiral—driven not by wages but by companies hiking prices. As she said:

> *Retail markups in a number of sectors have seen material increases in what could be described as a price-price spiral, whereby final prices have risen by more than the increases in input prices. The compression of these markups as supply constraints ease, inventories rise, and demand cools could contribute to disinflationary pressures.*

Companies made all sorts of excuses to raise prices during the pandemic and afterward. The rough state of the labor market and price hikes are intertwined in that inflation narrative.

#3 GLOBALIZATION

Globalization is the force that has enabled so many economies to prosper during the past few decades. It has facilitated greater trade, flow of money, idea exchange, and population movement, all of which contributed to bolstering global supply chains and competition. But now, everyone is freaking out in the postcovid era, which makes sense. There is talk of "reshoring"—bringing manufacturing back to one's own country—and "friendshoring"—shifting trade to politically aligned nations—that is reversing the global trade patterns that have existed since the end of the Cold War. This is a double-edged sword.

If countries such as the United States were to no longer participate in globalization activities, it would have significant implications domestically and for the entire world.

On one hand, globalization has allowed countries to leverage their comparative advantages in various industries. For instance, the United States has excelled in technology and innovation, while other countries, like China (a production powerhouse), specialize in manufacturing or agriculture. By trading and collaborating globally, economies have benefited from these specialized skills, leading to increased economic growth. Each country focuses on what it is best at producing, and then trades what they make with other countries that produce what they do not produce a lot of. Undoing globalization could disrupt these trade relationships and hinder overall economic efficiency, as countries cannot independently and domestically produce all of the goods they consume.

Imagine if Japan—a country that heavily relies on imports to sustain itself—suddenly stopped importing cotton, timber, uranium (for nuclear power), oil, dairy, and beef. As there is limited domestic supply of these resources, its entire textile (clothing) production, energy supply, and the delicious beef ramen and Japanese cheesecake industry would collapse—a mess that would unravel the entire Japanese economy and cause societal distress.

On the other hand, undoing globalization could provide countries with greater control over their supply chains. The covid-19 pandemic exposed vulnerabilities in supply chains, particularly in critical sectors such as medical equipment and pharmaceuticals. Reversing globalization could allow nations to bring essential production processes back within their borders. This would reduce dependence on foreign imports during emergencies, an instrumental factor for managing inflation amid global crises—a pretty good thing!

#4 ENERGY MARKETS

In 2022, Europe felt the consequences of the global energy supply chain breakdown when Russia invaded Ukraine. Europe imposed heavy trade sanctions on

Russia to condemn the attack, which resulted in Europe getting cut off from a key source of energy—liquefied natural gas (LNG). This was very concerning as 40% of natural gas and 25% of oil imported into the EU was from Russia—not to mention that 40% of residential heating used Russian gas. Germany, in particular, heavily relied on the Nord Stream pipeline, which connected Russia and Germany underground through the Baltic Sea. This led to higher inflation and the European energy crisis.

Being a preeminent global LNG exporter and the largest energy partner of the EU, the United States rapidly responded to the crisis by tripling LNG exports to the EU in 2022 and enforcing additional export sanctions on Russia. As a result, the EU became the largest importer of U.S. LNG exports, constituting more than half of traded U.S. LNG at 52%. However, the entire process was still difficult to achieve and buried under a lot of bureaucracy and geopolitical tension. As we know, energy is the common denominator of economic activity, and when energy prices are high, everything hurts (economic frostbite!).

In summary, as Jerome Powell said in 2022, "I think we now understand better how little we understand about inflation." The certainty is being uncertain.

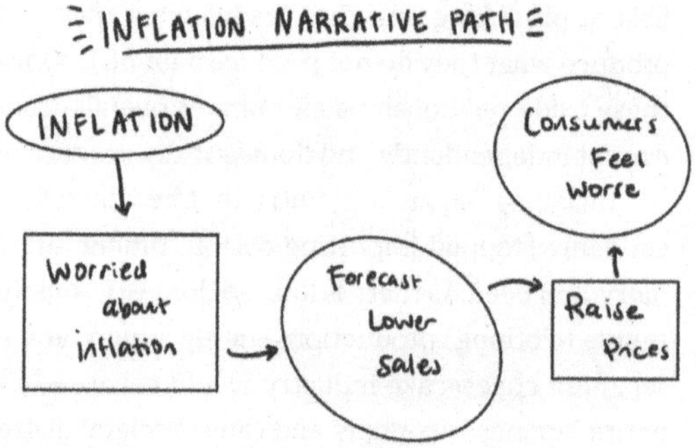

OTHER TYPES OF FLATIONS

DEFLATION

But we also have to be wary of deflation, the opposite of inflation. This is when the prices of goods and services fall, which sounds okay! Who wouldn't want things to be cheaper, right?

Right. But also wrong. Deflation is harmful to the economy in the long term in the same way that high inflation is harmful. It discourages spending and investment because people are like, "The thing I want to buy will be cheaper tomorrow, so I'll wait until then," and then tomorrow never comes. It can lead to lower economic growth because the demand for goods and services falls as people sit on their hands instead of spending money, which can lead to higher unemployment rates as companies say, "No one is buying our stuff! Goodbye, employees." Lower incomes and decreased economic activity put pressure on everyone.

Furthermore, deflation also can increase the real burden of debt! Which isn't great. If you borrow $50,000 to buy a house when inflation is at the Fed's target of 2 percent and then deflation hits and takes the inflation rate to -2 percent, that's a 4 percentage point change in the inflation rate—and a 4 percent increase in the real value of the debt that you took out for your house. Each dollar of those $50,000 is now more valuable in real terms because of deflation, which makes it more difficult to pay back that debt.

So, yeah, it's like Goldilocks: There needs to be just enough inflation to keep the global economy running and people happy. And the "keeping people happy" part is key! A lot of the success of a policy depends on people *believing* in the policy. The Federal Reserve's credibility is one of its most powerful assets. If it loses that, its job will become infinitely harder.

HYPERINFLATION

What happened in the Weimar Republic, the post-World War I successor of the German Empire, in the 1920s, is a great example of the importance of maintaining fiscal credibility—and the havoc that ensues when credibility is lost.

From 1921 to 1923, the Weimar Republic—now modern-day Germany—experienced hyperinflation. This is when inflation gets completely out of control and prices rise uncontrollably. A cup of coffee could cost $1 at 8:00 A.M. and $4.50 at 9:00 A.M.—hourly price increases in the hundreds or thousands of percent.

The German Empire had funded World War I through borrowing and was saddled with a massive amount of debt when it lost. The Treaty of Versailles—which formally ended WWI—imposed a huge reparations debt on the Weimar Republic that could be paid only in gold or foreign currency. In order to pay these debts, the government decided to print a lot of money (number one no-no in economics), leading to hyperinflation and uncontrollable price increases. At the peak of hyperinflation, the country was experiencing approximately 29,500 percent inflation per month and the deutsche mark was worth one-trillionth of its original value. It was worth so little that Germans were burning the deutsche mark instead of wood to stay warm.

Inflation was fine with politicians because it kept unemployment low. The Germans were happy (for a bit); the German stock market tripled (until it fell by

97 percent in 1922). People started taking out money; they figured they might as well buy a place to live (a hard asset) with the depreciating currency and have their debt inflated away.

But the war debts still had to be repaid. As the government continued to print more money to repay its debts, tax revenues fell to zero, and the government had become illegitimate in the eyes of the people. The citizens didn't want to pay their taxes, because why would they pay money to a government that no longer worked? The government responded by issuing more bonds and printing even more money, which only exacerbated the problem. People realized that their money was rapidly losing value, so they tried to spend it quickly, leading to even higher prices and a vicious cycle of inflation.

The loop was broken when farmers stopped accepting the inflated currency for their crops.

Hyperinflation "works" only when a currency is considered viable; once farmers, the people who feed us, strike, game over. The connectors—consumers and businesses—have to play the game in order for the game to work. In 1923, the Weimar Republic changed its currency to the rentenmark, which was backed by bonds indexed to gold. The government had to revalue the currency, pay some more reparations, and reissue government bonds.

However, the main problem was the loss of government credibility, and the government using inflation as a way to pay for its functionality. This underscores the importance of monetary policy in maintaining balance in the economy and how consumers and businesses need to be involved for such a policy to work. Even the best policies and technology can't fix a broken system if the people involved stop participating.

This happens in the modern day, too. Zimbabwe's hyperinflation in the early 2000s offers another dramatic example. It was a period when the government's excessive money printing in response to an economic crisis resulted in astronomical inflation rates, peaking at an almost unfathomable 79.6 billion percent month-on-month increase in mid-November 2008.

Argentina has been plagued by recurring cycles of hyperinflation, notably during the late 1980s and early 1990s. One of the most severe instances occurred in 1989, when the annual inflation rate surged to over 3,000 percent, primarily due to excessive money printing and fiscal mismanagement. This period was characterized by rapid devaluation of the Argentine peso, skyrocketing prices, and widespread economic instability that severely impacted the living standards of Argentinians.

We are all a part of the puzzle, for better or for worse, and that's especially true for how we manage and deal with inflation.

CHAPTER 9

The Labor Market

Satisfaction with family life and health are the strongest predictors while satisfaction with income and leisure time are the weakest predictors of overall life satisfaction for both genders.

—STEFANI MILOVANSKA-FARRINGTON AND STEPHEN FARRINGTON

WHAT IS THE LABOR MARKET?

The labor market. It's really important, because having a job (that pays enough to stay alive, provides some form of healthcare, and enables a person to live the life they want) is really important. And the post-pandemic world was a turning point for how we think about work.

As the dust of the pandemic began to settle, workers began to rise up. As the calendar flipped to 2022, a seemingly paradoxical labor landscape unfurled across much of the world. With headlines screaming about the "Great Resignation" on one hand, and soaring job openings on the other, a central question reverberated: "In an era post-covid, with all its lessons and losses, what do workers really want?"

Millions, whether by choice or circumstance, were reevaluating their place in the working world. Mass resignations, surging strikes, demands for better wages and working conditions, and an amplified quest for work-life balance became the anthems of this labor movement. From Amazon warehouses to Hollywood sets, workers demanded more than just paychecks. They sought respect, flexibility, and a redefined sense of purpose. As industries scrambled to recalibrate, the power dynamics of employer-employee relationships were thrust into the spotlight.

The labor market runs on supply and demand, with employees supplying skills and employers paying for them. Our economic prosperity, bargaining power, and ability to find meaningful work flow from the state of the labor market. It's a linchpin in how the rest of the economy functions, but of course, it's in constant flux.

Shiny new jobs pop up thanks to technological advancements, and old jobs are aged out by those same technological advancements (looking at you, AI!). This chapter explores how the health of the labor market is measured, who pulls its strings (and what strings they *should* be pulling), and the myriad ways it impacts our economic prosperity and well-being.

When I interviewed Mary Daly, the president and CEO of the Federal Reserve Bank of San Francisco, about the labor market in March 2023, here's what she told me.

> **Mary:**... *The best thing we can do for Americans is provide a sustainable path of growth that gives people opportunities to change jobs, to find the career that matches their interest, to grow their careers over time, but then to bring that paycheck home week after week and be able to afford things that they afforded last week. And right now we can't do that. So I think that's the point of balancing the economy. You balance the economy to give people a full slate of options, not just a positive here and a take back there.*

What President Daly was saying matters for how we talk about the labor market, because the Fed shapes so much of how the labor market functions. The Fed is focused on giving people optionality—so that they are able to afford being alive (by getting inflation down) and that people are able to get a job (by supporting the labor market). But the labor market is weird, riddled with anomalies and strange dynamics, especially in the postcovid era. There are a lot of ways to slice and dice the labor market. There are a few main ways to measure it, such as asking people if they have a job and asking companies if they are hiring. The analysis process is broad and often reveals gaps between private and public data, openings and quits, and survey response rates.

KEY LABOR MARKET METRICS

THE UNEMPLOYMENT RATE

The total labor force is calculated as the number of unemployed people actively seeking work plus the number of employed people (around 166 million people in early 2023, a complete recovery from the April 2020 figure of 156 million people).

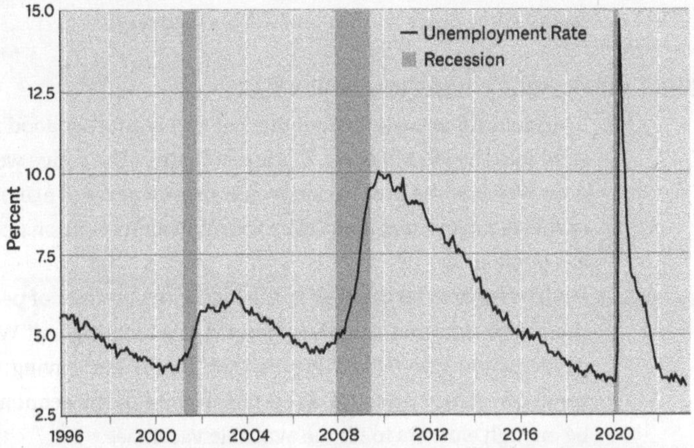

Source: U.S. Bureau of Labor Statistics; NBER

There are two things to know about the unemployment rate:

1. **Discouraged Workers:** The unemployment rate doesn't capture individuals who have become discouraged and given up on actively seeking work due to a lack of job opportunities or other factors. These discouraged workers are often considered "marginally attached" to the labor force. They would like to work but have stopped actively searching for jobs and, therefore, aren't in the labor force.
2. **Underemployment:** While the unemployment rate focuses on whether individuals have a job or not, it fails to account for the quality of those jobs or whether they match the educational attainment or skills of the workers. This can include overqualified people working in low-skilled jobs (like a doctor working at a coffee shop), part-time workers who want full-time employment, or workers in temporary positions.

A low unemployment rate (3 to 4 percent) is generally considered to be good! It means that the labor market is strong, employees are moving and grooving, and job opportunities are widely available. A higher unemployment rate (6 to 7 percent) represents a weaker labor market, indicating that job opportunities are not as plentiful and wages will tick lower.

In early 2023, the total labor force was around 166 million people, representing a complete recovery from the April 2020 figure of 156 million people.

The unemployment rate is the number of unemployed people divided by the total labor force. The unemployment rate was at a near record low in early 2023, peaking at 14.7 percent in April 2020 and hovering around 3.4 percent nearly three years later—an incredible recovery!

THE LABOR FORCE PARTICIPATION RATE

The labor force participation rate (LFPR) is another good metric to give us insight into the labor market. It is an estimate of the active workforce of the economy, which is the number of people sixteen years of age or older employed or seeking employment divided by the total noninstitutionalized civilian working-age population.

The higher this number is, the higher the number of people who are part of the population that is actively working. Which is good! When the labor force participation rate falls, it means that people are leaving the workforce. This trend can create pressure on certain sectors of the economy, as there may not be enough workers to fill the available vacancies.

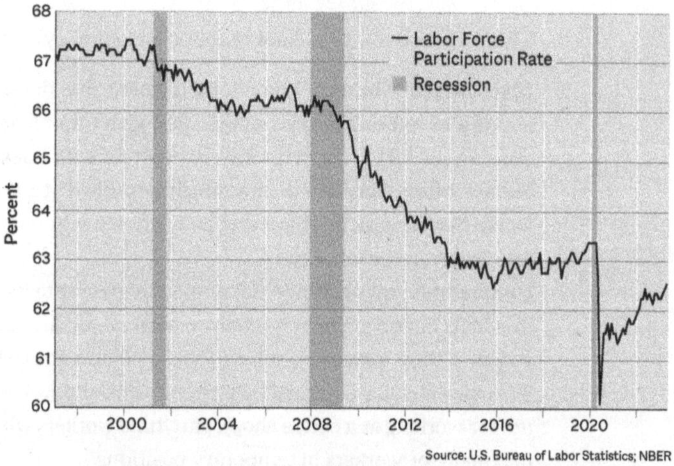

The LFPR was around 62.6 percent in early 2023, which was still relatively low historically (it was closer to 70 percent in the early 2000s but never fully recovered after the 2008 crash). It's also improving, which has bolstered the broader economy in the post-pandemic era, but part of the reason that it has not fully recovered is due to the aging population. This demographic shift means a larger proportion of the population is retiring, leading to a natural decrease in labor force participation.

SURVEYS AND MEASUREMENTS

There are two main surveys that tell us if people have a job:

- **Current Population Survey (CPS).** This monthly survey asks approximately 60,000 households if they have a job to estimate the number of employed people in the population as a whole.
- **Current Employment Statistics (CES) survey.** This survey asks approximately 122,000 businesses and government agencies how many people they have on payroll to estimate the number of jobs in the population as a whole.

The two surveys diverge, mostly because the household survey has a broader definition of employment and is more prone to sampling error because it surveys only 60,000 households (which can be more than one person). However, both surveys are revised regularly, and there are a number of statistical processes to make sure that the metrics capture what they are meant to.

Household and payroll survey employment, seasonally adjusted, January 1994 to August 2023

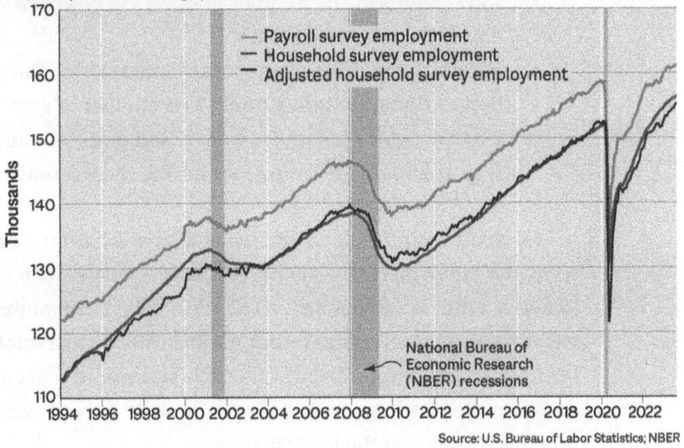

The Employment Situation Summary, which is published by the Bureau of Labor Statistics once a month, incorporates both surveys and focuses on a broad view of the labor market. When combined, the two surveys tell us about:

- **Nonfarm payrolls:** The number of paid workers in the United States, excluding farm workers, private household employees, and nonprofit organization employees

- **Unemployment rate:** The percentage of the labor force that is unemployed
- **Labor force participation rate:** The percentage of the working-age population (sixteen years of age and older) that is employed or actively seeking employment
- **Average hourly earnings:** The average wage earned by workers on an hourly basis
- **Average workweek:** The average number of hours worked by employees in a week
- **Employment by industry:** Employment data by sector, such as manufacturing, construction, retail, and healthcare

There are a variety of other measurements, too, including:

- **Job Openings and Labor Turnover Survey (JOLTS).** This report, published by the Bureau of Labor Statistics once a month with a two-month lag (so the June report is published in August), focuses on the demand for labor and the flow of workers. It includes:
    - **Job openings:** The number of open job positions on the last business day of the reference month
    - **Hires:** The number of employees hired during the reference month
    - **Separations, including quits:** The number of employees who left their jobs during the reference month and quits (the number of employees who voluntarily left their jobs during the reference month)

So there is all this data, and we still have a hard time figuring out exactly what the labor market is doing. As Jerome Powell, the chair of the Federal Reserve, said in November 2022, "We talk a lot about vacancies in the vacancy-to-unemployed rate, but it's just one, it's just another data series. It's been unusually important in this cycle because it's been so out of line. But so has quits. So have wages. So we look at a very wide range of data on unemployment—on the labor market."

As Preston Mui, an economist at Employ America, explained the difference between quits and job openings: "Job openings, as measured by JOLTS, don't tell the whole story. Crucially, they don't contain any information about recruitment efforts."

The job openings figures are strange, because they're survey based. Employ America has long argued that metrics such as the quit rate, or how many people have quit their job, are much better indicators of the health of the labor market than the number of job openings available. Quits and hires data are cleaner than job opening data because they aren't reliant on the inherent bias that comes with people responding to surveys.

It therefore provides good (but not great) insights.

The numbers can be manipulated, too. A March 2023 *Wall Street Journal* article reported that some companies were leaving job openings up on websites to make it look as though they were growing, even when they had no intention of hiring. There's also a gap between what the Bureau of Labor Statistics reports for job openings (the aforementioned JOLTS) and what is reported by private companies like ZipRecruiter, which base their reports on listings on their sites.

The data we see aren't always representative of reality. We all engage with the labor market, whether it be directly or indirectly, as it's how most of us stay alive. And, of course, we can't talk about jobs without talking about wages.

WAGES

The labor market has changed a *lot* in recent years. In the past, it was possible for baby boomers to buy a new house right out of college, work for the same company for forty years, and raise 2.5 kids on their 9-to-5 salary. That isn't true anymore. Instead, it's become clear that workers are really not respected in many different ways.

In the United States, the cost of childcare has skyrocketed, there are essentially no parental leave options, and wages haven't kept up with inflation for

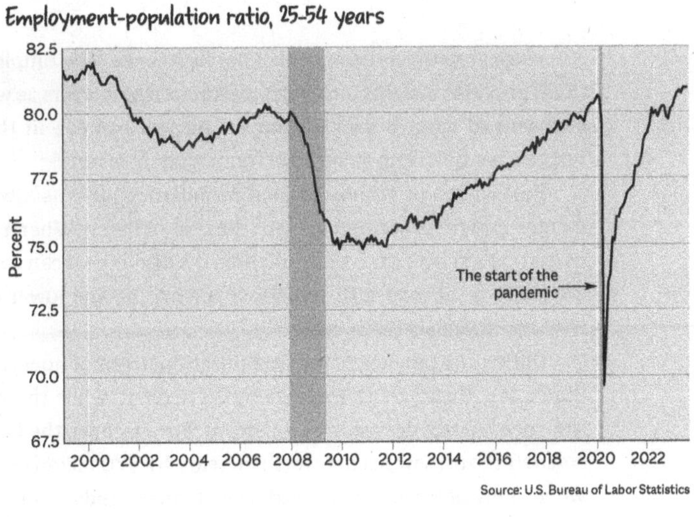

many people. One can moan and say, "Companies need to maintain their profit margins, therefore they really shouldn't pay people a living wage," but, like, come on. Also, the "nobody wants to work anymore" trope is a straight-up lie. People *do* want to work; the employment rate of twenty-five to fifty-four-year-olds who have full-time jobs is back at pre-pandemic levels, but nobody wants to work for $7 an hour.

People want to be compensated via wages and benefits for the work they do. According to a McKinsey & Company survey, the main reason people leave their jobs is due to limited opportunities for career advancement and development; they want to work and grow, but there are no options to pursue this.

Top reasons for quitting previous job, April 2021–April 2022, as a percent

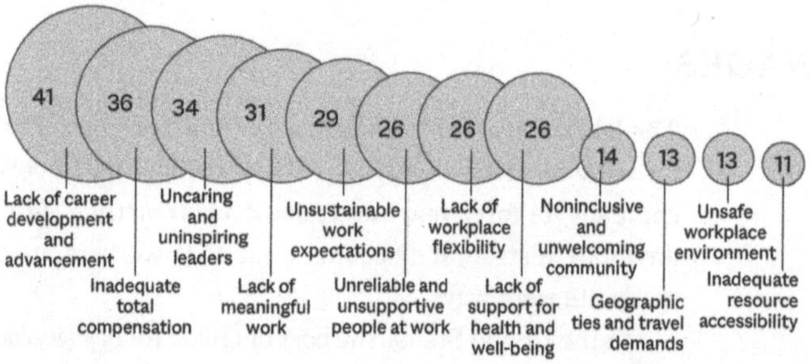

Source: Subset of respondents from McKinsey's 2022 Great Attrition, Great Attraction 2.0 global survey (n=13,382) including those currently employed and planning to leave (n=4,939), those currently employed and planning to stay (n=7439), and those who quit their previous primary jobs between April 2021 and April 2022 (n=1,154)

Wage growth has been kind of flat for a while. The Employment Cost Index (ECI) provides insights into cost pressures on employers as well as wage growth and general labor market dynamics. As you can see in the following chart, wages have ticked up since 2021 (nominally, at least).

Real wages, or wages adjusted for inflation, give us a better sense of how income growth is keeping up with the cost of living. When real wages stagnate or grow at a slower pace than inflation, the disconnect can contribute to income inequality as it erodes the ability of the middle and lower classes to keep up with continuously rising costs.

During the pandemic, the wealthiest 1 percent of households in the United States saw their wealth increase by 35 percent, while the bottom 50 percent saw their wealth decrease by 4 percent. For example, the former CEO of Amazon, Jeff Bezos, saw his net worth increase by $70 billion during the pandemic, while many of his employees struggled to make ends meet.

Wages and salaries and benefits for state and local government, 12-month percent change, not seasonally adjusted

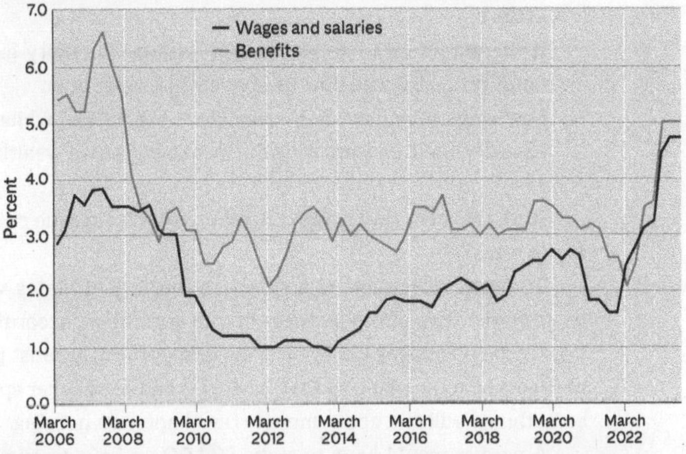

Source: U.S. Bureau of Labor Statistics

The situation has gotten worse over time. As Carter Price and Kathryn Edwards noted in their 2020 paper "Trends in Income from 1975 to 2018," if income growth since 1975 had remained as equitable into the 2000s, the aggregate income would have been $2.5 trillion higher—or enough to double the median income, equating to roughly $1,000 more a month in pay for the average employee.

Such disparities in real wages—and the concentration of wealth—create a lot of problems for social mobility and exacerbate economic inequality. Depressed wages are harmful for many, many reasons.

THE MINIMUM WAGE

In the United States, there is a federal minimum wage, the legally mandated minimum hourly wage that employers must pay to employees. It has remained stagnant for a long time at $7.25 an hour, as of late 2023, but the state minimum wage varies from state to state.

- 76.1 million Americans, or about 55 percent of the labor force, earn hourly wages, according to the 2021 BLS report "Characteristics of Minimum Wage Workers, 2021."

- Throughout the 1960s and 1970s, the minimum wage—in terms of 2019 dollars—was well above $8.00 per hour and peaked in 1968 at $11.69, which is well above the current minimum wage of $7.25 (where it has stayed since 2009).
- If the minimum wage had moved with productivity growth (as it did up until 1968), it would now be about $24.00 per hour.
- Low-wage jobs have *increased* since the 1970s, while middle-wage jobs have declined, exacerbating the increasing gap in wealth distribution.

With this historical context in mind, what is the true cost of a too-low minimum wage?

To begin with, there is no place in the United States where a minimum-wage worker can afford a two-bedroom apartment, according to the National Low Income Housing Coalition. This is important, as most people need a two-bedroom at some point, as they have kids and seek larger spaces to grow into—something I will talk about more in the chapter on housing.

A worker would have to make $24.00 an hour to comfortably (aka have enough income for food, healthcare, housing, and so on) be able to afford a two-bedroom (funnily enough, right in line with the aforementioned "productive wage") and $20.00 an hour to afford a one-bedroom. That leaves a gap of about $17.00 and $13.00, respectively, per hour, which can only be filled by working two more minimum-wage jobs. With the current minimum wage, they would have to work nearly a hundred hours per week to be able to afford a two-bedroom and nearly eighty hours per week for a one-bedroom.

"At least they have a job!" some people might say. We tend to miss the forest for the trees, especially when discussing the unemployment rate. As Martha Ross, a senior fellow at the Brookings Institution, explained, "[The unemployment rate] is important, and we shouldn't lose it. [But] if wages aren't enough to support yourself, then the low unemployment rate doesn't mean that people are doing well."

"If we pay them too much, they are going to get fired!" other people might say. If workers start demanding more money, companies might decide that it is cheaper to let them go. But modest, gradual wage increases actually don't result in a reduction in employment. As Dale Belman and Paul Wolfson highlighted in *What Does the Minimum Wage Do?*, a review of fifteen years of research into the minimum wage, "There is little evidence of negative labor market effects [from an increase in wages]. Hours and employment do not seem to be meaningfully affected." They continued, "While not a stand-alone policy for resolving the issues of low income in the United States, the effectiveness of moderate increases in the minimum wage in raising earnings with few negative consequences makes it an important tool for labor market policy."

If someone can't afford a stable place to live, life becomes very hard. When there is a disconnect between security and existence, it becomes much more difficult to function. If people's basic needs aren't being met, they can't focus on much else. With more time to think and more time to process, they make better choices and their stability increases. Safety delivers returns. Security creates growth. It is imperative to invest in people—and that begins with paying them a living wage.

THE SKEWED WAY WE SEE WAGE GROWTH

We've been able to ignore the necessity of a living minimum wage because we have had a lot of services subsidized during the era of extremely low interest rates. In the world of venture capital and excess funding, we were able to have bonkers things such as fifteen-minute grocery delivery and rideshare services straight to our door without having to pay for what those services truly cost. Companies such as Uber and DoorDash provide us with on-demand delivery and transportation services despite being unprofitable, resulting in the perception of affluence.

This feeling of being rich and mighty because we can have burgers dropped off outside our house has somewhat offset the perception of wage stagnation, as Sarah O'Connor of the *Financial Times* wrote:

> *In the decade after the 2008 financial crisis when wage growth was fairly stagnant for many, perhaps these apps gave us a sense we were wealthier than we really were, albeit with some hidden long-term costs. Laziness might have been democratised—but not for long.*

The availability of subsidized services provided by venture darlings created a sense of wealth that made everyone feel richer—even though no one (except maybe the founders of those companies) actually got wealthier from them.

Tipping culture is a bit similar to the distortion that zero-interest-rate companies created. Businesses should, of course, pay their employees fairly, but that would create a gap between the prices we expect to pay for things and what things cost to make, which would make it clear that a lot of people can't really afford what they want. A 2023 *New York Times* article by Kellen Browning explored the math of Uber Eats and DoorDash, interviewing workers, and reported:

In the United States, Mr. Kravchenko has marveled at the gaudy displays of wealth. But he is constantly flummoxed by the stinginess of some customers.

"I don't understand how somebody can have a $5 million house and pay $3 to $5 a tip," he said in Russian, sitting in his car next to the dumpster in the Pacific Palisades alley. He switched to English: "I guess, the more money, the more problems."

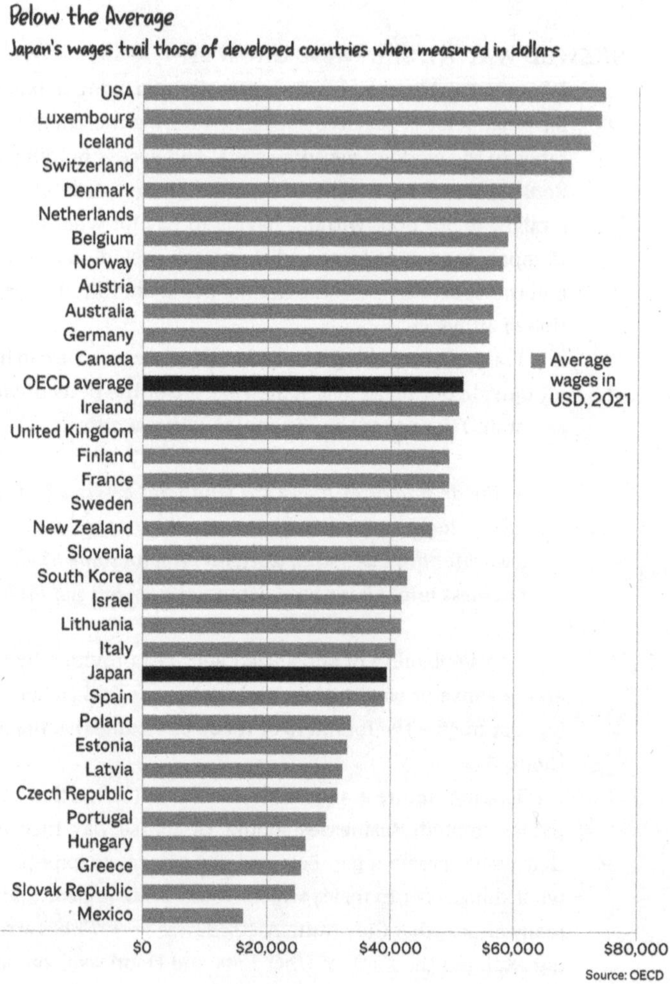

Tipping culture is becoming increasingly pervasive because most employers don't pay their employees enough. But part of the reason that tipping culture exists is that we don't love paying for what things really cost—and one of the easiest ways for businesses to reduce their expenses is to pay their employees less.

THE INTERNATIONAL IMPACT OF LOW WAGES

The idea of comparative advantage, where one country is better at producing something than others, is often based on lower wages. Lower wages in a country can lead to lower production costs, giving it a competitive edge on the global market in certain industries. This cost advantage allows such countries to specialize and export these cost-effective goods, while importing goods that are costlier to produce domestically. As the Nobel laureate Robert Solow said in a 2000 press briefing with President Bill Clinton, "China will compete for some low-wage jobs with Americans. And their market will provide jobs for higher wage, more skilled people. And that's a bargain for us."

Growth in annualized real family pre-transfer income by quantile

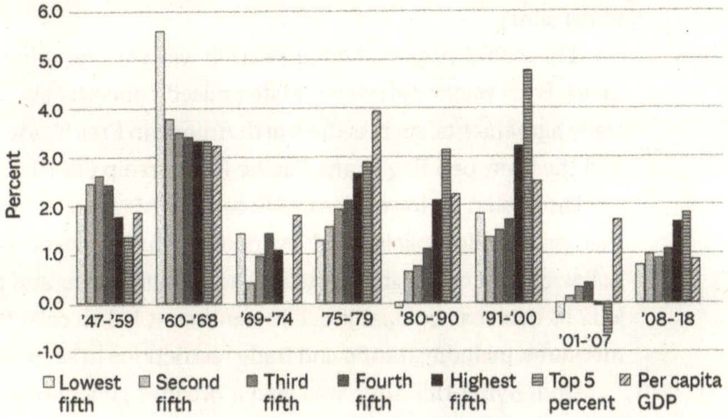

Source: Authors' calculations from U.S. Bureau of the Census, Current Population Survey, Annual Social and Economic Supplements. Tables F-2 and F-7

But Michael Pettis, a senior fellow at the Carnegie Endowment and finance professor at Peking University, argues that this sort of mindset is "bad competitiveness"—that a world that relies on suppressed wages ultimately ends up relying on huge amounts of debt to maintain demand and production levels. The theory is that the same level of output is produced by paying $20 for labor in America and $2 for labor in China; the difference just increases the profit that the producer is able to capture for itself. Pettis wrote, "The purpose of international trade should be to maximize overall productivity and, with it, to increase welfare. It should not allow individual countries to maximize domestic production at the expense of their trading partners."

Pushing low-paying jobs into other countries is not the best way for the world economy to grow. Instead, focusing on production, innovation, and more balanced trade is the best path toward an increase in wealth for everyone.

For decades, free trade was the favored policy approach of both major political parties in the United States. Everyone was excited for its potential to boost domestic economic growth, foster innovation, and lower consumer prices, so the general consensus in Washington was toward embracing global markets and reducing trade barriers.

However, the early twenty-first century saw a growing skepticism about the supposed unbridled benefits of globalization. A series of economic shocks, coupled with concerns over trade deficits, intellectual property theft, and the decline of domestic manufacturing, began to reshape the narrative that everyone had purported for years. The financial crisis of 2008 only heightened these worries, as many Americans faced job losses, stagnating wages, and economic uncertainty.

The 2016 U.S. presidential election was very revealing of the shifting sentiment. Both major party candidates raised concerns about the impacts of free trade agreements, such as the North American Free Trade Agreement (NAFTA) and the then-pending Trans-Pacific Partnership (TPP).

Discussion of downsides began to grow. Many in Washington began to argue that past trade policies had overlooked the domestic costs, particularly the hollowing-out of certain industries like manufacturing and the loss of well-paying jobs to overseas companies. This sentiment led to calls for more protectionist measures, including tariffs and trade restrictions to keep production local.

Underlying this shift was also a broader geopolitical strategy. The rise of China as an economic powerhouse posed challenges to the United States in terms of trade balances, technological competition, and global influence. This rivalry further complicated the free trade debate, as policymakers grappled with how to ensure U.S. economic security and global competitiveness, while still tapping in to international trade.

In 2022, post-Brexit—itself a function of the worries over trade and equitable international arrangements—Andrew Bailey, the governor of the Bank of England, told Britons not to ask for a pay raise to help fight the cost-of-living crisis. Of course, he makes more than £575,000 ($727,000)—eighteen times the U.K. average for a full-time employee. That generated a lot of animosity among Britons, who are mostly just trying to get by. To have someone tell them, "Just be happy with less while everything costs more" was a painful experience. The United Kingdom does have minimum wage rates, which vary depending on the age of the worker, and a relatively robust social safety net. But again, these push-and-pull wage dynamics highlight the importance of policy.

HOW WE VALUE WORK

The way we value work, especially in developed nations, is uneven. We often separate work into "white-collar" jobs (e.g., office jobs involving staring at an Excel spreadsheet) and "blue-collar" jobs (jobs that require some sort of manual labor). We are a knowledge-based society, so we place a higher premium on jobs that require a "good education" than on jobs that require a depth of physical knowledge (and oftentimes still require a good education!).

This is similar to G. K. Chesterton's thoughts about the miraculous nature of the dandelion, in which he wondered what he must have done to earn the privilege to see a dandelion—and reflects on how little we respect that privilege:

> *There is a way of despising the dandelion which is not that of the dreary pessimist, but of the more offensive optimist. It can be done in various ways; one of which is saying, "You can get much better dandelions at Selfridge's," or "You can get much cheaper dandelions at Woolworth's."... merely sneering at the stinginess of providing dandelions, when all the best hostesses give you an orchid for your buttonhole and a bouquet of rare exotics to take away with you.*

One could draw a line from Chesterton's thoughts on dandelions to the way we tend to treat certain aspects of blue-collar work—whether through lower wages, longer working hours, or simply a societal nose sniff at the jobs that most need to be done. He continued:

> *These are all methods of undervaluing the thing by comparison; for it is not familiarity but comparison that breeds contempt. And all such captious comparisons are ultimately based on the strange and staggering heresy that a human being has a right to dandelions; that in some extraordinary fashion we can demand the very pick of all the dandelions in the garden of Paradise; that we owe no thanks for them at all and need feel no wonder at them at all; and above all no wonder at being thought worthy to receive them.*

Construction, a blue-collar job, is one of those weird dynamic things. It is the foundation of the economy, meaning that it's an indicator of the health of the broader macrosphere. When residential construction employment falls, it ends up dragging down total employment (it's that powerful). As Eric Basmajian, the founder of EPB Research, pointed out:

- Building permits, the legal permission from the government to build something, are very sensitive to changes in monetary policy because builders freak out—they don't want to build during a recession!
- Building permits, these permissions to build, lead units under construction. So if there is a drop-off in permits, the number of buildings being built is going to fall, too.
- And of course, if the number of units under construction falls, so does construction employment.

When the number of housing permits issued goes down, trouble is coming for construction employment—and the rest of the economy.

WORKER POWER

If there was any possible silver lining to the inflation of the early 2020s, it was that workers were finally able to demand higher wages.

Worker power grew stronger. Even those who lost their jobs in 2022 were able to quickly get new interviews for new positions, often leading to higher pay. The reservation wage, or the lowest average wage that people were willing to accept for a new job, was $75,811 in March 2023, a substantial increase from $73,667 in November 2022, according to the Federal Reserve's Survey of Consumer Expectations Labor Market Survey. Being laid off helped a lot of people find jobs in companies that would actually value them.

The upward trend in reservation wages is primarily driven by employed respondents

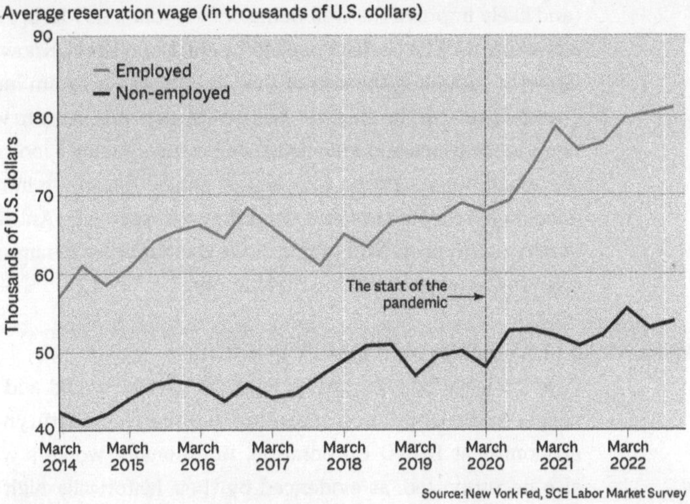

As the journalist Bryce Covert wrote on The American Prospect website:

> *What did happen when Americans got better unemployment benefits is that they were freed up to think about what kind of job they really wanted, and to pursue getting it. The labor shortage was more of a reset: People re-evaluated their relationships to work, facilitated by being able to make ends meet in the meantime.*

When we give people space to process things that happen around them and to them, they can make better decisions. When they make better decisions, they are able to do cooler things. Social safety nets are not bad things; they enable people to grow into what they have the potential to be.

HOW CAN THE LABOR MARKET BE IMPROVED?

Demographics are key, too. We have to be mindful of the aging population; about 2 percent of the fall in the labor force participation rate in the United States can be attributed to people getting older and retiring. That means we need more workers—and more ways to support them.

IMMIGRATION

Improving U.S. immigration policy would do wonders for economic growth (and likely improve the well-being of everyone). As Maria Prato of Yale University wrote in "The Global Race for Talent: Brain Drain, Knowledge Transfer, and Growth," "doubling the size of the US H1B visa program increases US and EU growth by 9% in the long run, because it sorts inventors to where they produce more innovations and knowledge spillovers." Taking a look at history can shed some additional light on this. Highly skilled Byzantine immigrants to Europe encouraged the Renaissance, according to research by Andreas Link of the University of Erlangen-Nuremberg. If we want another Renaissance, we need to be open to the ways of making that happen!

PARENTAL LEAVE AND DISABILITY POLICIES

Parental leave policies can be improved, which would add around 3.5 million people to the labor force, according to research by Kathryn Anne Edwards, an economist at RAND Corporation. Additionally, workers with disabilities can also be supported, as evidenced by their historically high employment rates during the work-from-home era of the pandemic, according to a 2022 report by the U.S. Department of Labor's Office of Disability Employment Policy. Tapping into these demographics, who are eager to work but need that extra push from policy to do so, can seriously bolster the LFPR!

RETHINKING OWNERSHIP

We can also rethink how wealth is generated in the labor market. A 2022 report by Oxfam found that the world's billionaires saw their wealth increase by $3.9 trillion between March 2020 and March 2021, while at the same time, workers around the world lost $3.7 trillion in income.

The United States has been battling wealth inequality for a long time. According to data from the Federal Reserve, the top 1 percent of households in the United States held ten times more wealth than the bottom 50 percent in 2022.

Money begets more money. And what happens when you become really wealthy is that you get into investing. Though most Americans' net worth is tied up in their homes, the very wealthy hold a majority of their wealth in stocks and private businesses. In fact, the top 10 percent of households in the United States own 84 percent of all stocks, while the bottom 50 percent own just 0.5 percent. This disparity in stock ownership has widened in recent years, with the top 1 percent of households owning 53 percent of all stocks as of 2020.

In 2023, Talmon Joseph Smith published a *New York Times* article, "The Greatest Wealth Transfer in History Is Here, with Familiar (Rich) Winners," which focused on the inheritance passed from the wealthy to their children and made a few key points: Total U.S. family wealth is now at $140 trillion, up from $38 trillion in 1989. High-net-worth families (about 1.5 percent of the population) hold 42 percent of the $100 trillion expected to be passed down (of which they will pay a mere $4.2 trillion in taxes).

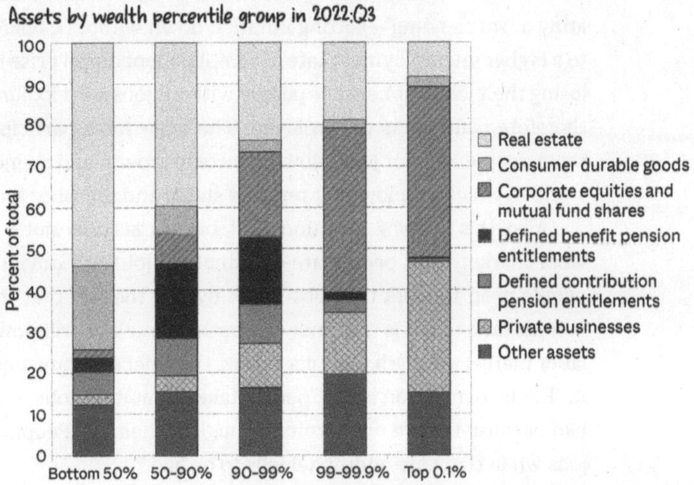

Source: Survey of Consumer Finances and Financial Accounting of the United States

Wealth is about ownership and equity. So we can talk about wage-price spirals, minimum wage, and other topics, but a key part of stabilizing the labor market might involve giving people shares in the companies they work for. That could do a lot to improve labor market incentives and wage imbalances and to help reduce wealth inequality. Other solutions involve progressive taxation, improved social safety nets, and worker ownership programs.

Publix is one example of a company that has implemented a worker ownership program. It has an employee stock ownership program (ESOP) that allows employees to buy Publix stock through their paycheck. This enables workers to hold shares in the company and therefore benefit from Publix gaining in value! The total value of the plan is north of $4 billion, with the average employee owning $22,000 in Publix stock. That's amazing!

Workers who hold stock in a company have a stake in what they make and are more likely to feel invested in the company's success. They aren't working to make billions of dollars for five dudes in suits in a boardroom somewhere; rather, they are working to make money for themselves. This enables them to build wealth over time and creates a much more inclusive and equitable economy.

BUILDING

The labor market is confusing.

There is a way for unemployment to go up that isn't bad. The policy of creating a "soft landing"—getting inflation down without causing a disaster—leads to a higher unemployment rate. Unemployment doesn't rise because people are losing their jobs but because people without jobs start looking for work and are therefore counted as unemployed. The labor force participation rate rises as more people look for jobs, slowing income growth and spending, and creates a world in which employment remains stable and the labor force grows.

Also, this is going to sound wild, but it's actually not a bad thing (for the labor market) that people are working two jobs. It's obviously not great that people need to work two jobs to get by, but the fact that they are *able* to get more than one job is a (somewhat bothersome but still powerful) indicator of labor market strength. As Julia Pollak, the chief economist at ZipRecruiter, put it, "Public perception is that people take on multiple jobs when the economy is bad because they're not earning enough in their job. People take on additional jobs when there are additional jobs to be had."

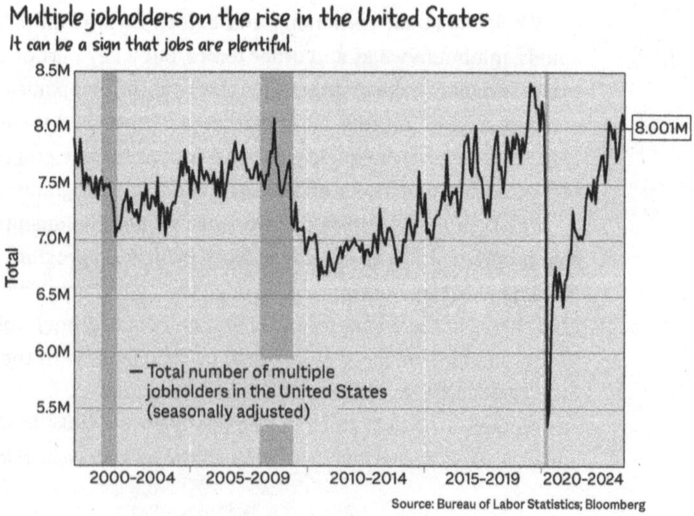

The economist Adam Ozimek published a piece in *The Atlantic* in 2023 that basically boiled down to "We don't have to destroy the economy in order to fix it," which is an incredibly important point. There's nuance, of course (rate hikes helped, as the economy needed a bit of a slowdown), but the general idea that we don't need a rise in unemployment to cause a recession to sucker punch inflation is really good; we don't need to suffer excessive pain to see progress.

There is a lot we can learn from nature when we think about how to make work and the broader labor market better. For example, trees in a forest are part of a beautiful, intricate system in which they channel various nutrients to one another, caring for one another through connection. It's an underground world, a support system that makes all the trees better. I do think we could learn from that, creating a collective world that doesn't see other people as enemies but as fellow humans, a space in which helping others is not a transaction but an equal exchange of selfless giving.

The labor market is going to be shaken up by various events over the coming years. For example, Artificial intelligence (AI) is speeding toward us at an unimaginable pace. That's terrifying, and we don't know the full extent of its repercussions yet. It's part of the reason things feel so weird right now. We never really know what the future is going to look like, but man, it sure does feel uncertain.

CHAPTER 10

The Housing Market

THE AMERICAN DREAM

The American Dream, as defined by James Truslow Adams, is "the dream of a land in which life should be better and richer and fuller for everyone, with opportunity for each according to ability or achievement." It's no secret that the American Dream (at least the way Adams saw it) is no longer what it used to be.

A lot of younger people think that we need a total market reset so they can get access to a home—otherwise, that dream (or, let's be real, any shred of stability) will never be theirs. Jerome Powell, the chair of the Federal Reserve during the 2020s housing bubble, even said that a housing market recalibration of sorts was necessary! A few things are going on with the housing market, including soaring home prices, a lack of housing in major cities, and private equity snapping up homes, leading to a housing crisis and, subsequently, a crisis for the American Dream.

THE HOUSING CYCLE IS THE BUSINESS CYCLE

Currently, a house costs 4.5 times the median family income, whereas, historically, it was 3 to 3.5 times the median family income. Housing has now become unaffordable.

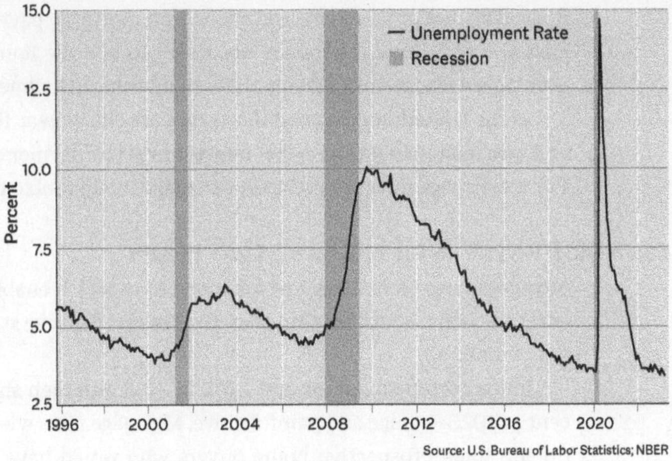

This is a supply and zoning issue. Edward Leamer, an economist at NBER, argued in his brilliant paper titled "Housing Is the Business Cycle," "Housing is the most important sector in our economic recessions and any attempt to control the business cycle needs to focus especially on residential investment." Weakness in housing sales is a core indicator of a recession, mostly because the world is driven by consumers, who are directly impacted by the cost of housing! As Leamer wrote, "it's a consumer cycle, not a business cycle." Residential investment (expenditure on constructing, renovating, or purchasing residential properties such as homes and apartment buildings), a key part of GDP, is important because people are important. But we forget that the world is made up of people and that capital appreciation (the increase in the value of something over time) isn't the core point of everything, ever.

HOW TO BUY A HOUSE

There are two ways to buy a home:

1. Put down all cash. (In July 2022, nearly one-third of all home purchases were made in cash up front.)
2. Finance the home through a mortgage.

If you finance a home, the total cost of the home is a function of the price you pay for it plus the mortgage that you have to pay off.

A mortgage is a loan specifically for buying real estate, requiring some cash up front (usually about 20 percent of the home price), known as a down payment. The rest of the house is covered by a mortgage payment. A mortgage allows you to borrow the money necessary to buy the house, and you repay it over time with interest, usually through monthly installments.

In the United States, most mortgages are thirty-year fixed-rate mortgages, so if you're able to lock in a low interest rate, the payments won't be that bad. But if mortgage rates skyrocket, it can make it impossible to finance a home.

MORTGAGE RATES OVER THE PAST TWO YEARS

Mortgage rates were really low for a long time, which enabled a lot of people to enter the housing market. But then the Federal Reserve started hiking rates to fight inflation.

Rates bottomed out around 2.5% in 2021 and then shot up to over 8 percent in 2023—a huge and painful move. Mortgage rates wield significant power, pricing some prospective home buyers who would have previously been allowed in out of the market. That also gave all-cash buyers, who are usually older and already have accumulated wealth, an advantage.

In 2020, the thirty-year mortgage rate was 2.87% and the average new home price was $405,000. By 2022, the thirty-year mortgage rate had risen to 6% and the average new home price was $547,000. That resulted in a $28,000 increase in the necessary down payment, assuming that a prospective buyer put 20 percent down, and a 96 percent increase in average monthly payments from $1,343 to $2,628—and this comparison doesn't include property taxes, insurance, utilities, and home repairs!

Over two years, monthly payments increased by almost $1,000 for a thirty-year fixed-rate mortgage. Eighteen million people were knocked out of the housing market because affordability disappeared so quickly.

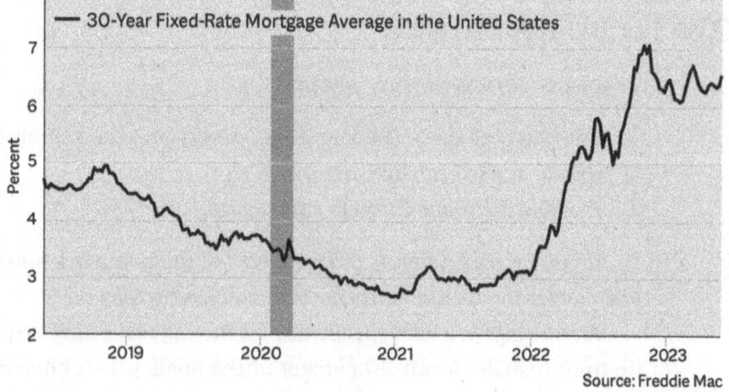

Those who were able to get in won the game. Nearly two-thirds of outstanding mortgages in the United States have an origination interest rate of 4% or less—and 39 percent of homeowners have no mortgage, equating to roughly 32 million people (mostly boomers) who are free and clear.

This creates issues across the board.

As interest rates have gone up, fewer people have wanted to invest in mortgage-backed securities, because the risk of defaulting (being unable to pay) on real estate loans has also gone up—not an attractive proposition. The effect? Mortgage providers are charging higher interest rates!

The flip side of 18 million people unable to afford owning a home is that they have to rent, which pushes rental prices up. Compound that with Millennials forgoing homeownership, and the demand can easily outpace the available supply of rental spaces—exacerbating the housing crisis more.

WELL, WHY DON'T WE HAVE ENOUGH HOMES?

So, yes, we do not have enough housing. For a few reasons (note: this list is not exhaustive):

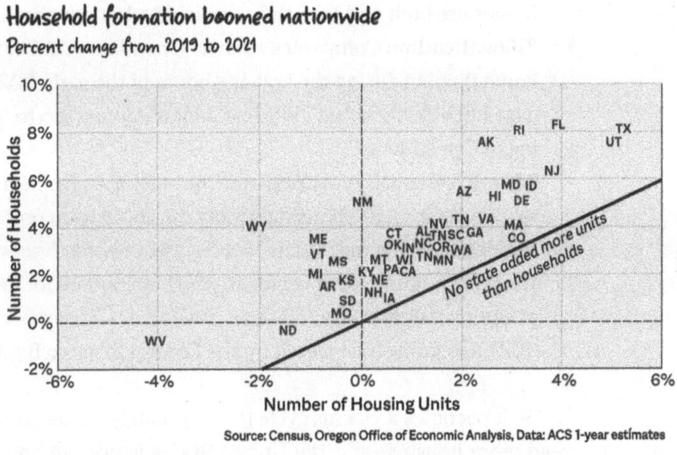

- **Regulation:** Zoning policies and obstructions to construction put into place by state and local governments make it much more difficult to build homes.
- **Types of homes:** One in twenty new homes are now built for the purpose of rental living rather than homeownership (it was closer to one in fifty during the early 2000s). According to research by CoreLogic, the percentage of

new single-family homes less than 1,400 square feet dropped from 70 percent of builds in the 1940s to less than 10 percent in 2020, so if you want to buy a starter home, tough luck. Sales of houses priced under $300,000 have fallen substantially since 2010, when they made up 70 percent of sales, to less than 10 percent in 2022.

- **Supply chains:** During the early 2020s, there were also significant issues in supply chains and labor resources, with many homes sitting idly, waiting to be finished. Paint, coating, and adhesives were in short supply due to overseas production challenges (globalization!), making building and decorating homes incredibly difficult. During the pandemic, not a single state added more housing units than new households, as reported by the American Community Survey.
- **Money:** Investors, mostly private equity firms, buy up a significant amount of real estate; according to ProPublica, they accounted for 85 percent of the biggest apartment deals by the Federal Home Loan Mortgage Corporation, also known as Freddie Mac, over the past decade. Investors have bought more than one in every ten homes sold over the past decade—twice the number before the 2008 housing crash. Capital allocators (the private equity firms and other institutions that are buying up real estate) decide how homes are built and who they are sold to, both metaphorically and literally.
- **Zillowification:** Companies such as Opendoor and Zillow were pioneers of home flipping during the housing boom of the early 2020s, but when mortgage rates skyrocketed, they lost a lot of money (up to $175 million, according to Opendoor).
- **Airbnb:** Over half of Airbnb's current listings have been added since 2020, further limiting the housing supply via short-term rentals.
- **Pandemic overhang:** Much of the surge in home prices is attributed to the work-from-home era of covid-19, which accounted for more than 60 percent of the overall increase in house prices from November 2019 to November 2021, according to research by the Federal Reserve Bank of San Francisco.

So it becomes a vicious cycle that ultimately circles back to the fact that we need more housing—and the United States is not the only country struggling with this.

HOUSING IN OTHER COUNTRIES

The crisis is actually worse in other developed nations for several reasons. The most common form of mortgage in the United States is now a thirty-year fixed-rate mortgage, but in the United Kingdom, variable-rate mortgages are often available—meaning that if the Bank of England raises interest rates, a buyer's monthly mortgage payments will increase!

In Australia, housing affordability is a big challenge due to zoning laws, land release, planning regulations, and other factors. These problems also exist in other nations. The perfect storm of climbing interest rates and expensive housing, exploding demand, and not enough housing is reverberating across the global economy.

Canada is in a league all its own. Its banks issue variable-rate mortgages. This differs from those in the United Kingdom in that U.K. banks provide more flexibility in prepayment options, while Canadian banks impose stricter penalties and Canadian borrowers have more options for longer-term fixed-rate mortgages. This means that borrowers' mortgage payments vary as the Bank of Canada raises or lowers rates, unlike payments on the United States' typical thirty-year fixed-rate mortgage—with *fixed* being the key word here.

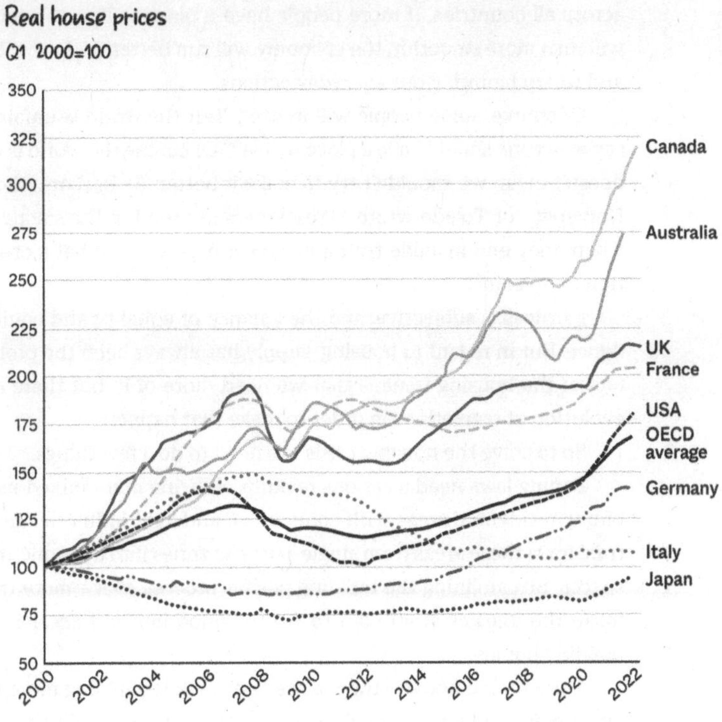

Source: OECD

FIXING THE PROBLEM

We see home equity as the way to a comfortable middle-class life. That's problematic! People shouldn't have to become real estate speculators in order to live a comfortable life. The Argentinian economics blogger Maia Mindel has written extensively about how housing is an investment opportunity—and the perceived catastrophe of home prices going down in developed nations: "By allowing the already rich to prevent the value of their [housing] investments from ever going down, the developed world has sleepwalked into an unenviable situation: one of stratified incomes, reduced opportunities, and worse outcomes for everyone."

Using a home as an investment vehicle isn't great, because it creates a vampiric housing market built on value extraction. When it gets bubbly, it gets inflationary, too. According to a report from the Federal Reserve, home price gains in the early 2020s created $9 trillion in wealth, and could have driven roughly a third of the increase in inflation during the 2020–2022 time frame.

Making sure that everyone has a place to live should be a high priority across all countries. If more people have a place to live, the economic wheels will turn more smoothly, the economy will run better, and we will have less fear and worry haunting our everyday actions.

Of course, some people will mutter, "But the world is unfair. How can you say everyone should have a place to live?" Of course the world is unfair, but that doesn't mean we shouldn't try to make it better. As Barbara Alice Mann of the University of Toledo wrote, "Westerners are fond of the saying 'Life isn't fair.' Then, they end in snide triumph: 'So get used to it!' What a cruel, sadistic notion to revel in!"

Fairness is subjective, and the balance of equality and equity is a delicate dance. But in regard to housing, supply has always been the problem. The core fact of the housing issue is that we need more of it, but there needs to be an evolution of regulations in order to make that happen.

So to solve the housing crisis, we need to do a few things.

Zoning laws need a serious revamp, allowing more mixed-use spaces combining residential areas with commercial and light industrial areas. It's time to transform these areas from single-purpose zones into dynamic, multifunctional spaces. Streamlining the building permit process so it's more transparent can make the journey from plan to reality smoother and accelerate the pace of building homes.

More prefab homes—they're the fast track to building more homes quickly and efficiently, blending modern aesthetics with practicality. Moreover, various cities are enacting policies to help expand their housing supply. For example,

South Bend, Indiana, offers preapproved house plans that can easily be built to produce more supply and support neighborhood infill. This is great!

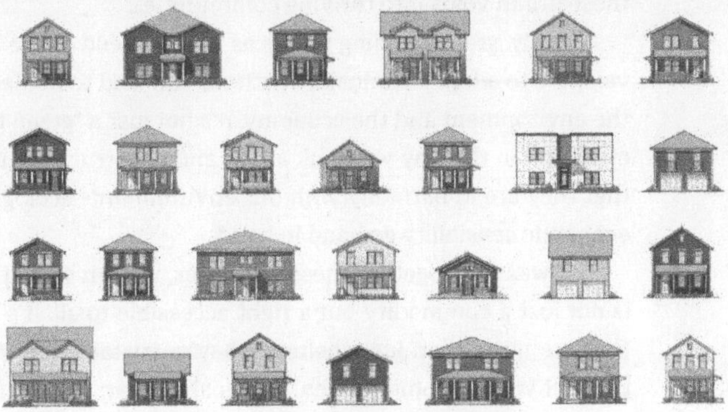

SOUTH BEND NEIGHBORHOOD INFILL
Preapproved, ready-to build housing

HOW DO MONTHLY PAYMENTS WORK?

An amortization schedule is one of the most important parts of home ownership. If you take out a $400,000 loan at 6% on a thirty-year mortgage, you will pay a lot in interest. Yet a home is one of the only things that people can buy with leverage, putting up only some of the money and borrowing the rest, and potentially see a healthy return on their investment after many years.

How payments change over the life of a 30-year loan

As the term of your mortgage progresses, a larger share of your payment goes toward paying down the principal until the loan is paid in full at the end of your term.

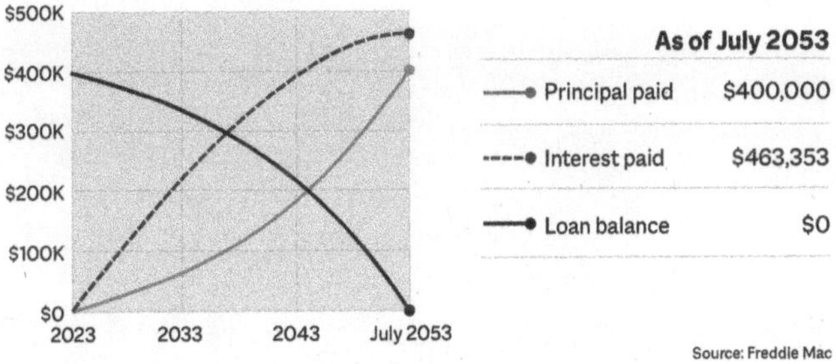

Source: Freddie Mac

When you first start paying off a traditional fixed-rate mortgage, a larger portion of your monthly payment goes toward paying off the interest, not the principal. This is because the interest is calculated based on the remaining balance of the loan, which is highest at the beginning.

As you continue to make payments, the principal amount reduces. Thus the interest calculated on this decreasing principal also reduces. Over time, a greater portion of your monthly payment goes toward the principal, allowing you to pay off the loan more quickly as you advance through the mortgage term.

Cities are peppered with underutilized spaces—let's transform these into vibrant residential areas. Offering incentives for infill development can turn these urban voids into thriving communities.

Finally, green building practices are the need of the hour. Encouraging developers to adopt sustainable methods can lead to homes that are kind to both the environment and the economy. It's not just a "green trend" but a necessary evolution in the way we think about and construct our living spaces, ensuring that they are in harmony with our environment—ecological responsibility and economic sensibility go hand in hand.

By weaving together these strategies, we can craft a future where housing is not just a commodity but a right accessible to all. It's about creating spaces that are more than just shelters—they're sustainable, affordable, and integral parts of vibrant communities. The goal is clear: to not only build more homes, but to build them smarter, more sustainably, and with a vision for the future. Let's make the dream of affordable, sustainable housing a reality for everyone.

CHAPTER 11

Stock Market

Markets can remain irrational longer than you and I can remain solvent.

—GARY SHILLING

WHAT ARE MARKETS?

Markets serve a main function as corporate financing instruments. They play a crucial role in helping companies and individuals raise money to meet their financial needs. Here are just a few examples (note: this list is nowhere near exhaustive! Markets range from the simplicity of a local farmers' market to the complexity of an "Offshore Secondary Collateralized Synthetic Derivative Futures Exchange").

- **The stock market.** Here, companies sell shares or ownership stakes in their business to the public. Investors buy these shares, and in return acquire a share of ownership in the company, becoming part owners. The money companies raise through the stock market can be used to invest in new projects, research, and development or to pay off debts.
- **The corporate bond market.** This market is a bit different. It's an opportunity for companies to borrow money from investors by issuing bonds. When a company needs funds for expansion, research, or other projects, it can issue bonds as a way to raise that money. A bond is like an IOU: The company promises to pay back the money it borrows, plus interest, to the investors who buy the bonds. The corporate bond market has different types of

bonds including "high-yield" or "junk" bonds. These bonds are riskier for investors because they are issued by companies with lower credit ratings, but they often provide higher returns if the company succeeds.

- **The venture capital market.** Venture capital (VC) is a type of financing provided to startups and small businesses that have high growth potential. Venture capitalists invest money in these companies in exchange for a share of ownership. The investment enables the startups to grow and expand their operations.

Markets also help to mitigate risk.

RISK TYPES IN MARKETS

There are several types of risk, some of which are:

- **Equity risk.** This is the risk of fluctuations in the prices of individual stocks and the broader stock market, which can be impacted by company performance (such as when Apple has a bad day) as well as trends across industries, broader economic conditions, and how people are feeling (investor sentiment).
- **Interest rate risk.** If the Fed moves rates, all sorts of things begin to topple. It can put pressure on stock valuations, as higher rates reduce the value of future cash flows.
- **Systemic risk.** If a bank fails, the market is going to have to think about what that means. Systemic risk includes everything from bank failures to broader recessions to regulatory failures—anything that could remove a Jenga block from the overall market stack.

Managing risk is all about making things more stomachable. The stock and bond markets help distribute company risk to investors, the housing market diversifies risk across homeowners, renters, and builders, and the labor market accommodates employees and employers forming the foundation of the economy. Just as the value of money is a collective belief, the behavior of every market is determined by the collective decisions of millions of investors based on their perceptions of reality. Markets reflect the foibles (and triumphs!) of human behavior and decision-making.

STOCK MARKET VERSUS ECONOMY

That being said, it's important to distinguish between the stock market and the economy. People often conflate stock market numbers going up with the success of the broader economy—but they are two very different beasts.

- **The stock market** is the physical manifestation of the performance of individual companies. The market determines how money moves throughout the economy and shows how corporations are using money in their business decisions, such as leveraging capital for certain projects or deploying assets in new markets to try to make more money.
- **The economy** is measured primarily by growth of the GDP, a measure of consumer spending, government purchases, investment, and net exports.

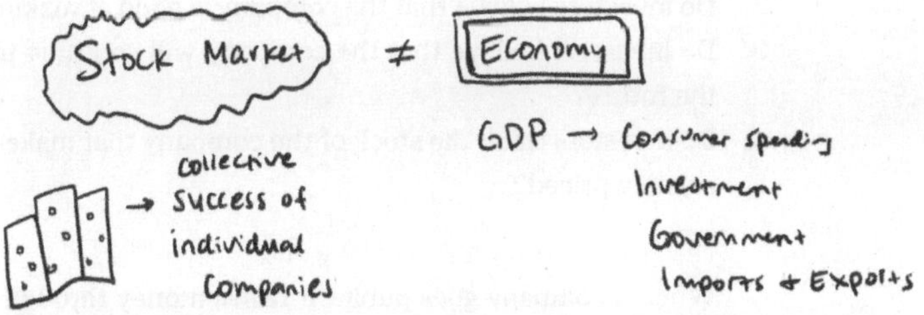

The stock market is a high-risk, high-reward game. What is sort of funny about the stock market of the early 2020s is that most of the giant companies are really ad salespeople masquerading as big tech. As Ethan Mollick, a professor at the Wharton School, has pointed out, "Compared to industrial giants of the past, Meta, Twitter, & Google are very specialized: they are overwhelmingly advertising firms. Even after all of Google's new initiatives, it is still 85% ad sales."

We can think of the stock market as being like an apple tree: Each company is an apple, and each slice of that apple is a share of the company's stock. So when you buy stock in a company, you are essentially buying a slice of its apple. You own a tiny piece of the company, and when the company makes money, you should make money, too. Ideally, your apple slice will go up in value over time, and one day you will be able to sell it for more than you bought it for.

At the most basic level, a company's stock is the reflection of the answers to four questions:

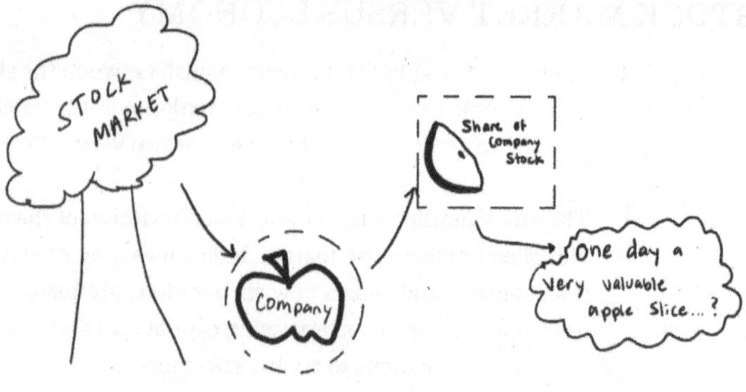

1. Do investors believe that people want the thing (or things) a company makes?
2. Do investors believe that the company is good at making the thing?
3. Do investors believe that the company will continue to make the thing in the future?
4. Do investors think the stock of the company that makes the thing is appropriately priced?

When a company goes public, it raises money through an initial public offering (IPO). That's when it sells its apples to everybody in a public marketplace: the stock market. Privately held companies, especially startups, generally provide employee stock options, but those are not accessible to the general public.

A higher share price doesn't necessarily mean that a company is worth more overall than other companies. A company's valuation is the share price multiplied by the number of shares outstanding (the number of shares of company stock that have been issued and are held by shareholders), which equals the market capitalization, or market cap. This is what the company is *really* worth—the valuation.

VALUATION EXAMPLE

Let's say that Microsoft stock is trading for $250 and has 8 billion shares outstanding, while Starbucks stock is trading for $100 and has 1 billion shares outstanding. To get the true valuations of the two companies, we need to multiply the share price by the number of shares outstanding:

- Microsoft market cap = $250 × 8 billion shares = $1.8 trillion
- Starbucks market cap = $100 × 1 billion shares = $100 billion

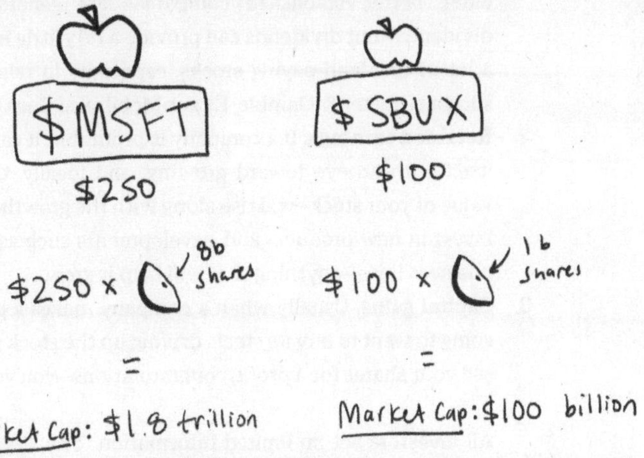

So even though they are kind of close in stock price, Microsoft is a *much* bigger company and therefore has a much bigger market cap.

Share prices fluctuate! Microsoft might trade all the way down to $100 or all the way up to $400—sometimes in the course of one day but usually over the span of a few weeks. Stocks move around so much because of investor sentiment, or how people are feeling about the companies.

- If investors think that Microsoft is going to do amazing things, more of them will buy the stock, pushing the stock price up.
- If they think that Microsoft earnings are going to be underwhelming, they're more likely to sell their existing shares or even short the stock (bet that the stock price will go down), which is the opposite of owning it. This pushes the stock price down.

Individual stock picking is difficult. A number of unpredictable factors can impact a company's performance. A natural disaster, fraud, or a pandemic can all result in a company's share price cratering. The market is not a moral compass, so it doesn't always respond to fraud or disaster or pandemics the way we think it will. On the flip side, a company's introducing new products, making an acquisition, or changing its leadership can trigger a run-up in its share price.

When you own a stock, that slice of the apple can make you money in a few different ways:

1. **Dividends.** When the company makes a profit, it often pays a portion of it to its shareholders; this is called a dividend. Not all companies do this—older, better-established companies are generally the ones that pay dividends—but dividends can provide a tidy little income stream if you own a lot of dividend-paying stocks, especially in relatively stable companies such as Procter & Gamble, ExxonMobil, and Coca-Cola.
2. **Retained earnings.** If a company is profitable, it can reinvest its profits into itself with an eye toward growing; and ideally, the share price—and the value of your stock—will rise along with the growth of the company. It might invest in new products and developments such as new buildings and new business lines—anything that will help it grow.
3. **Capital gains.** Usually when a company makes a profit, a lot of people are going to want to buy its stock, driving up the stock price. If at that point you sell your shares for a profit, congratulations—you've just made capital gains.

All investors act on limited information. The stock market is the price of hopes and dreams. A couple factors can influence how confident investors feel about realizing their dream of making a profit:

- **Company performance:** Four times a year, every public company has to report to its owners (the shareholders) how things are going. It reports how much money the company has made (revenue), how much money it has made after deducting costs (profit), and what the company team thinks will happen in the future (forecasts).
- **Target prices:** A lot of the success of certain parts of the finance industry is based on trying to predict how companies' share price will move ahead of the earnings report being published; analysts will often release share price targets, or what they think will happen to the stock price based on what they think will happen with the earnings report. Analysts trot out all sorts of valuation models, but most of the time, they make educated guesses based on vibes and their gut feeling.

When I worked at Capital Group, I spent a lot of time building valuation models. There are several valuation models; two of the most common are a discounted cash flow model, which estimates a company's value based on expected future cash flows, and comparable analysis, which compares financial ratios and multiples such as price-to-earnings ratio or enterprise value to earnings before interest, taxes, depreciation, and amortization, or EBITDA, across similar companies. Even for professionals, it can be challenging to figure out what growth rate makes sense based on past data and future expectations. Investment advisers publish the numbers—what they expect Microsoft's revenue to be, for instance—and if the company misses the target, it can negatively impact the stock price. If the company beats the target, it can positively impact the stock price.

In the long run, a lot of this is noise—a basket of diversified companies known as ETFs is usually the best path for most people to go to profit from the stock market (not investment advice!).

EXCHANGE-TRADED FUNDS

Stocks can be bundled into various financial instruments, such as exchange-traded funds (ETFs). These are baskets of stocks that track various indices, commodities, and asset classes. They reduce the risk of holding any one security. For example, farmers plant multiple crops to safeguard against the failure of a single crop, and many companies offer more than just one product in order to manage risk and achieve balanced outcomes. ETFs serve a similar function by offering diversified investment exposure to hedge against uncertainty.

IS BLACKROCK RUNNING THE WORLD?

ETFs are funny because a lot of people think that BlackRock, one of the top ETF providers, is secretly running the world because it is invested in so many different companies. But BlackRock, although it is powerful, is not telling the companies in its portfolio what to do. It owns a huge number of shares in the largest companies in the world, trillions of dollars' worth of assets, so many people believe that surely it controls all those companies, right? Well, no. The shares represent its clients' money; the ultimate owners of the shares that BlackRock or, as another example, Vanguard has in various companies are the people who invest with BlackRock or Vanguard.

In 2022, Vanguard, one of the top ETF providers, was the top holder of 69 percent of the companies in the S&P 500. That doesn't mean that it is directly managing 69 percent of all companies; it just means that it is holding the stock of those companies in investment products that it then sells to investors. Its officers are on the boards of directors of those companies, helping make strategic decisions and whatnot, but they usually vote for what the company wants to do.

INDEX PROVIDERS

Index providers, such as MSCI, FTSE Russell, and S&P Dow Jones, are extremely important, too, and they work closely with ETF providers. They have a symbiotic relationship, wherein the index providers create various indices to gauge the performance of various markets and the ETF providers use the indices to manage their ETF products. This is important! In November 2017, Bloomberg journalists Tracy Alloway, Dani Burger, and Rachel Evans published an article titled "Index Providers Rule the World—for Now, at Least," exploring the power of the companies that determine which companies are put in their baskets. As they wrote:

> *Something else that might be described as imbalanced: the growing clout of index providers such as MSCI, FTSE Russell, and S&P Dow Jones Indices. In a market increasingly characterized by passive investing, these players can direct billions of dollars of investment flows by reclassifying a single country or company, effectively redrawing the borders of markets, shaping the norms of what's considered acceptable in international finance, and occasionally upsetting the travel plans of government ministers.*

Instruments called *passive vehicles*, which replicate indices, generate huge amounts of inflows for the index providers. It's the simplest way for most people to get exposure to the market. But it creates problems because the index providers decide which company's stocks are invested in. As Peru's former finance minister Alonso Segura Vasi put it, "Investors' decisions to invest in the market are significantly guided by their decisions, whether they put you in the index or do not put you in the index. They do control the fates of companies' and countries' access to capital markets."

Markets, stocks, ETFs, and other instruments are meant to trade on fundamentals or trade like the company (or bundle of companies) they are tracking profitability-wise, expense-wise, cash flow-wise, and so on; that's the theory, at least. The discounted cash flow model creates a valuation of the current share price that is based on a certain set of expected cash flows that a company *should* produce based on its profitability and earnings, a discount rate is calculated, and all of that indicates a present value at which the asset is ultimately priced.

PASSIVE VERSUS ACTIVE

The addition of Tesla, Elon Musk's electric vehicle company, to the S&P 500 as a large weight was a seminal moment for passive investing—investment strategies that aim to replicate the performance of a market index such as the S&P 500. Active investing is actively choosing which stocks to invest in based on educated guesses based on research with the goal of outperforming rather than simply matching performance.

Tesla's addition to the S&P 500 index was a notable event due to the company's high market capitalization and its prominence in the electric vehicle industry. As a result, when it was added to the index, many passive index funds that tracked the S&P 500 had to buy Tesla shares to align their portfolios with the index. That led to increased demand for Tesla stock and a surge in its price, contributing to the so-called Tesla effect. So there was a lot of volatility and trading activity as people bought Tesla stock, leading to a lot of attention to the stock on the part of media, analysts, and retail investors.

But this is where markets get funky. From a performance standpoint, passive indexing has demonstrated its effectiveness over time. Many studies have shown that a significant majority of active fund managers consistently fail to beat their respective benchmark indices, such as the S&P 500. In fact, Morningstar's U.S. Fund Fee Study reported in 2021 that only 23 percent of active funds outperformed their counterparts from 2010 to 2020.

As a result of the inefficacy of active investing, investors have increasingly turned to passive index funds and ETFs as a way to achieve broad market exposure at a lower cost and with greater diversification. But passive investing creates a sort of loop. As more investors shift toward passive investing strategies, the prices of the stocks included in the popular indices are influenced primarily by the flow of funds into passive funds, rather than the companies' individual merits. This can lead to price movements that are driven more by market flows than by fundamental factors—and result in a circus.

THE STOCK MARKET IS SEVEN COMPANIES

The industry has also become very concentrated, leading to more circus-ry. Financial markets have gotten really, really big, driven mostly by a few key companies, especially in the United States. According to Jamie Dimon, the CEO of JPMorgan Chase:

> *I have written before about the diminishing role of public companies in the American financial system. They peaked in 1996 at 7,300 and now total 4,600. Conversely, the number of private U.S. companies backed by private equity firms has grown from 1,900 to 11,200 over the last two decades. And this does not include the increasing number of companies owned by sovereign wealth funds and family offices. This migration is serious and worthy of critical study, and it may very well*

increase with more regulation and litigation coming. We really need to consider: Is this the outcome we want?

As of 2023, the stock market is dominated by tech companies, including Apple, Meta (formerly known as Facebook), Nvidia, and others. Seven stocks—Apple, Meta, Nvidia, Amazon, Tesla, Microsoft, and Alphabet Inc, Google's parent company—were 26% of the S&P 500 as of 2023 and made up more than 110% of its gains. Without those seven companies, the S&P 500 would have been down 0.8% versus *up* 7% on the year through May 2023. Concentration risk is the highest it's been in decades because the S&P 500's largest companies make up a significant portion of its overall value—meaning that if those companies fall, so does the market.

S&P 500: Weighting of top holding (annual, 1980–2023)

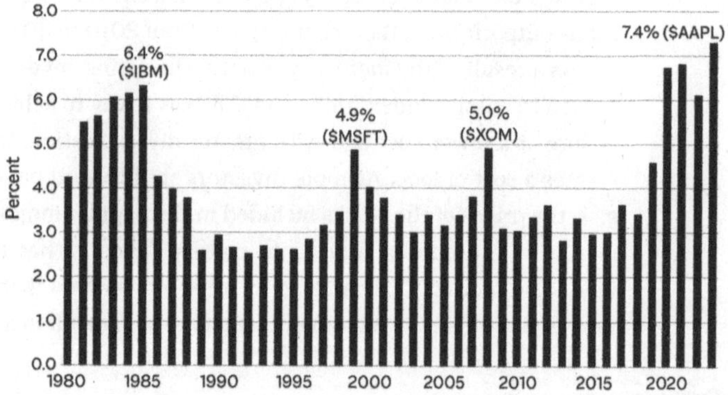

Source: S&P Dow Jones

Small companies tend to remain private, because, as Dimon highlighted in the letter, "the governance of major corporations is evolving into a bureaucratic compliance exercise instead of focusing on its relationship to long-term economic value. Good corporate governance is critical, and a little common sense would go a long way."

Markets are bloated. As Michael Pettis tweeted:

Financial markets have grown so large relative to the underlying economies that regulators have no choice but to intervene to protect failing banks, even though this only reinforces further growth in the financial system. Perhaps the solution is not to keep saving the banks, nor even to let them fail, but to take longer-term measures to cut down the size and importance of the financial system in the US and global economies. Banks should be cut down, different sectors of the financial system segregated, financial transactions taxed, and capital controls implemented that limit massive hot money flows. Critics will say that these measures will reduce the efficiency of the financial system, and they are right, but increased efficiency in the financial system has long ago stopped meaning increased efficiency in allocating capital productively, and has meant instead increased efficiency in financial flows.

You can see this trend in the chart of market capitalization versus GDP shown below, also known as the "Buffett Indicator," a number that Warren Buffett prefers to look at to get a sense of where valuations stand at any given moment. This is the total market value of all publicly traded stocks within a country divided by that country's gross domestic product, and as you can see, it's high. The market is overvalued relative to GDP, and the stock market is growing faster than the economy.

Wilshire 5000 to GDP ratio

Total value of all publicly traded stocks/GDP ratio (Dec 1, 1970–Jul 27, 2023)

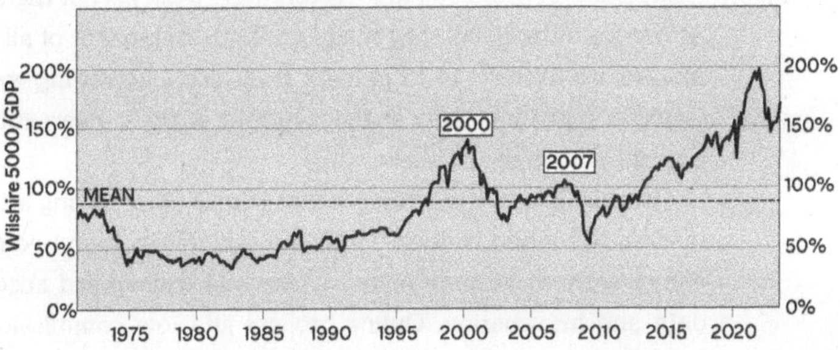

Source: Longtermtrends.net

The unfortunate thing about markets is that they have sort of devolved into a "vibe fest," deviating from their original purpose. They were designed to be practical—yet relatively boring—tools for people to get money to do useful economic things. But they've largely separated from that, making concepts like intrinsic value and the efficient markets hypothesis mostly useless.

EFFICIENT (AND INEFFICIENT) MARKETS

The efficient market hypothesis, formulated by Eugene Fama in the 1960s, states that prices reflect all available information, stocks always trade at their fair value, and the only way to outperform the market is through accepting higher risk.

However, the stock market is a game that increasingly reflects our artificial interests. Back in 2021, companies such as GameStop and AMC Entertainment Holdings exemplified this phenomenon. The two companies' business models didn't have any inherent value, but their stock price was bid up for speculative purposes (investors knew that the companies would never be profitable, but it's a fun game to play).

In 2021, reality evaporated from pretty much all markets. There was no concept of fundamentals or company valuations based on the earnings the companies produced or the cash flows they achieved. The stock market was instead based on internet points and social media fervor.

We can see this in zero days to expiration (ODTE) options activity, put-and-call options on individual stocks that expire within twenty-four hours—basically, a gauge of speculative activity based on earnings releases or economic data reports. As the number spikes, it means that more speculative activity is occurring.

The year 2021 was a very speculative cycle, in which the stock market was treated like a casino. Retail investors were a big part of the memefication story. At one point in 2020, they made up 20 to 25 percent of all value traded in the market, up from 10 to 15 percent from 2019, according to Citadel Securities. GameStop put investors at the forefront of the conversation, giving them the power to move the market.

It was clear in the numbers that people were paying attention to the stock market. Robinhood added 6 million users in less than two months. Call option values were at all-time highs. There was widespread accessibility to margin debt and information. Online brokers and low commissions facilitated flow. Elizabeth Lopatto, a senior editor at The Verge, explained it this way:

> *Are there any people under the age of 40 who have ever thought markets were something besides a casino? Meme trades aren't the cause of widespread distrust, they're the symptoms of it. And those people under 40 who think finance is for gambling? They're the lucrative part of Robinhood's user base. Legal issues aside, it seems like Robinhood has a good business model for monetizing financial nihilism—which is the kind of thing investors might get excited about.*

GameStop and AMC are a perfect example of reflexivity and animal spirits. Their story is emblematic of how confusing markets can be and how nothing

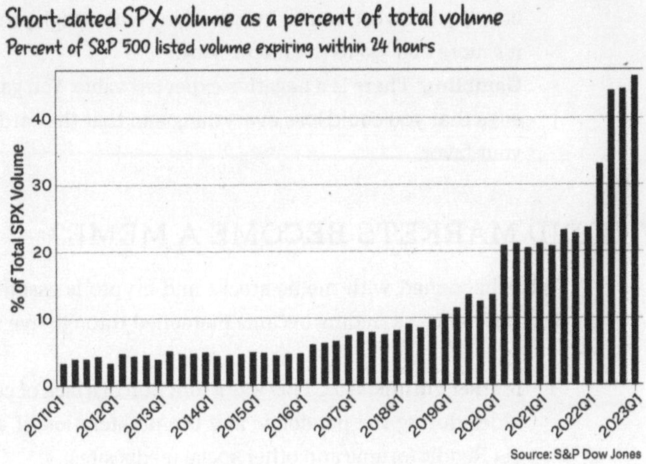

makes sense if you think of "sense" in the traditional terms of logic and knowledge.

WHAT HAPPENED IN 2021?

Speculation is a key element of our human nature. Collective belief is the driver of asset value in a lot of cases! If people believe that a stock or crypto token should go up by X percent and funnel their dollars into it, more people will be like, "What's going on over there?" (this is reflexivity, which I talked about earlier!) and then—*boom!*—its price will go up.

In 2021, a lot of the value drive was based on "But what if this [enter random stock or cryptocurrency] becomes very, incredibly valuable?" Our human brains love speculation—think about how many people play the lottery or gamble. We have FOMO. We have a collective belief in memes. We have the idea that if you aren't playing the game, you won't win, so you might as well toss a few coins into the ring.

And our society has a get-rich-quick mindset, which increases the likelihood of our speculating instead of investing. There is a difference between investment and speculation and gambling, based mostly on the probability of success.

- **Investing:** If you put your money into Apple stock with the reasonable expectation that Apple will continue to be an okay company and make money.
- **Speculation:** There is a positive expected value: When you speculate on the markets, you put $50 into Dogecoin with the hope of making $500 mil-

lion. If you invest money in something with a high probability of failure and it's more of a "go to the moon" vibe.

- **Gambling:** There is a negative expected value: You gamble with the knowledge that you could lose everything and that the cards will likely not fall in your favor.

WHY DID MARKETS BECOME A MEME?

What happened with meme stocks and crypto is essential to understanding this difference as trading became memefied through five main factors:

1. **Market enthusiasm.** This was a function of a lack of consumption opportunities during the pandemic and the proliferation of access to information via Reddit forums and other social media sites.
2. **Risk-on sentiment.** There were a lot of you only live once (YOLO) vibes during the pandemic because everyone was stuck at home and the concept of life was absurd.
3. **Liquidity.** About 40 percent of stimulus checks went into the stock market, and of course, any sort of excess creates exuberance.
4. **Meme markets.** Special purpose acquisition companies (SPACs), NFTs, and GameStop are all "real" products that can be traded, but they were fueled by the power of memes rather than the power of reality.
5. **Globalization of markets.** For example, FUTU, a Chinese-based fintech company that operates an online brokerage platform that enables users to trade all sorts of financial instruments—specifically, retail investors in China to trade U.S. stocks and other assets—does a huge volume of business.

Financial instruments such as crypto, meme stocks such as AMC and GameStop (ticker symbol: GME), and the whole era of Elon Musk tweeting about random coins are an important lens into this weird era of speculation. There were a lot of people who made life-changing money by investing a few dollars in things such as SHIB coin or Bed Bath & Beyond stock. One of my friends opened a bar with the profits from his trades! And all of this was driven by a collective belief in the value of an asset.

As we saw with GME/AMC/the meme stocks, sometimes things don't trade purely on the basis of fundamental factors such as financial performance but rather on the basis of speculation and hype. The efficient markets hypothesis bears out only in a perfect world.

CHAPTER 12

Bond Market

THE BOND MARKET

The bond market and stock market are sort of similar; both are platforms for companies to raise money and allow people like you and me to participate in the process.

Bonds are a vast, complex network of financial instruments that form a cornerstone of modern finance, but outside Wall Street, they aren't really talked about a lot! Bonds are the undercurrent of the rivers we all wade through, the backbone of the stock market, and the support system of most of the businesses we interact with every day.

Most people who want to buy a car, a house, or anything else that is big and expensive need to take out a loan. Companies, as well as governments and financial institutions, have to do the same if they want to finance a really big project. But rather than going to a bank, they go to the bond market.

WHAT ARE BONDS?

Bonds represent the debt of a company, government, or municipality. When you buy a bond, you are lending money to one of those entities for a certain amount of time so it can carry out various projects or finance certain activities, and in return it pays you interest over that time period. Bonds tend to have a lower risk than stocks because they have regular payments called coupon payments that they pay out to investors on a set schedule—and bond investors are paid before shareholders if the company ends up going under.

The bond market facilitates the flow of money between entities that need it (borrowers) and those that have it (lenders). For example, Kansas City, Missouri, approved an $800 million infrastructure repair program, financed by General Obligation bonds. The goal was to repair streets, bridges, sidewalks, and more as part of their GO KC Program. It would normally enlist a broker/dealer to help sell these bonds to investors such as mutual funds. Bonds have a lot of complex components.

BONDS BETWEEN FRIENDS

For now, think of it as being like borrowing $10,000 from a friend. "I'll pay you back in two years," you promise them; they become the lender and you the borrower. To make sure they know that you're not going to dip out before paying them, you tell them that you'll pay an annual interest rate of 1% with semiannual payments: $100 a year, paying $50 twice a year. The yield (the return generated by the investment over a period of time) on the bond is 1%; because the bond isn't trading on the open market, the market value and the face value are the same. This is a simplified example—and bonds are different from regular loans. Bonds are issued by governments, municipalities, and corporations (not by regular people) and are often traded on markets (loans usually aren't, unless they are packed into the MBSs or CDOs I talked about before).

This underground bond sale that you and your friend are entering into has a few components:

- **Maturity date.** This is the two-year time frame that the two of you entered into, the time in which the face value, or total value of the bond ($10,000) will be repaid.
- **Coupon rate.** This is the 1% interest that you're paying annually. This is usually a fixed percentage of the face value of the bond, which is $100, or $50 twice a year.
- **Number of periods.** You entered into a two-year agreement by which you're going to be paying your friend four times (semiannually ends up being four payments over two years), so this is four.
- **Yield to maturity.** The future value of coupon payments is discounted via this rate—the rate of return investors would get if they reinvested every

coupon payment from the bond at a fixed interest rate until the bond matures, which is quite a chore to calculate. To simplify, we can just assume that it is 2%.

This is where things get mathy, but that's okay!
First, let's calculate the present value of the semiannual payments:

$$50/(1.01)^1 + 50/(1.01)^2 + 50/(1.01)^3 + 50/(1.01)^4 = \$195.09$$

Now we'll calculate the present face value of the bond:

$$10{,}000/(1.01)^4 = \$9{,}609.80$$

Added together, we get the total value of the bond = $9,804.89.

So if you want to trade your bond on the market (or if your friend wants to trade it on the market after they buy it), this is what it would trade for. We calculated the present value of the bond's expected value based on the coupon payments you promised your friend for sticking around.

Stocks are valued in sort of the same way—the net present value of future cash flows—but bonds return interest payments, plus the loan principal when the bond finally reaches maturity, so the valuation model for bonds and stocks is actually quite different.

There are two more important things to know about bonds:

1. **Bond prices and interest rates are inversely correlated.** That means when interest rates go up, bond prices go down, because they usually were issued with a lower rate. So if you have a bond paying 2% and then interest rates tick up and all the new bonds are paying 3%, your bond is going to fall in value because people are like, "There is *no way* I am paying a lot to take on that lower yield!" It's the opposite when interest rates decrease. If rates fall and all the new bonds are paying 1%, your 2% bond is going to look superhot, leading to it trading at a premium because everyone is like, "*Please* give me the yield."
2. **Duration determines bond movements in relationship to outside factors.** Duration is how a bond's price sensitivity to a 1% change in interest rates is measured. When you have a longer-term bond, like thirty years, it's going to be pretty sensitive to changes in interest rates because it has to exist for such a long time, with a lot of future cash flows. A shorter-term

bond has less exposure to interest rate fluctuations because it isn't around as long.

Of course, as when anyone owes anyone else money, there is risk! The risk here is that bondholders might not be able to make their payments to you; this is known as the default risk.

A *bond rating* is the measure of the creditworthiness of a corporation, organization, or institution based on its profitability and the stability of various projects it is working on.

BOND RATINGS

Starbucks, for example, has a rating of BBB+ from Standard & Poor's (one of the two main ratings agencies) and a rating of Baal from Moody's (the second main rating agency), which is an assessment of Starbucks' credit risk and ability to pay back the bond. Both of those ratings are low investment grade, meaning the agencies think that Starbucks can pay its loans back perfectly fine and isn't at too high a risk of default but may be susceptible to adverse economic conditions or changes in the business environment.

Companies with a higher credit rating (usually those that are better able to repay their debts) are going to have a tighter spread than companies with lower credit ratings. There are other things that influence credit ratings, including the amount of collateral a bond issuer puts up. Bond issuers *love* when they can possess collateral in the case of default—so if a borrower can put up an asset to make sure everyone is feeling good, that helps a lot.

AAA bonds have the most immaculate vibe, are "investment grade," and pose the lowest risk to investors. "High-yield" bonds (those rated BB and below) are riskier, but they also (usually) pay higher rates of return because of that risk.

HIGH-YIELD FRIEND

Let's say you have a friend who is a bit loose with their budget. They're constantly asking you to loan them a little money, and they don't always come through on their promise to pay it back. So you wise up and become more hesitant to lend them money—maybe even charge them interest on the money they still need to repay you. They are risky relative to your other friends. The friend spread is wide.

That same story plays out in the bond market!

If the spread is wide—meaning that the company is wildly risky relative to government securities—lenders will begin to demand higher interest rates.

If your friend said, "Hey, I need to borrow a hundred dollars, and I will give you my laptop as collateral," that's even better. You might even charge them a lower interest rate because if they *don't* repay you, you get to keep the laptop.

> **WHAT IS A SPREAD?**
>
> The most important thing to know about bonds is how they move (in terms of interest rates) relative to other bonds. How bonds are moving relative to other bonds relative to how U.S. Treasury bonds are moving is called the ***credit spread.*** This is the price of corporate bond risk relative to that of "risk-free" U.S. Treasury securities.
>
> For example, let's say the ten-year Treasury bond is trading around 3% and a ten-year corporate bond is trading with a yield of 4%. The spread between the two is 1%, or 100 basis points (1 basis point equals 0.01%). That 1% yield is what you get paid for taking on corporate risk (the corporation's risk being greater than the government's).

TREASURY BILLS, NOTES, AND BONDS

U.S. government bonds are usually considered to be risk free, because historically, and in an ideal future world, the U.S. government is very unlikely to default on its debt. One of the most critical ingredients of asset prices is the price of safety, or the assurance of risk-free investments, which is represented by the yield on risk-free assets such as three-month Treasury bills, which are assumed to have very little (if any) default risk. You might say, "The U.S. government seems pretty risky to me!" Risk is relative. The term *risk free* implies three main things:

1. SAFE: The U.S. government is unlikely to default on its debts.
2. LIQUID: The Treasury market is liquid, meaning that there are usually a lot of willing buyers of government debt: foreign governments, investors, and others.
3. STABLE: The short term minimizes rate movements, meaning that over the short term (say, three months), rates aren't going to bounce around too much.

The risk-free rate is crucial because it's used to value all other assets, including stocks, bonds, and the rates people pay on their mortgages. For example, an increase in the risk-free rate puts pressure on stock valuations because it raises the discount rate I talked about earlier, which bites into the expected market return because future cash flows will be worth less. The term *risk-free rate* in the bond world is somewhat like the North Star of the finance world. When the risk-free rate moves, it's like a domino effect: Everything from stock prices to corporate bonds and even your neighbor's mortgage rate feels the impact. It's a baseline that tells investors what they can expect to earn without taking on excess risk.

TREASURY MARKET

So Treasuries are meant to be the safest asset in the world. These are the underlying forces powering the global market ecosystem because they are the bonds that the U.S. government sells in order to raise money and finance its activities. There are three types of Treasuries:

1. **Treasury bills.** These range in maturity from one month to one year.
2. **Treasury notes.** These have two-, three-, five-, seven-, and ten-year maturities.
3. **Treasury bonds.** These mature in twenty to thirty years.

Treasury yields, particularly the ten-year yield, are seen as a useful indicator of how people are feeling about the economy. The relationship between Treasury yields and investor sentiment is complex—but higher yields on long-term

Treasuries can sometimes be associated with positive investor sentiment and optimism regarding economic expansion and increased business profitability.

What is really important is how yields relate to one another across something called the yield curve, the relationship between bond yields and maturity dates.

- The yield curve should generally be *upward sloping;* you should be compensated more for holding thirty-year bonds than ten-year bonds because there is more uncertainty (and hopefully economic growth) on the thirty-year horizon.
- However, sometimes the yield curve *flattens.* This means that investors in the bond market don't see a lot of economic opportunity over that timeline; essentially, they feel, the market in ten years will be relatively the same as the market in thirty years.
- Also, sometimes the yield curve *inverts.* This is bad. This means that the bond market is *not* happy—investors don't expect economic growth in the future. An inverted yield curve normally signals a recession.

But as economists at the Federal Reserve wrote, "It is not valid to interpret *inverted term spreads* as independent measures of impending recession. They largely reflect the expectations of market participants." (Author's emphasis.)

What the heck, right? Expectations manifest reality! And before you ask, "Isn't this book about economics, not astrology?," let's just say that economics and astrology have more in common than not.

The basic takeaway is that the yield curve reflects economic vibes. When it inverts, vibes are bad. When it's upward sloping, vibes are good. But sometimes the vibes are confusing. Inversion of the yield curve does not always mean that a recession will follow; it just means that things are not looking hot.

The inverted yield curve has preceded recessions in the past, but it isn't a foolproof oracle of what is to come; nothing can be. We must understand why things go up, because that will tell us why other things go down. Treasuries are the foundation our economy rests on. Most countries hold them, most investors hold them, and they're the support beams of the entire U.S. economy.

So in the world of government bonds, U.S. Treasuries are often the poster child for stability and low risk. Each country usually issues their own sovereign bonds, with a different profile of risk and return. Some, like German Bunds or U.K. Gilts, are pretty stable. Others, from countries with less stable economies, like Argentina or Zambia, are much riskier. Just like U.S. Treasuries, these sovereign bonds are a reflection of a country's economic health and a good gauge of global financial currents.

MARKETS AS VIBE REFLECTORS

In his book *Reminiscences of a Stock Operator*, a lightly fictionalized account of Jesse Livermore, a legendary trader in the late 1800s who knew the game of market psychology and emotions all too well, Edwin Lefèvre wrote:

> *Nowhere does history indulge in repetitions so often or so uniformly as in Wall Street. When you read contemporary accounts of booms or panics the one thing that strikes you most forcibly is how little either stock speculation or stock speculators to-day differ from yesterday. The game does not change and neither does human nature.*

Livermore was incredibly good at predicting market movements and trends, shorting the market (betting that it would go down) before the 1906 San Francisco earthquake and the 1929 Wall Street crash. There's a list of investing rules published by Martin Zweig, another incredible investor and analyst, that echoes Livermore's credo, "There is nothing new on Wall Street."

SHEARSON HUTTON

Shearson Lehman Taxable Fixed Income Technical Analysis

The Market Technician's Association Monthly Meeting 4/11/90

Marty Zweig's Investing Rules

1) **The trend is your friend, don't fight the tape.**
2) **Let profits run, take losses quickly.**
3) **If you buy for a reason, and that reason is discounted or is no longer valid, then sell!**
4) **If the values don't make sense, then don't participate. (2+2=4)**
5) **The cheap get cheaper, the dear get dearer.**
6) **Don't fight the FED (less valid than #1).**
7) **Every indicator eventually bites the dust.**
8) **Adapt to change.**
9) **Don't let your opinion of what should happen, bias your trading strategy.**
10) **Don't blame your mistakes on the market.**
11) **Don't play all the time.**
12) **The market is not efficient, but is still tough to beat.**
13) **You'll never know all the answers.**

14) **If you can't sleep at night, reduce your positions or get out.**
15) **Don't put too much faith in the "experts."**
16) **Don't focus too much on short term information flows.**
17) **Beware "New Era" thinking, i.e., it's different this time because . . .**

All seventeen rules are based on managing emotions. That's been the schtick of this whole book, right? Vibes and feelings are much more important to how the economy (and stock market) functions than we give them credit for. The reason we tend to ignore the emotional aspects of these things is that they sound sort of silly. They make it difficult to plan policy. And of course, as Morgan Stanley wrote in an investor letter in 2023, "Price has driven narrative for generations. . . . Strong US growth, persistent EU inflation & a disappointing China reopening are all recent narratives supported by prices. But for all 3, the fundamentals look more complicated and face key near-term tests."

Price drives narrative. So parts of how we interact with the economy and markets are emotion, influenced by price, but it's very much which came first—the chicken or the egg? The price or the story?

Wasteland Capital, a popular Twitter account, tweeted in November 2022, "It's fascinating that finance professionals can look at exactly the same product, financials, data set, management team, facts and events, and draw completely opposite and entirely conflicting conclusions." The stock market is bizarre, because, as Wasteland Capital pointed out, no one really agrees with what is going down at any given point. The industry is based on making money off people disagreeing on what will happen and why.

There is a lot of speculation in markets. They haven't done what they need to do. As Martin Sandbu, the *Financial Times*' European economics commentator, wrote in July 2022:

> *Yet these past 20 years have been the era of lower-than-ever financing costs, first because of market exuberance, then thanks to central banks' ultra-lax monetary policy. And what do we have to show for all that cheap credit? Two lost decades for investment. . . . I think our failure to invest is profoundly political. . . . That is true in good times, when transfer payments, tax cuts and immediate public goods are all politically more attractive than capital investment. (Something equivalent is at work in the private sector: witness companies' choice to return cash to owners through share buybacks rather than invest in their own growth.) It has also been true in bad times, when investment is the easiest expenditure for belt-tightening governments and companies to cut.*

Society at large has gotten a bit lazy. We have sacrificed tomorrow for today, and the markets are a prime example of that. Sandbu highlighted companies that are conducting share buybacks, or buying shares to boost their stock price, rather than saying, "Maybe we should invest in our company for longer-term growth." That isn't great.

Market blowups, such as the 2008 financial crisis and the dot-com bubble, occur when people forget that they actually exist in reality, with real-world constraints that need risk management, and money becomes a religion of sorts. We get caught up in the game, and the game becomes us. We become defined by the money we make—the gains. When losses come, so does the loss of faith.

Markets are a pressure cooker, too. In 2023, a writer at Bloomberg published an article titled "Corporate America's Earnings Quality Is the Worst in Three Decades," which basically took the stance that corporate America was engaging in a little bit of accounting embellishment to make the numbers look better than they are. As Gregg Fisher, the founder of Quent Capital, said in the article, "The pressure on these leadership teams is intense. If you're getting ready to release your earnings and you can move a penny around somewhere from left to right, it just might tell a better story that as long as it's legal, they do it."

Part of the market dance is that hedge fund assets have gone parabolic, part of the dance is trying to appeal to markets, part of the dance is just to stay alive as a company—it's all a very delicate balance.

Value of assets managed by hedge funds worldwide from 1997 to 2023

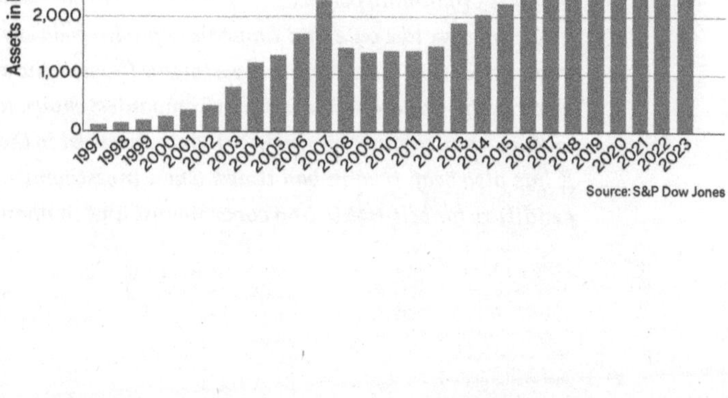

Source: S&P Dow Jones

We repeatedly learn the same lessons regarding markets, risk taking, and making educated decisions relative to what has happened historically, but it seems that each time we must process the knowledge differently. Things sort of change, but there is always the same underlying problem of exuberance or zero risk management, and because markets are based in human nature, we repeat the same errors over and over again.

CHAPTER 13

Cryptocurrency

Humans are drawn to challenges that echo the Darwinian struggle, where survival hinges on the dynamics of tribal allegiances and social ties. This competitive spirit underpins the allure of cryptocurrency. It's a realm where ownership, network effects, technological innovation, and financial interests converge.

Jamie Dimon of JPMorgan Chase has dismissed Bitcoin as "a fraud," while Nobel Prize–winning economist Paul Krugman has derided cryptocurrencies as "a techno-mystical bubble wrapped in libertarian ideology."

Cryptocurrency remains a paradoxical phenomenon. It was developed in the late aughts, surged to staggering popularity, waned, and then revived, all within the span of the last decade. Similar to all new markets, there's a ton of rug pulling, money grabbing, behind-the-scenes moves that make uneven markets—some are in the know, others aren't.

THE CRYPTOCURRENCY NARRATIVE

There are four different interpretations of the broader crypto narrative:

1. **Get rich!** Crypto is really just a parade of wealth, a bunch of rich people getting richer and leaving everyone else behind.

2. **Ownership, governance, and participation.** For some, crypto offers a unique proposition where users can buy tokens that enable them to own and vote on projects. The idea is that crypto is going to change how the economy functions through modifying how we work, play, and do things (however, what those *things* are is rather imprecise).
3. **Technological infrastructure.** Some see beyond its financial aspects, where crypto acts as an extension to the existing internet, leveraging blockchain to inject decentralization, transmutability, and transparency into digital spaces.
4. **Diffused networks.** Some lean really heavy into the lack of centralized control, with markets and interactions spread across a network of independent participants.

The narratives are always compounded by fear of missing out (FOMO). During the 2021 era bubble, this sentiment drove buyers to value assets like the non-fungible token (NFT) *Golden Fur Bored Ape* at $1.5 million or the EtherRock, an Ethereum Pet Rock JPEG selling for $1.3 million. Because, of course.

Crypto has always been prone to speculative activity. It's bubbly, similar to traditional markets in a lot of ways. As with most aspects of finance, there is an element of Ponzinomics in everything having to do with it. The more money that goes into the crypto industry, the better it is for the crypto industry.

It's all a bit... floofy. But one of the biggest complaints people seem to have with modern society is the financialization of everything—the increasing influence that the financial markets have on our daily lives. The financial sector has grown, advertising is ubiquitous, and it often feels as though shareholder rights supersede civil rights, as the *Financial Times* noted in 2023. That makes sense, right? Every time you turn around, some buy now, pay later company is trying to get you to pay four monthly installments for a pizza. Everything we do is a money sign, something to monetize or build a brand from.

There is a lot of debate in the federal government about the best way to approach cryptocurrency—whether it should develop its own central bank digital currency, or CBDC, and how to regulate it. (Is it a security? A commodity? Who's in charge around here?)

One big difference between crypto and dollars is that people don't invest in dollars. They can save them or use them to invest in other things, like stocks, but dollars are transactional agreements, not investment tools. The dollar is a government accounting device, not a speculative asset.

Tech faces a lot of issues, including centralization, data ownership, privacy concerns, and a lack of moderation. Finance grapples with similar problems, including widening wealth gaps and centralization of wealth in the top 1 percent. Crypto is presented as a solution to these challenges: decentralizing the centralized, redistributing data ownership through smart contracts, implementing privacy and moderation tools via the blockchain, and dispersing wealth.

But the problem of the rich getting richer remains unsolved. Crypto has the same problem that traditional finance has: People who have a lot of money have the greatest opportunity to make more money. And a lot of crypto solutions create more problems. There are a lot of scalability problems, and the industry is plagued by security issues, including hacks, attacks, and fraud. The high energy consumption associated with crypto is also a major concern. Cultural issues exist, too, with a focus on get-rich-quick schemes and an abundance of scams and bad actors.

Also—

It's inaccessible. "Gas fees," or the costs to transact on the blockchain network, can price people right out. The user interface isn't always great. Too many people ride the get-rich-quick bandwagon, and not enough people take advantage of the underlying "get-rich" possibilities.

Crypto is a deviation from traditional finance. It was originally designed to be a way to think about finance as a culture and a representation of a community. It's a weird, decentralized, tokenized world. Crypto is also a Swiss-type bank account (i.e., highly private and confidential) for people running from their governments who don't want to keep a stack of gold bars in their backyard. The monetary use case for crypto is that it is largely convenient and liquid and its value goes up as financial censorship increases. It's largely meant to shield assets from prying eyes.

But as I talked about previously, *crypto has always attracted speculative activity.* And there are a *lot* of ways to speculate in crypto: NFTs, tokens, DAOs, Bitcoin, Ethereum, SHIB coin, Dogecoin, Poopcoin. The list is endless. It's like a never-ending game of Jenga, and if you pull a block out, you could either make millions of dollars or lose everything on a picture of a cat.

The Securities and Exchange Commission (SEC) is trying to figure out how to regulate crypto. Because crypto trading is decentralized, there really isn't a main regulator saying, "Hey, no, don't steal millions of dollars."

The SEC seems to be trying to regulate the industry in the same way as securities (the courts might disagree, given what's been going on with the cryptocurrency XRP). It judges whether cryptocurrencies are securities by using the Howey Test, which labels financial instruments as said securities if there has been "an investment of money with an expectation of profits derived from the efforts of others." So most of the industry does tend to fall under the securities umbrella, which means that crypto issuers have a lot of paperwork to file with the SEC—which isn't great for the ethos of decentralization.

The crypto industry has a lot of components, including the following.

NONFUNGIBLE TOKENS

Nonfungible tokens (NFTs) are kind of like digital trading cards, unique digital assets that are owned on the blockchain. NFTs are funky. They can be used for digital content; creators, as opposed to platforms, own their work. They can also be used for purchasing domains and physical assets such as real estate and cars. Most important, though, an NFT is the pointer to an asset, not the asset itself. So when people say, "I took a screenshot, this monkey JPEG is mine!," that's not technically true. The value doesn't rest in the picture itself; it rests in where the picture sits on the blockchain, which is what the NFT points to.

An NFT is a function of status, identity, and belonging. It usually has one owner, and that's the goal because NFTs work best for assets or content or art that is unique and scarce and has proven ownership. No two NFTs are the same, and their existence in the public record gives each of them verifiability and credibility.

Of course, theory and reality can diverge.

IS DOGECOIN ALIVE OR DEAD?

When it comes to crypto assets, it's important to understand the difference between tokens and coins. Coins are native to their own blockchain and are often used as a form of currency or as a way to pay for transaction fees on the network. Examples of coins include Bitcoin and Ethereum. Tokens, on the other hand, are often built on top of an existing blockchain and can represent a variety of assets or functions within a network. For example, a token might represent ownership in a DAO or access to a specific application on a decentralized platform.

Shiba Inu (SHIB) coin is another example of speculation within the crypto universe, and it gets into the funky existence of a Schrödinger coin. SHIB is in the same land as Dogecoin, which is based on a picture of a dog. And it really is based on a meme rather than reality! But in 2021, someone made a *bunch* of money after investing $8,000 in SHIB in August 2020. By October 2021, their position was worth $5.7 billion. Gross!

This also showcases the inherent push-pull of speculation because liquidity is key to functioning markets. There is no way to pull $5.3 billion out of SHIB without causing it to crash. Much of crypto's value comes from new investments and guesses about its future. So, Dogecoins often change in price based on trends and popular internet jokes. Schrödinger coin shows the paradox of speculation. It's similar to the famous thought experiment of Schrödinger's cat, which exists in a superposition of states (is it real or not?) until it's actually observed, just as crypto exists in a superposition of states until it's bought or sold.

But if you can't get your money out, are you really rich? If you can't get the money, is it really yours? Is Dogecoin alive or dead?

There comes a point when you have to open the box and see what's inside. This means selling your crypto, right? But liquidity is key. If everyone who owns a cryptocurrency tries to cash out at once, the value of the currency will plummet, everyone will lose money, and the double-edged sword will stab everyone in the eye.

This is FOMO, the idea that if you don't throw your entire net worth into a meme coin, you'll never make the once-in-a-lifetime wealth that everyone else seems to be making. But ultimately, it's a dice roll, and memes get you only so far.

The "why wouldn't you?" is where the value comes from. But the reality is that there's no guarantee of what you will find when you open the box.

Of course, the natural inclination with a lot of the events that happen in crypto is to shout into the wind, *"well, I would never buy this stuff!"* And that's okay! Honestly, I wouldn't buy some of it, either. But someone will. And that's all that matters for keeping the industry alive.

FTX

I am going to touch on this briefly even though it's a bonkers situation that represents the perfect alignment of greed and grift. It's not quite a timeline but rather a representation of the vortex of the universe it's in. Many people believe they understand crypto, but the reality of what goes on inside crypto companies can be more like gambling than speculation.

FTX was fraught with stupid, big bets that worked until they didn't and financial engineering that morphed into (or always involved) fraud and beyond. There are four key things to know about FTX:

- **FTX was a very big player.** FTX was a powerhouse in the industry—so much so that it bailed out other crypto companies such as Voyager and BlockFi a few weeks before it collapsed (this would come to haunt its directors later).

- **FTX's tentacles were spread throughout the industry.** It was sort of associated with a hedge-fund-venture-capital-esque firm called Alameda Research but not technically, because it was kind of illegal to be too closely associated with it. So FTX's directors made sure to say, "No, we aren't that closely associated with Alameda," and everyone was like, "Sure, totally makes sense."
- **FTX's directors had no concept of risk management.** They also made sure to highlight excessively that there was zero downside to any of the things they were doing! No risk at all!
- **Sam Bankman-Fried was the face of the industry.** Sam Bankman-Fried, a cofounder of FTX (as well as Alameda, just to give you a hint of how messy this would get), was the regulators' darling; he was called to testify before Congress to help shape regulations for the crypto industry, giving out total OhBoyFounderGeniusExtraordinaire vibes, very similar to Mark Zuckerberg when he testified about Facebook.

But those four factors became a perfect nightmare. On November 2, 2022, Alameda's balance sheet was leaked by CoinDesk. And everyone was like, "Hey, why do you have, like, $3.6 billion of FTT and $2.16 billion of FTT collateral?" FTT is a token issued by FTX for trading fees, which meant that Alameda and FTX were very much intertwined—even though they really shouldn't have been.

Alameda quickly tried to stem the problem by saying, "Oh, noo, ha-ha, that's not our balance sheet, that's a figment of your imagination" (which was somewhat true, as some of its assets were imaginary). However, Changpeng Zhao, the CEO of Binance, another big crypto exchange, was like, "Buckle up." You see, Changpeng and Sam had a bit of beef. Sam, as the face of the industry in the United States, was helping design regulations that would hurt Binance (and the broader industry), so beef was warranted.

But their history went back farther than that. Binance had helped spin up FTX, had sold its stake about a year before, and in exchange, had received $2 billion of FTT, among other things. Changpeng said that he was going to sell his stake in FTT and opined, "I think that your firm is going to blow up."

That was a nuclear situation for FTX, so Caroline Ellison, the CEO of Alameda Research, tweeted at him on Twitter, "Hey, we can buy all your FTT for $22," and the market freaked out! Then a bank run happened (that was a theme of the latter half of 2022 into 2023!).

FTX was flailing, and so was Alameda. People took $6 billion out of FTX, which created a vacuum. FTX then paused withdrawals. Binance was like, "Hey, we can save you," but then saw the pit of Hell that was the balance sheet and quickly said, "Never mind!"

Meanwhile, Sam Bankman-Fried was tweeting wildly, assuring everyone that everything was fine and trying to find $9 billion to close the deficit, which, of course, is what we all do right before our company implodes. But things kept getting worse! Imagine that you are crawling around in a sewer and shining a light down side tunnels! That is this!

As it turned out, Alameda's directors weren't good at trading. They had gotten too aggressive with venture investments, had a large margin position, pledged illiquid collateral (money that they really didn't have) to do more bets—and were well-capitalized gamblers. FTX filed for bankruptcy—it and its 134 associated firms. John J. Ray III, the man who liquidated Enron, stepped in as CEO, threw his hands in the air, and let out a scream.

But then things got spookier, because it turned out that SBF had built some sort of backdoor so that Alameda could borrow an unlimited amount of money from FTX—Alameda's $1 million was FTX's $1 million, which is very illegal.

FTX's balance sheet was a nightmare, a Crayola crayon copy of some other dimension of reality. It was composed of tiers of liquidity: liquid, less liquid, and illiquid. That is not at all how a balance sheet should look; a balance sheet should *balance* assets and liabilities. Meanwhile, FTX had less than $1 billion in assets and $9 billion in liabilities, which was not good.

The company's *most liquid* asset was Robinhood shares and a hidden, internal "fiat@" account, which apparently was $8 billion accidentally sent to Alameda (who among us hasn't sent an accidental $8 billion to a friend?) and a token called TRUMPLOSE. Its two *biggest* assets were FTX and something called Serum, which is also something FTX helped create. Collectively, those were worth $10 billion before the crash—at least according to the balance sheet. And that gets back to Schrödinger coin—anything is worth $10 billion if you say it is! Like yes, your toaster is theoretically worth $10 billion until it's time to sell it—and then it isn't.

Then contagion occurred. A lot of big crypto companies have imploded this way. The speculation came to an end. The directors of the venture capital firms that had invested in FTX were like, "whoops," and just sort of shook their heads sadly, although they probably should have been very aware of what was happening.

The episode exposed the underbelly of the crypto universe in a really impactful way and woke everyone up to what was actually going on with FTX, the darling of the crypto universe. It likely caused irreparable harm. It also showed how important it is to pay attention to companies' decision-makers.

WHERE CRYPTO WENT WRONG

Despite its potential, there's substantial resistance to crypto. It's meant to be an anchor of hope, yet the crypto world often doesn't seem inclusive for everyone. Open source for whom? Collaborative with whom? Decentralized by whom?

Crypto was meant to be a reimagining of how the world works, taking things from Web2, taking other things from finance, and putting them into a hodgepodge package based on decentralization, ownership, and a bunch of other buzzwords.

Of course, governments are paying attention and have partially tolerated blockchain because it's a useful technology. Central bank digital currencies, or CBDCs, are digital versions of a country's regular money created and regulated by the government. In March 2021, the Bank of Japan explored a digital yen program to see how a CBDC could be used in payment and settlement systems. In April 2020, the Bank of England published a paper that talked about the monetary policy use case for a CBDC.

And of course, blockchain technology, known for its secure and transparent nature, has been considered for some CBDC projects because it could reduce fraud and enable quicker and cheaper cross-border transactions as well as make it easier for central banks to implement policies, control interest rates, and manage the money supply in real time.

In July 2023, the U.S. government established FedNow, a digital payments system, finally catching up to where the rest of the world had been ten years before. Most countries seem interested in the concept of a CBDC, which provides seamless transactions and a microscope on what people are doing, but how long they will take to implement the tech is another conversation entirely.

We want to own things. We want to build things. Crypto provides tools to do that, but it might have lost its soul in the euphoria. Either way, owning the online (how do people who use the internet benefit from the upside of the internet, versus Big Tech capturing all the value?) will be a theme as we become increasingly embedded in the digital world, and crypto is an early iteration of a solution for what that could look like.

CHAPTER 14

Recessions

A global recession would be an expensive waste.
—ADAM TOOZE

RECESSIONS AND ECONOMIC DOWNTURNS

Recessions occur when the economy shifts from a period of expansion to contraction, and it can be a technical nightmare to figure out if we are in one.

Even when the economy is technically *not* in a recession, high gas and food prices can make it feel like one. Recessions, an unfortunate economic reality, are some of the scariest things we have to deal with. They're one of those eco-

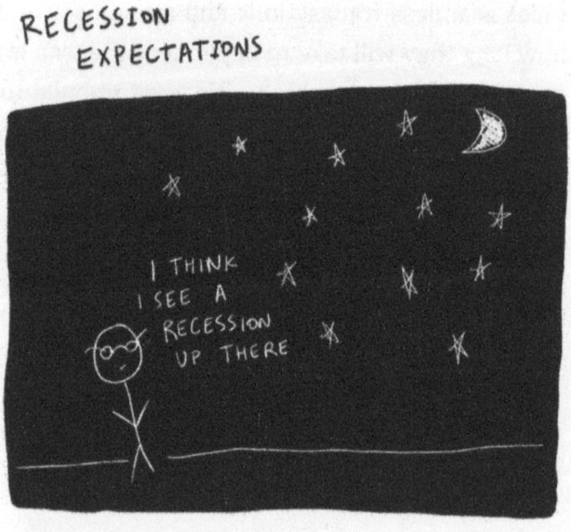

nomic maladies that plague us because of the boom-bust cycle of our economic systems.

The world is cyclical, and the economy fluctuates between periods of economic expansion and contraction due to changes in government policy, consumer sentiment, spending, and business investment. The markets love "line go up," which creates a lot of incentives for things to go up in the broader economy! And to go up way too fast! Eventually, all of it—the economy, markets, and everything in between—will come crashing down.

THE SEMANTICS OF A RECESSION

The strangest thing about recessions is that we usually don't know if we are in one until *after* it's happened. In the United States, recessions are determined by the National Bureau of Economic Research (NBER), a nonprofit organization that uses various metrics to figure out where we are in the economic cycle. They take into account a whole slew of economic data, including:

- Total nonfarm employees
- Employment level
- Industrial production
- Real manufacturing and trade-industry sales
- Real personal income excluding transfers
- Real personal consumption expenditures
- Gross domestic product (GDP)
- Gross domestic income (GDI)
- The average of GDP and GDI

There isn't a fixed rule to determine when recessions happen; it's just a combination of the above data points and the general vibe that NBER gets from the economy. It looks at depth, diffusion, and duration (the three D's).

- Depth: how much economic indicators deteriorate
- Diffusion: how broad that deterioration is across the economy
- Duration: how long the deterioration lasts

For example, we had a recession from February to April 2020 when the covid-19 pandemic began. Twenty-one million jobs were lost in two months—the *depth* was there, as production levels, employment levels, retail sales, spending, and personal income all collapsed. The *diffusion* was there, too, with economic weakness across almost every single industry. *Duration* was a little different, as the recession was only two months, but it was so deep and widespread that the amount of time didn't matter.

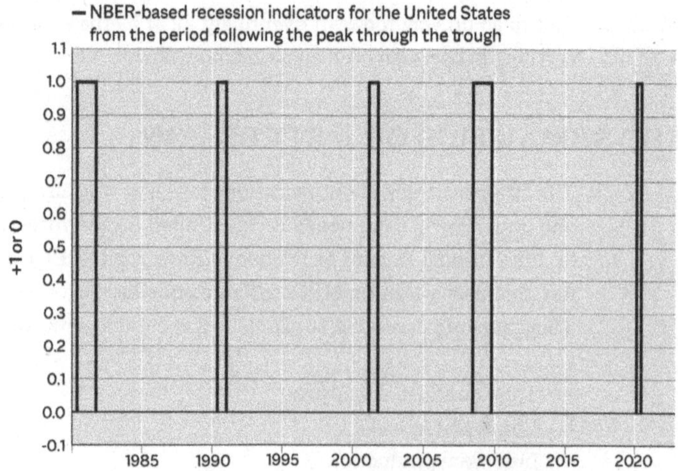

Source: The Federal Reserve Bank of St. Louis

However, there is an element of subjectivity in determining if we are actually in a recession. As James Hamilton of the University of California at San Diego wrote:

> *The NBER's dates as to when U.S. recessions began and ended are based on the subjective judgment of the committee members, which raises two potential concerns. First, the announcements often come long after the event. For example, NBER waited until July 17, 2003 to announce that the 2001 recession ended in November, 2001. Second, outsiders might wonder (perhaps without justification) whether the dates of announcements are entirely independent of political considerations. For example, there might be some benefit to the presidential incumbent of delaying a declaration that a recession had started or accelerating a declaration that a recession had ended.*

NBER is pretty subjective—it takes its sweet time and isn't immune to politics (just like any other institution).

The crucial thing about all this is how people perceive and experience their circumstances. If we are in an economic slowdown, it doesn't make it any better by defining it as a recession or not. The most important thing is how we move forward. The lens through which we view our world quantitatively is archaic. For example, the inverted yield curve is one way that markets will attempt to signal if we are in a recession. However, the yield curve is not always accurate and works only within a pretty small sample size.

Yield-curve inversions have been a reliable recession indicator

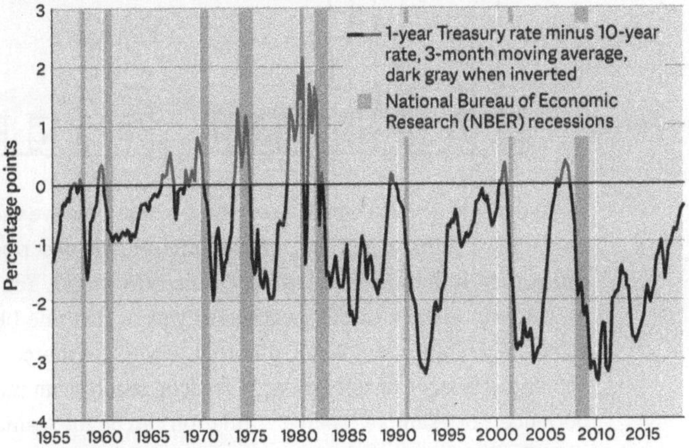

Source: Federal Reserve Board; NBER

The term *recession* is largely semantic. This might sound silly, but *recession* is a label more than anything else. It's good to know when and why a recession happens, but when we are in one, we could call it a potatocession and it would still have the same impact. What really matters is wage growth, unemployment, opportunities, and so on.

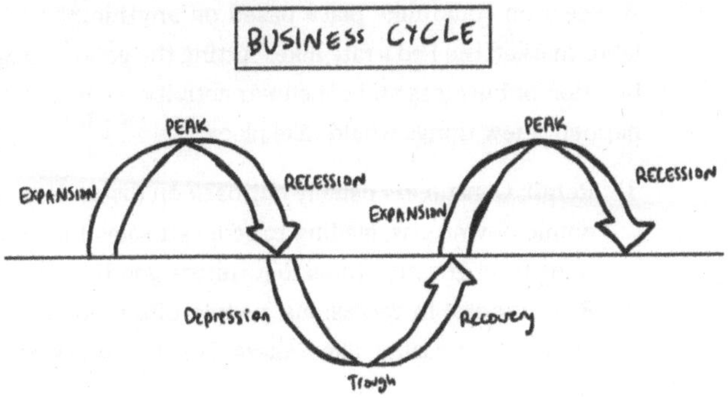

In the words of the gaming expert known as Cheesemeister on Twitter, "Mario games teach us that even if something is essentially the same, psychologically it can be completely different. This example is very easy to understand."

We live in a world where everything is not what we thought it was going to be (which I think is just life), so the differentials described above matter because they influence how we experience the world. You can be at the same height with a stack of blocks beneath you or just one block floating—it's the same height, but a completely different way to get there.

The economy, despite its wide-ranging reach, is an incredibly personal experience. For example, 5 percent inflation can be the "same" for everyone but is actually completely different because 5 percent means a lot of different things to different people. If you read that inflation is at 9.1 percent but feel as though it's more than 20 percent because of your experience of shortages at the grocery store and your rent going up $1,000, that creates pain. This can feel like a recession, but it isn't. Technically.

WHAT DOES A RECESSION LOOK LIKE?

A recession could take place based on anything from a slowing down in the labor market, the Fed's rate hikes hitting the economy in a big way, or any combination of business and consumer activity coming to a halt. If a recession did happen, a few things would take place:

1. **Retail:** Consumers usually cut back on discretionary spending during economic downturns, leading to reduced sales for retailers, impacting everything from grocery stores to furniture goods.
2. **Restaurants:** In recessions, people often cut back on dining out to save money. Fast-casual, like Panera Bread, and luxury dining establishments,

like Salt Bae's restaurant in Las Vegas, might be particularly vulnerable, though fast food sometimes proves more resilient.

3. **Travel/Tourism:** This industry is highly sensitive to economic downturns. Business travel can decline when companies look to cut costs, and leisure travel drops as households tighten their belts. The 2020-2021 period really highlighted the vulnerability of this sector to external shocks (like the covid-19 pandemic).
4. **Leisure/Hospitality:** This sector, closely related to travel and tourism, would likely see reduced revenues. Hotels, resorts, and other destinations would experience declines in bookings, and entertainment venues, like cinemas and theaters, might see fewer patrons as everyone tries to save money.
5. **Service Purveyors:** Professional services, especially those deemed nonessential, could see decreased demand. For instance, luxury services or elective medical procedures might see reductions.
6. **Real Estate:** Housing markets can be impacted in several ways during a recession:

    a. **Residential:** Potential homebuyers might delay purchasing due to economic uncertainty, leading to a decline in sales and potentially in prices.

    b. **Commercial:** As businesses contract or shut down, demand for office and retail spaces might decline (exacerbating the already strange state of commercial real estate due to people working from home).

    c. **Manufacturing/Warehouse:** These sectors are closely tied to consumer demand. As people buy less, there's less need to manufacture goods or store them in warehouses. Also, global disruptions can impact supply chains, affecting manufacturing operations.

HISTORIC RECESSIONS

There are real economic downturns that have lasting, devastating consequences. The recessions of 2008 and 2020-2021 are two such examples. Both downturns greatly impacted people's lives and left lasting scars, but they were completely different from each other.

2008 RECESSION

The 2008 recession played out over many years. A slew of bad decisions compounded to create a massive tower of financial instability. The housing market boom was the best-known part of this. Lenders were like, "Oh, yeah, this is what I want. I am going to lend to anyone and everyone," leading to a series of loans to people who were likely to be able to pay them back as well as loans to people who were unlikely to pay them back. The biggest problem in 2008 was that people expected home prices to go up forever. As Antoinette Schoar, an economist at the MIT Sloan School of Management, saw it:

> *The problem with the banks was less a misalignment of incentives or deliberate misselling of loans to people who couldn't afford it, and more, if you want, stupidity. It was this belief that house prices could only go up, and so it didn't matter whether the person who was buying a particular house might lose his or her job and default on their payments. The bank would be holding valuable collateral and everything would be fine.*

The problem was the belief in "home prices go up forever": optimism about the cyclical housing market on the part of the banks and people buying homes.

The mortgages were packaged into financial products known as mortgage-backed securities (MBSs). The securities were then sold to investors worldwide, who were like, "Let's get some exposure to the *very strong* housing market in the United States and the American Dream! That's always been a good and stable thing!"

It was not a good and stable thing! The housing market started to cool off, home prices began to decline, and everything began to fall apart. A lot of borrowers found themselves unable to repay their loans, leading to a bunch of foreclosures on homes across both prime and subprime mortgages. That was devastating, not only for the people who were being foreclosed on but also for the value of the mortgage-backed securities, which became essentially worthless.

To make things worse, a lot of the mortgage-backed securities were insured through credit default swaps, a type of financial instrument. By protecting investors from the risk of people defaulting on debt obligations, they were supposed to insure the investments against loss—so if they did become worthless, investors would still be okay. But because everything went so bad so quickly and so many people were affected, the insurance companies couldn't meet all the claims.

Everyone freaked out. There was a credit crunch, when the banks were too spooked to lend money, which is necessary to boost business investment and consumer spending; that made it hard for the economy to function. A global recession ensued. No one could really do anything because the intricate, delicate financial system was cratering.

2020 RECESSION

The recession of 2020-2021 was a little bit different; it was due to a global pandemic. When covid-19 began to spread around the world, lockdowns followed, with social distancing put into place. No one could go anywhere. Global supply chains broke. Nothing could get anywhere. There were all sorts of shortages, from toilet paper to lumber. Prices skyrocketed for certain goods because nothing was where it needed to be. That all happened in a matter of weeks! The financial crisis of 2008 played out over months before it became severe, but the effects of the pandemic were immediate.

In April 2020, the price of oil went negative as oil demand plummeted due to the lockdowns (no one and nothing were going anywhere). There was a shortage of places to keep the oil, so oil producers were like, "Someone has to take this off our hands!," and they ended up paying buyers to buy the product. It was a very weird supply-and-demand situation, and it highlighted the new world that the pandemic had catapulted us into. Financial assets sold off across the board, with all sorts of liquidity issues as people tried to figure out what was going on. E-commerce, healthcare, and technology all did great during that time, but airlines, travel, and energy were brutally beaten up due to uncertainty and fear.

The recovery after the 2008 recession was also different from the recovery after the 2020 recession. In 2008, the government created the Troubled Asset Relief Program (TARP), and in 2009, Congress passed the American Recovery and Reinvestment Act (ARRA), which helped stabilize the financial sector and stimulate the economy (at a cost). TARP was all about bailing out the banks and taking toxic assets off their balance sheets. But soon it was pouring money into banks and bailing out General Motors. People got pretty mad about that! The ARRA was meant to help create jobs and provide infrastructure spending to try to spur the economy in the right direction, but it was slow to work. And TARP was so big.

They were tactics of bailout capitalism and initiated much of the action we see today. There is a lot of support for businesses, and this makes sense! Businesses employ people, and people are the economy, so it makes sense to support people where they work. But businesses don't always distribute the help.

If businesses become reliant on government interference, it creates all sorts of problems, such as zombie companies—companies that should die but don't because there is always support for them!

ZOMBIE COMPANIES

Zombie companies, as defined by Ryan Niladri Banerjee and Boris Hofmann in their paper "The Rise of Zombie Firms: Causes and Consequences," are firms that are "unable to cover debt servicing costs from current profits." They don't make enough money to be successful but remain afloat mostly through borrowing money and seeking government aid. Think of WeWork, which seemingly stays afloat out of sheer willpower, and GameStop, which subsists on meme fumes, Reddit posts, and rocket ship emoji.

But zooming out here, targeted government intervention can sometimes prevent systemic collapse (as we saw during March 2020), preserve jobs, and provide economic stability during times of crisis.

In 2020, trillions of stimulus dollars were injected into the economy, including direct payments, expanded unemployment, small-business loans, and more. People were mostly okay. They were not okay during 2008.

The pandemic was, of course, global. The rapid spread of covid-19 impacted every country on Earth, triggering a global recession and impacting businesses on all continents. India went through a severe downturn, with millions of workers losing their jobs. The United Kingdom experienced a notable decline in GDP. In Brazil, the already existing economic challenges of high unemployment rates and income inequality were exacerbated. Germany experienced a large contraction in industrial production and export volume. Every nation had to grapple with bankruptcies, layoffs, and supply chain disruptions. Governments and central banks had to step up quickly with giant stimulus packages and monetary intervention.

But the world emerged from the 2020–2021 recession rather rapidly due to governments and banks doing so much. In the United States, the recession officially ended in April 2021, according to the NBER overlords. But for the rest of 2021 and into 2022, we were flirting with a different kind of recession: a vibecession.

THE VIBECESSION

A *vibecession* is a period of temporary vibe decline during which economic data such as trade and industrial activity are okay-ish. There is, of course, an element of *reality* to our existence: policy decisions, manufacturing output, gas prices, and other factors that cannot be modified by our feeble human minds (at least right now).

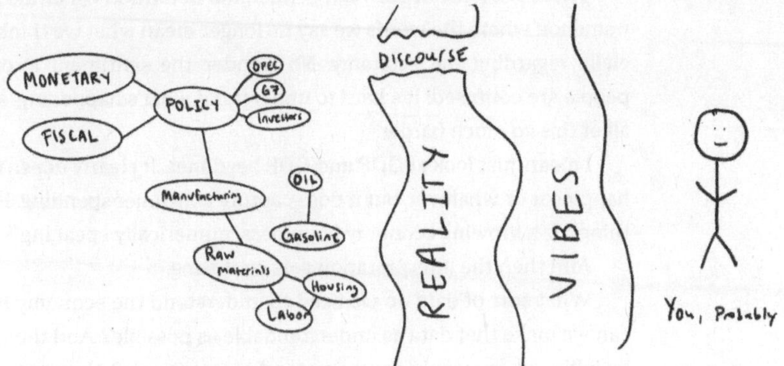

But those decisions do affect normal, everyday people who generate the vibes that do most of the work in determining how we feel. We take experience and evidence and shape our expectations, which warps our perception and acts as a forcing function for interpretation—and that is how you feel (in the most simplistic sense possible).

That feeds back into discourse and discussion, which also influences vibes and thus feelings. How you feel compounds into how everyone feels, and that is consumer sentiment. Of course, consumer sentiment is *everything* because consumer spending is such an important component of GDP growth.

Experience and evidence shape perceptions, which end up molding an interpretation of the future, which results in our collective reality, as discussed in the Vibe Economy chapter. Another hurdle that we are running into is language—we don't have the words to describe what is going on, especially with the advent of digital technology.

We speak to one another using words that have evolved over and through time, so that we know what one is talking about when they reference a doorknob or a pencil. But there is currently a battle between words and concepts.

For example, the number of Americans that support "spending on the poor" is 71%, but if you call it "welfare" that number drops to 30% according to the National Opinion Research Center at the University of Chicago. There is no difference beyond that of words! Yet that makes all the difference. We have three different definitions of what it means to live "paycheck to paycheck" as reported by Matt Darling, senior employment policy analyst at the Niskanen Center, yet endless headlines proclaim that x percentage of people are living paycheck to paycheck.

There is a tension between definer and definition which also creates a phenomenon where the words we say no longer mean what we think they do, especially regarding the economy. No wonder the sentiment is off! No wonder people are confused! It's hard to understand what's happening, and that makes all of this so much harder.

I mean, just look at GDP and GDP headlines. It clearly doesn't really capture happiness or whatever, but it does capture consumer spending. Is that the same thing? Is a growing economy happiness, numerically speaking?

And then the interpretation gets confusing.

What sort of data do we need to understand the economy better and how can we make that data as understandable as possible? And then, what would it look like when people do understand the economy? How can we help people make better decisions?

Of course, as I have talked about throughout the book, there are many real problems with the economy. We have a structural affordability crisis. A housing crisis. A healthcare crisis. A childcare crisis. The list is endless and nothing can hide anymore. The things to be anxious about are numerous. The geopolitical warfare. The walls of any sense of economic safety caving in. The endless political theatrics.

But we don't even have the words to talk about it with one another.

THE BENEFITS OF RECESSIONS

With all that being said, recessions suck. But there are also opportunities! A lot of companies actually experience growth during downturns—Amazon, Netflix, Walmart, McDonald's, and others all grew during the 2008 financial crisis because of strategic business decisions:

- **Walmart (2008 financial crisis):** As the world's largest retailer, known for its low prices, Walmart benefited during the 2008 recession as consumers became more price-conscious. Walmart's sales and earnings grew during this period.
- **Netflix (2008 financial crisis):** As consumers cut back on more expensive entertainment options, such as going to movies or taking vacations, many turned to affordable at-home entertainment. Netflix saw subscriber growth and solid performance during the recession.

- **Amazon (2008 financial crisis):** While many retailers suffered during the downturn, Amazon's emphasis on low prices, convenience, and a broad selection helped it capture market share.
- **McDonald's (2008 financial crisis):** McDonald's is often seen as a recession-resistant company because people turn to cheaper dining options during economic downturns. The fast-food giant posted strong sales during the 2008 recession.
- **General Mills (2008 financial crisis):** People often eat at home more during recessions to save money. Companies that produce consumer staples, like General Mills with its cereal and other products, can and did see stable or increased sales.
- **Microsoft (2001 dot-com bubble burst):** Despite the tech sector being hit hard by the dot-com bubble burst, Microsoft, with its diversified products and strong balance sheet, navigated the period effectively.
- **Dollar Tree & Dollar General (2008 financial crisis):** Discount stores generally do well during recessions as consumers look for bargains. Both of these chains expanded and saw increased sales during the recession.
- **Procter & Gamble (various recessions):** As a producer of consumer staples, such as laundry detergent, toothpaste, and toilet paper, P&G often maintains steady sales even in economic downturns.
- **Ross Stores & TJX Companies (2008 financial crisis):** These discount apparel retailers saw strong sales and expanded their store count while other retailers struggled, because they are a discount option for apparel and other goods that people like buying (and people always really like buying goods!).

There is always opportunity, even in the scariest times. As Aristotle said, "It is during our darkest moments that we must focus to see the light."

It's human nature to want to assign blame, to identify a definitive, central cause behind a problem. It's easier that way! Of course, it's easy for me to say, "Ah, yes, many are at fault, therefore we must be kind in distributing the blame." But that's the reality of the strange era we live in. People often want validation of their feelings that things are bad, and this can lead to a sort of vibes-based recession (the aforementioned vibecession).

This is why the debate over what a recession is or is not can become just a matter of semantics. If people are feeling bad about their economic prospects, that's a real data point. If people aren't happy with the economy, we risk spiraling into some sort of vibes-based recession as a result of the vibes-based model influencing the vibes-based narrative that influences the vibes-based economy.

As former Secretary of Defense Donald Rumsfeld once said, "There are known knowns: these are things we know we know. We also know there are known unknowns: that is to say we know there are some things [we know] we do not know. But there are also unknown unknowns—the ones we don't know we don't know."

No one really knows what is going on.

The only certainty is uncertainty, the only conviction is lack thereof, and the only path forward is blindfolded.

We may simply be consuming far too much information for our brains to process. We are not built to be bombarded by all of the news, all of the time. But we are, and the resulting overwhelm becomes the narrative.

The answers we have about the economy oftentimes just lead to more questions. And I think that inquiring tone at the end of a sentence as people ask what's going on tells us more about the economy than any report ever will. The worry of a recession should not be discounted, especially considering how fast the economy can turn, given things like geopolitical conflict and global pandemics. There are also lagged effects. So if the Federal Reserve or the U.S. government does something, like raise rates or cut taxes, that impact will take time to show up.

However, Bloomberg Economics predicted a 100 percent chance of a recession by the end of 2022, and that never happened. But that doesn't mean it never could happen.... And in general, the tension is thick (something I'll get into in later chapters) and it rings of Toni Morrison's words in *The Source of Self-Regard*:

> *Fascism talks ideology, but it is really just marketing—marketing for power. It is recognizable by its need to purge, by the strategies it uses to purge, and by its terror of truly democratic agendas. It is recognizable by its determination to convert all public services to private entrepreneurship, all nonprofit organizations to profit-making ones—so that the narrow but protective chasm between governance and business disappears. It changes citizens into taxpayers—so individuals become angry at even the notion of the public good. It changes neighbors into consumers—so the measure of our value as humans is not our humanity or our compassion or our generosity but what we own. It changes parenting into panicking—so that we vote against the interests of our own children; against their health care, their education, their safety from weapons. And in effecting these changes it produces the perfect capitalist, one who is willing to kill a human being for a product (a pair*

of sneakers, a jacket, a car) or kill generations for control of products (oil, drugs, fruit, gold).

There's a scene in the movie *Before Sunrise* in which one of the characters says:

> *I believe if there's any kind of God it wouldn't be in any of us, not you or me but just this little space in between. If there's any kind of magic in this world it must be in the attempt of understanding someone, sharing something. I know, it's almost impossible to succeed, but who cares really? The answer must be in the attempt.*

The answer must be in the attempt. We get so caught up in what happens at the end that we forget to simply exist. And maybe availability and optionality could both be solved if we were just more present in the moment. More reflective. More there for one another.

Of course, the thing we have to remember is that people are the economy. As we try to figure out how to integrate AI into our lives, manage wealth inequality, and try to maintain our labor market, we have to remember that people are everything.

PART IV

How Money Moves

CHAPTER 15

Fiscal Policy

It is better to be roughly right than precisely wrong.

—JOHN MAYNARD KEYNES

WHAT IS FISCAL POLICY?

Fiscal policy, the mighty tool wielded by governments, utilizes federal spending, taxation, and borrowing to influence individual and corporate financial decisions, maintain the economy's delicate balance (or attempt to), and ultimately, shape the destiny of nations. This chapter will walk through how the government wields its financial power through spending programs and tax policies to manage the country's overall economic stability. Let's start by getting a few misconceptions out of the way.

- **Government spending is to blame for inflation.** Productive government spending is quite good for the economy. Think public transit (not the *one more lane bro* for highways but actual investment in subways and light rails), education, healthcare, environmental protection, and scientific research. If the government is spending on things that aren't useful (say, sending billions of taxpayer dollars toward maintaining empty buildings), that's another story.
- **Government deficits are always irresponsible.** It's okay for the government to spend more than it makes, or run a deficit, especially when it is spending on the aforementioned productive investments. Think of it as in-

vesting in a class to become a certified electrician—a necessary up-front expense for a benefit that will pay off down the road.

- **Trade deficits are bad for the economy.** Again, it's not inherently bad for a country to import more goods than it exports—to buy more things from other countries than it sells to other countries. What's important are capital flows. As long as a country with a trade deficit continues to attract investments in its stock and bond markets, the overall balance remains in check.

When we are in an economic downturn or are anticipating a recession (basically when things look dicey), the government's go-to move is to spend money—pouring funds into infrastructure projects or education or dispersing stimulus payments as we saw in 2020, accompanied by tax cuts and strategic borrowing of bills, bonds, notes, and more. This *should* unleash a wave of economic energy, creating jobs and fueling the demand for goods and services. The atmosphere transforms, consumer confidence rises, and the economic vibes grow stronger. The party is in full swing. But if the government borrows too much—and isn't careful with how it spends the money—it can lead to high inflation, which we know can be a problem!

When the government tightens its purse strings (its default response to high inflation), through either tax increases or a slowdown in borrowing, the once lively gathering loses its momentum, bringing an abrupt end to the festivities. The flow of money, which is vital for people and businesses, becomes restricted, affecting their spending capacity.

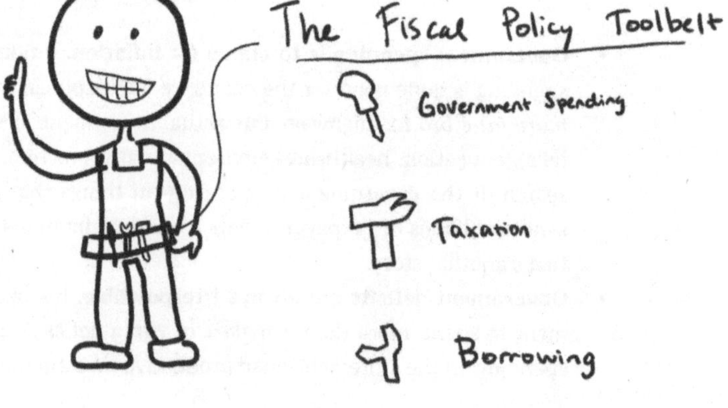

WHAT DOES THE GOVERNMENT SPEND MONEY ON?

The government spends money on a lot of things, including:

1. **Social programs.** These include social welfare programs such as housing assistance, unemployment benefits, educational programs, food assistance, and other forms of social safety nets.
2. **Defense and security.** This is all about military, national defense, and homeland security. It covers the costs of maintaining armed forces, defense infrastructure, weapons, and equipment, as well as funding military operations and initiatives.
3. **Infrastructure development.** This includes spending on public assets, including roads, bridges, airports, railways, public transportation systems, water supply networks, and other critical infrastructure.
4. **Public services.** This covers the cost of government operations and services to the public including government agencies, administrative functions, law enforcement, and firefighting.
5. **Debt interest payments.** These are funds to service government debt obligations. This spending includes interest payments on outstanding government debt issued through bonds and other securities, financial instruments used to help fund various operations.
6. **Research and development.** This includes investment in research and development that supports scientific advancements, technological innovations, and initiatives to address societal challenges that are meant to encourage innovation.
7. **Subsidies and grants.** These support specific industries, businesses, and individuals to promote economic growth and job creation and to foster specific sectors and projects.
8. **Foreign aid.** This is financial assistance or resources to other countries to support their development, address humanitarian crises, and foster good diplomatic relations.

All of these things are partially funded by taxes.

TAXES

In the United States, the tax system, like the monetary system, is based on the full faith and credit of the United States. In other words, people are going to pay taxes only if they believe in the system collecting them. There would have to be a catastrophic level of loss of faith for them not to, and there is a reason that the government has to maintain the trust of the people it serves! Democracy fundamentally depends on the belief and engagement of its citizens; without their trust and active participation, it risks transforming into a different system entirely, where power is concentrated in the hands of a few. Without public belief in the integrity and ability of the government to serve the nation's best interests, the foundation of democracy becomes shaky. When people stop believing in the government's ability to make responsible decisions, there is a risk of widespread disillusionment, political apathy, and social unrest. So taxes are more than just a tool to raise money; they are a social consensus mechanism that enables civic engagement and shapes societal priorities (sort of).

Unlike the United States, which pulls in most of its money through income taxes, more than 170 countries, including all those in Europe, collect a value-added tax, or VAT. It's seen as a way to generate money for the government without all of the burden falling on individual taxpayers; it also simplifies income tax filing, provides a consumption-based tax versus income-based tax, and is an evenly distributed burden because the tax is added to the price of goods and services at every stage of production and distribution.

But let's talk about the burden facing the individual taxpayer. If you're American, you pay a percentage of your income to the government, collected by the Internal Revenue Service (IRS). The government uses a progressive income tax system, which means that the more money you make, the higher the percentage of your income you pay in taxes (usually, that is; some people know how to do some fancy accounting so that they pay less). There are seven tax brackets, with rates ranging from 10% to 37%. How much each individual pays is a bit complicated—but it's all about margins. You don't pay 37% on all of your income, just on the amount above the previous tax bracket. Here is the tax table for 2023:

Marginal tax brackets for tax year 2023, single individuals

TAXABLE INCOME	TAXES OWED
$11,000 or less	10% of the taxable income
$11,001 to $44,725	$1,100 plus 12% of amount over $11,000
$44,726 to $95,375	$5,147 plus 22% of amount over $44,725
$95,376 to $182,100	$16,290 plus 24% of amount over $95,375
$182,101 to $231,250	$37,104 plus 32% of amount over $182,100
$231,251 to $578,125	$52,832 plus 35% of amount over $231,250
$578,126 or more	$174,238.25 plus 37% of amount over $578,125

Marginal tax brackets for tax year 2023, married filing jointly

TAXABLE INCOME	TAXES OWED
$22,000 or less	10% of the taxable income
$22,001 to $89,450	$2,200 plus 12% of amount over $22,000
$89,451 to $190,750	$10,294 plus 22% of amount over $89,450
$190,751 to $364,200	$32,580 plus 24% of amount over $190,750
$364,201 to $462,500	$74,208 plus 32% of amount over $364,200
$462,501 to $693,750	$105,664 plus 35% of amount over $462,500
$693,751 or more	$186,601.50 plus 37% of amount over $693,750

Credit: Table: Gabriel Cortes/CNBC
Source: IRS

In Canada, the federal government also uses a progressive income tax system, but the tax brackets and rates are different from those in the United States. There are currently four federal tax brackets, with rates ranging from 15% to 33%. Similarly to the United States, it's tiered, so if you make $70,000, you'll pay 15% on the first $50,197 and then 20.5% on the remaining.

Finally, in the United Kingdom, the income tax system uses a progressive system with various tax brackets and rates. There are currently four tax bands, with rates ranging from 20% to 45%. In March 2023, Chancellor of the Exchequer Jeremy Hunt froze the personal allowance until April 2028. The idea is that pay raises will move people into the higher tax brackets. But taxpayers in the United Kingdom still pay a decent amount in national income, VAT, and council tax and rates.

How income tax levels in England, Wales, and Northern Ireland* will change from April

BAND	CURRENT	NEW	RATE
Personal allowance	First £12,570 earned**	Frozen until 2028	0%
Basic rate	£12,571 to £50,270	Frozen until 2028	20%
Higher rate	£50,271 to £150,000	£50,271 to £125,140	40%
Additional rate	Over £150,000	Over £125,140	45%

*Scotland sets its own bands and rates
**Reduced by £1 for every £2 earned between £100,000 and £125,140

Each of these tax systems has pros and cons. The United Kingdom's tax system funds the National Health Service, providing free healthcare, and contributes to a substantial social safety net and public education. But the tax rates are high, and the entire economy has been funky since Brexit. In Canada, the healthcare benefit situation is similar, and tax revenue is also used to help combat climate change. But Canada also has regional disparities and a housing crisis. United States taxes fund healthcare, with an increasing percentage going toward Medicare and Social Security.

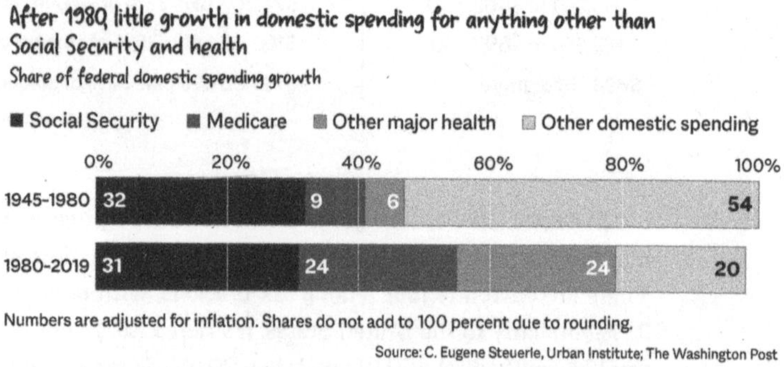

BONDS

The government makes the lion's share of its money through individual income taxes (federal, state, and local), with a healthy stream coming in from payroll taxes for Social Security and Medicare, corporate income taxes, and a trickle coming from fees, fines, and assets it sells off (lighthouses, seized homes, and other property). But usually, taxes, fees, and fines don't quite cover what the government needs to fund its programs, so it issues bonds.

Bonds, as discussed in the Stock Market chapter, are a promise to pay money back at some point in the future, and markets (usually made up of foreign governments, like China's and Japan's, mutual funds, depository institutions, state and local governments, pension funds, insurance companies, and others, like individuals, banks, and corporate businesses) say, "Ah, yes, we will buy that from you." The government is then able to execute on public infrastructure, social spending, and other projects.

There are different types of government debt. Bonds, known for their stability and low risk, are backed by the full faith and credit of the U.S. government. Municipal bonds are issued by state and local governments to fund projects such as schools, highways, and utilities. Corporate bonds, which enable companies to raise money by borrowing money from investors, provide varying levels of risk and return potential for investors, depending on the creditworthiness of the issuing corporation.

TYPE OF BOND	ISSUER	PRIMARY PURPOSE
Treasury Bonds	U.S. Federal Government	Fund federal government operations and obligations.
Municipal Bonds	State or Local Governments	Fund public projects like roads, schools, and infrastructure, or cover general operating expenses.
Corporate Bonds	Corporations	Raise capital for business operations, expansions, or other corporate initiatives.

THE DEBT CEILING

This brings us to the debt ceiling, a cap on how much the government can borrow to pay for things such as roads, public schools, and the military. It's set by Congress and is often compared to a credit limit, but for the government. In 2023, Congress fought the battle again—and the government narrowly evaded collapse.

It's stressful to have the government almost collapse every few months because it can't pay its bills. People are furious, and they should be. Why are our elected officials allowing federal workers to be repeatedly threatened with mass furloughs and hiring freezes, and endangering crucial programs and services like WIC, the special supplemental nutrition program for Women, Infants, and Children? It's stupid. But that's why we need to understand it.

The goal of the debt ceiling is to give Congress more control over government spending. It was intended to limit the amount of debt the government could take on, but over time, it has become more of a political football than a useful tool for moderating government spending—something used to try to extract political concessions or virtue signal to legislators' bases in an era of dysfunctional bipartisanship (not to mention of wasting everyone's time and money).

The original intention of the debt ceiling was to promote fiscal responsibility, but we have strayed far from that. It's a flawed mechanism that exacerbates partisan gridlock and threatens the nation's financial stability. Rather than fostering prudent fiscal management, it has turned into a tool of political posturing, with politicians using it as leverage to advance their own agendas, often at the expense of the nation's well-being.

Abolishing the debt ceiling would be a step toward restoring fiscal sanity and promoting rational decision-making! By eliminating this arbitrary limit on government borrowing, Congress could focus on more substantive debates about spending and revenue without having to resort to brinkmanship and theatrics. The debt ceiling is also ineffective at controlling government spending; it doesn't even look at the underlying causes of deficits or encourage long-term fiscal planning.

The debt ceiling's original purpose has been overshadowed by its adverse consequences, making it a detrimental relic of the past. Abolishing it would signal a commitment to pragmatic governance and demonstrate a willingness to tackle the nation's fiscal challenges with seriousness and deliberation. By doing away with this counterproductive mechanism, Congress could pave the way for a more stable, transparent, and effective fiscal policy.

Congress is almost always battling over the debt ceiling; it has moved the debt ceiling seventy-nine times since 1960, and every time the government approaches the limit, anxiety spikes about the prospect of its hitting it and being unable to meet its financial obligations. In recent go-arounds, conversations have sounded approximately like this:

Republicans do not like the level of spending Democrats want for programs to improve education, transportation, housing, scientific research, and environmental protection (which is what the government is designed to do at a base level). Both parties are guilty of trying to score political points at the absolute worst moment, because there is a potentially severe fallout from not solving the debt ceiling problem.

What would the consequences of breaching the debt ceiling be?

- **The Treasury would stop functioning.** If the Treasury can't keep money flowing back and forth and the government shuts down, payments to federal workers, agencies, Social Security beneficiaries, and Medicare providers would be delayed, financial markets could panic, and public confidence in our political institutions would be (justifiably) shaken. Even though the government has technically hit the debt ceiling limit before, the Treasury has always bought enough time for Congress to strike a deal by using cash on hand (a limited supply of money that's ideally supposed to be kept on hand) and what it calls "extraordinary measures" (aka creative accounting maneuvers). If the government does default, lenders will become highly reluctant to lend to the United States, and those who do will demand higher interest rates. This would result in even more of the government's budget allocated toward interest payments.

- **The United States could go into default.** This would be unprecedented, and the cascading effects would be catastrophic—including a downgrade by credit rating agencies, higher borrowing costs, and a recession, creating problems both for everyday consumers and for the United States as a global power. For the time being, the U.S. dollar is the premier reserve currency of the world (meaning that it's the currency most commonly held by central banks and major financial institutions around the world) because the United States is currently King Daddy of the world and has the biggest economy. A default would shatter global trust in the U.S. government at a very delicate geopolitical moment—and make everyone question the strength of the United States and the dollar.

The United States is one of the only countries that has a debt ceiling; Denmark does, too, but it isn't weird about it like the United States is. Other countries are concerned about their debt loads (Switzerland and Norway have virtually no debt, so not them), but the United States is the only one that uses it as a political football and puts the fate of the country at risk every few years. Other countries, including Germany, Italy, Poland, and Switzerland, have balanced budget provisions. Germany has a debt brake, or *Schuldenbremse,* which puts a limit on the structural deficit the government can run. France has a fiscal rule called the "golden rule," which sets a limit on the structural budget deficit.

The debt ceiling is bad. It is simply, objectively, bad. Not only because it's glorified paper pushing, but also because it undermines confidence in the U.S. economy, makes market expectations go haywire, and creates unnecessary stress for us all—especially federal employees, who have to worry about whether they'll be paid if there is an extended impasse and the Treasury runs out of cash to fulfill its obligations. The debt ceiling comes into conversation only because the government is funded by us, the taxpayers.

THE UNITED KINGDOM SHOWS THAT FISCAL POLICY IS AN ART

How the government decides to handle taxes, government spending, and borrowing is key. The United Kingdom ran into this head-on with Prime Minister Liz Truss, who in September 2022, during a period of inflation, announced a "minibudget." The budget included increased tax cuts and a lot of government spending, which was very fiscally loose. Misplaced tax cuts, just like loose monetary policy, are inflationary, and the inflationary pressures contributed to Truss famously having a shorter shelf life as PM than a head of iceberg lettuce from the supermarket.

The introduction of the minibudget (and subsequent market reaction) caused the price of government bonds (called "gilts" in the United Kingdom) to collapse. The market deemed the minibudget irresponsible because in the inflationary environment, it was very much not the time to be cutting taxes! People were like, "It's insane to be doing fiscal easing in the middle of an inflationary crisis because you're going to cause more inflation."

Once the sell-off began, it was assumed that the Bank of England would step in and fix everything: do an emergency rate hike, buy bonds, anything. But it didn't. In one example of the extremity of market moves, the yield on thirty-year U.K. inflation-linked bonds jumped by more than 250% (meaning that they *fell* 250% in price) after the Bank made the announcement that it was not going to intervene.

The reason that the Bank ended up going all in was that there was a liquidity crisis in liability-driven investment (LDI) funds that were very invested in gilt-edged securities, the government Treasuries. Gilts, of course, were selling off. So the LDIs were not doing that well. And it turned out that pension funds, which people use for support in retirement, owned a lot of LDIs. So the pension funds were at risk of blowing up.

The Bank had to do something. So it stepped in. It bought bonds! However, the move was ineffective because it functioned as a quantitative easing program about a week after the bank had announced quantitative tightening (I will discuss the specifics of that later) with almost 10 percent inflation as the backdrop.

There were so many things going on! The U.K. government had an expansionary fiscal policy that was largely inflationary, freaking everyone out because inflation was already so bad. Then the Bank of England had to step in to save the government from itself!

That crisis revealed the political limits of fiscal policy, at least during times of high inflation. It threw the United Kingdom into austerity, constraining both bad and good economic plans. It also underscored the power of monetary policy—and how influential our central banks have become.

LESSONS FROM THE EUROZONE

The eurozone debt crisis, which began in 2009, is a good example of the importance of a certain level of debt management. Several countries using the euro as their currency, including Greece, Ireland, Portugal, Spain, and Italy, faced severe financial difficulties, with high levels of public debt, soaring borrowing costs, and struggling economies. The crisis led to concerns that the eurozone might break up, which could have had profound consequences for global financial markets and the world economy. Ultimately, the eurozone was saved by the creation of the European Financial Stability Facility (EFSF) and the European Stability Mechanism (ESM), the European Central Bank (ECB) intervening with liquidity support, a banking union, bailout packages provided by the IMF, and, most important, by Angela Merkel, the German chancellor, agreeing to support the euro.

Basically, Germany needed to run a deficit to help save all the other European countries, specifically Greece (George Papandreou, its prime minister at the time, had agreed to a massive sovereign default that had sent the country's economy into a downward spiral) and Italy. Merkel wanted nothing to do with it. When asked by U.S. president Barack Obama and French president Nicolas Sarkozy to increase contributions to the eurozone "firewall," "to the astonishment of almost everyone in the room, Angela Merkel began to cry. 'Das ist nicht fair.' That is not fair, the German chancellor said angrily, tears welling in her eyes. 'Ich bringe mich nicht selbst um.' I am not going to commit suicide."

Germany ended up contributing, saving the euro. There were lessons in there about the balance of austerity— the fact that some government spending is important and, as Mark Dow of Behavioral Macro, put it, "There should be no doubt by now that markets, economists, and pretty much everyone for the past generation has underrated the power/utility/capacity of fiscal policy, and overrated the power/utility/capacity of monetary policy."

CAN THE GOVERNMENT SURVIVE?

A government's decisions on spending, taxation, and borrowing not only have immediate effects on the economy but also shape the trajectory of society over time. Policymakers have an ethical responsibility to consider the interests of both present and future generations when formulating fiscal strategies.

There are a lot of questions about what is going to happen with entitlements, support, and deficits at a certain point, especially considering all the noise about Social Security running out by 2030 in the United States, pensions potentially drying up in the United Kingdom, and so on.

It makes sense to worry about this stuff. My grandma worked at one company her whole life (and worked very hard), retired in her sixties, and is still living off her pension in her nineties. That is likely not going to happen for the younger generations. Populations are aging, and life expectancies are increasing. In 1940, there were forty-two workers per retiree, but that number has fallen to three to one, meaning that there are not nearly enough workers to support Social Security beneficiaries.

Japan is a good example of a real-time fiscal and monetary experiment in the face of challenging demographics. Japan has one of the world's most rapidly aging populations. This demographic trend has resulted in a declining workforce and a rising number of retirees. As a result, Japan's public debt-to-GDP ratio is among the highest in the world as the government has run a huge deficit over the years in an attempt to support the population. So it has passed various fiscal stimulus packages to boost demand, mainly through spending on infrastructure projects and social programs, as well as a lot of support from their central bank, the Bank of Japan.

Basically, governments are running a lot of fiscal experiments in real time.

FISCAL POLICY IS GOOD, ACTUALLY

Alex Williams, an economist at EmployAmerica, developed something he called a "Frying Pan Chart" to describe the idea that the 2010s are over or the concept that fiscal spending is not always a bad thing. The chart that follows looks like a frying pan—you can see the dip during 2010, when fiscal austerity, the government spending less, was a popular ideology. But during both the Trump (mostly in the form of tax cuts) and Biden administrations, government spending was *big*, including the CHIPS Act of 2022, the Inflation Reduction Act of 2022, and the Infrastructure Investment and Jobs Act of 2021.

The Frying Pan Chart bolsters the idea that the government can—and should—spend money. The fact that we didn't during the 2010s because of the idea that governments shouldn't spend money was net harmful.

As the early-twentieth-century economist John Maynard Keynes said, "Anything we can actually do, we can afford." Governments exist to spend money.

Borrowing money is okay! It really is! A lot of people scream about deficits, but red ink in the federal budget isn't cause for alarm the way it would be in say,

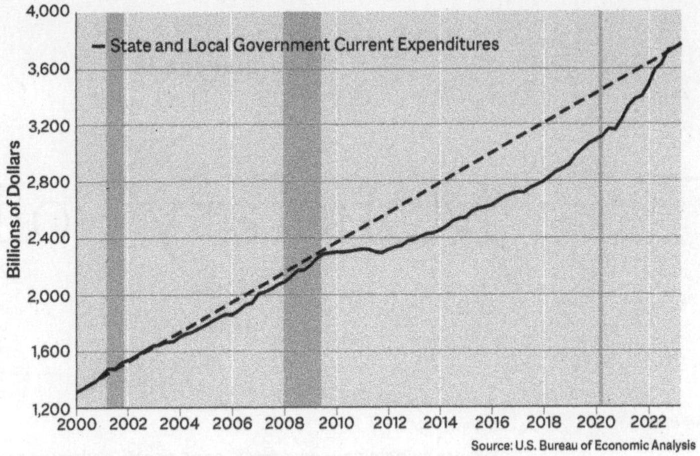

a family's budget, especially if the borrowing is being spent on productive things such as infrastructure or education. Olivier Blanchard, a former chief economist at the International Monetary Fund (IMF), argued that there are benefits to high levels of government debt in a low-interest-rate environment—not an argument for more public debt, just an acknowledgment that debt isn't always a bogeyman.

That being said, interest rates skyrocketed in 2022 and 2023 as the Fed raised them to fight inflation, creating higher interest payments for the U.S. government. But the real problem comes when a country borrows money to pay for the money that it's already borrowed—that's a real debt-death-doom loop.

CHAPTER 16

Monetary Policy

We are spinning our own fates, good or evil, and never to be undone.

—WILLIAM JAMES

Monetary policy is powerful. Central banks are everywhere! Most countries have one, except for some unique cases such as Andorra and Monaco (which lean on the European Central Bank for support). The big players, such as the Federal Reserve, the Bank of England, the European Central Bank, the Bank of Japan, and the People's Bank of China, wield significant power and influence in their respective domains. Each central bank has to find the sweet spot between stimulating economic growth and curbing inflation.

So what's their game plan?

Let's concentrate on the Federal Reserve as an example. Although it focuses on domestic policy, its actions often send ripples around the globe. It's a high-stakes game, and its decisions can have far-reaching consequences that extend beyond the nation's borders.

WHAT DOES THE FED DO?

What exactly does the Fed do? It has a dual mandate—a tightrope walk at best.

The Fed wants to make sure that people have choices: that they are able to pay their living expenses and to get a job.

1. **Mandate 1: Price stability.** How can inflation be managed? How can the panicky "prices are rising" narrative be prevented from becoming a self-fulfilling prophecy? (More on that vicious cycle later.)

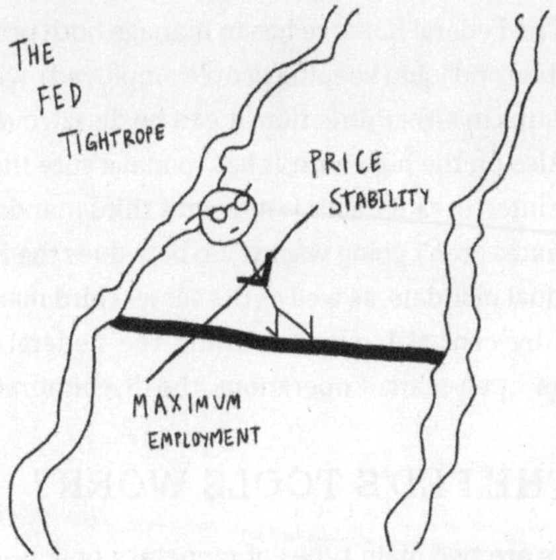

2. **Mandate 2: Maximum employment.** This the Fed's second big focus in theory, though it's hard to achieve when it's hell-bent on keeping inflation down. The metric of maximum employment is about inclusion, diversity, and a job market for everyone.

The Fed has a tough walk on this dual-sided tightrope: It doesn't want to overreact by moving rates too much and having the economy respond negatively, but it also doesn't want to underreact and have the economy react even more negatively.

This is a delicate balance to maintain. It's very much like Goldilocks and the porridge. Monetary policy is a big decision with a teeny tiny hammer, and there is a lot of gray area that the Federal Reserve has to be mindful of. Inflation can't be too hot or too cold—it has to be just right, a Goldilocks zone.

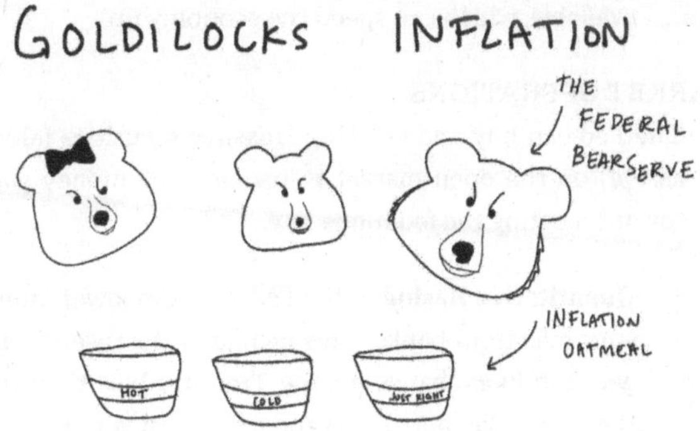

The Federal Reserve has to manage both price stability (keeping prices reasonable) and jobs (keeping people employed), which is very difficult to do. If the scale tips in either direction, it can be disastrous.

Also on the high wire, it has to make sure that it maintains long-term, moderate interest rates. This is its secret third mandate, which translates to "making sure rates aren't going wacky." So how does the Fed make sure that it is meeting this dual mandate, as well as the secret third mandate? The most common tools used by central banks (including the Federal Reserve) are reserve requirements, open-market operations, the discount rate, and the fed funds rate.

HOW DO THE FED'S TOOLS WORK?

There are two main types of monetary policy—contractionary and expansionary. Contractionary policy (raising rates, shrinking the balance sheet) is used when the Fed wants to slow the economy down. Expansionary monetary policy (cutting rates, increasing the balance sheet) is used when the Fed wants to speed the economy up.

RESERVE REQUIREMENTS

The reserve requirement is the minimum amount of money that a bank must hold in reserve to make sure that it has enough money to supply its customers' demands. The Fed sets this number by mandating the percentage of a bank's total deposits (including checking accounts, savings accounts, and money market accounts) that it's required to have on hand overnight.

- When the Fed increases the reserve requirement, it can reduce the amount of funds that institutions have available to lend, which slows the economy down.
- When the Fed decreases the requirement, it increases the amount of funds available, which can speed the economy up.

OPEN-MARKET OPERATIONS

The Fed can buy and sell U.S. Treasury securities (along with other financial assets) on the open market to regulate the money supply and nudge banks toward meeting the fed funds rate.

- **Quantitative Easing:** If the Fed wants to lower interest rates, it buys Treasury bills from banks. This increases the reserves for banks because they get cash in exchange for the Treasury bills they sell to the Fed, enabling them to make more loans and more money to enter into the economy.

- **Quantitative Tightening:** If the Fed wants to raise interest rates, it does the opposite by selling Treasury bills to banks. This decreases banks' reserves and allows less money to enter the economy, thereby slowing things down.

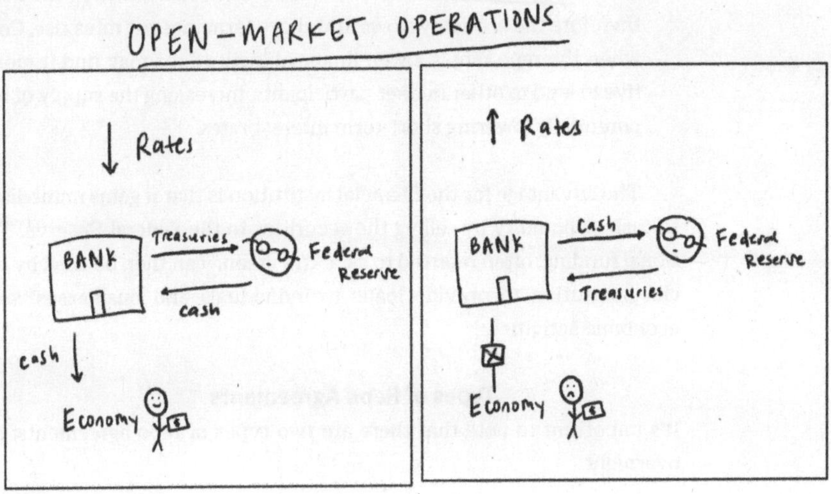

REPO AGREEMENTS

The Federal Reserve engages in various market operations, including term and overnight repurchase (repo) agreements. These serve as short-term borrowing arrangements between financial institutions and central banks. The primary purpose of these agreements is to provide liquidity, which refers to access to cash or assets that can easily be converted into cash.

Here's how repo agreements work:

1. The Federal Reserve buys securities, such as Treasury bonds, from financial institutions.
2. However, this purchase is not permanent. Instead, there is an agreement between the two parties that the financial institution will repurchase the same securities from the Federal Reserve at an agreed-upon date later on.
3. This repurchase arrangement acts as a collateralized short-term loan.
4. The key feature of a repo agreement is that the sale price of the security is higher than the repurchase price, creating a price difference between the two, which effectively represents the interest earned by the Federal Reserve. This difference in prices is known as the "repo rate."

5. By setting the repo rate, the Federal Reserve can change short-term interest rates in the financial markets. A *higher* repo rate encourages financial institutions to participate in repo agreements with the Federal Reserve rather than lending to other banks or entities in the private market—which means they have less money available to lend to others in the market and therefore the economy slows and short-term interest rates rise. Conversely, when the repo rate is lower, financial institutions may find it more attractive to lend to other market participants, increasing the supply of funds and potentially lowering short-term interest rates.

The advantage for the financial institution is that it gains immediate access to cash or liquidity by selling the securities to the Federal Reserve. This additional funding, often referred to as "extra green," can then be used by the financial institution to provide loans to individuals and businesses, supporting economic activities.

Types of Repo Agreements

It's important to note that there are two types of repo agreements: term and overnight.

- Term repo agreements have a longer duration, lasting a few days or weeks.
- Overnight repo agreements are very short term, lasting only one day.

Institutions use repo agreements to meet daily liquidity needs—if they don't have enough money on hand, they can enter into an overnight repo to cover the deficit. Term repos are used for longer-term liquidity need or project financing.

The Fed also has a tool called the Standing Repo Facility (SRF), which helps keep the money market stable. It provides liquidity to banks if they need it, giving them access to short-term funding through repurchase agreements (repos) with a central bank. This ensures that markets can function properly and provides money in case any banks need it. This is really important because if the money market goes haywire, it can cause big problems for the broader economy. The SRF helped keep things under control during the financial crisis of 2008, when lots of people were pulling their money out of money market funds—short-term investments that are supposed to be low risk. Basically, the Fed acts as the firefighter of the economy, putting out financial blazes before they turn into infernos.

THE DISCOUNT RATE

The discount rate is the interest rate that the Fed charges on loans made through the discount window. It's set above the fed funds rate to discourage borrowers from using it. Institutions normally borrow from the discount window if they desperately, desperately need money—it serves as a safety net for stability, particularly during times of financial stress.

But the discount rate is more than just a way for the Fed to make money off loans; it's actually a signal that tells us what the Fed is thinking about the economy. Think of it as a traffic light for the economy.

- When the light is green (the discount rate is low), banks are free to borrow and lend money more easily, and the economy can speed along.
- But when the light turns yellow (the Fed raises the discount rate), banks know they need to chill out because borrowing money just got more expensive.
- And when the light turns red (the discount rate is really high), banks know they need to stop and reevaluate their strategies because borrowing money is just too costly.

THE FED FUNDS RATE

The point of this rate (referred to as the bank rate in the United Kingdom, the refinancing rate in the European Central Bank, and other names in other nations) is to make it more or less expensive to be alive—to change the cost of money. Central banks set a target range for the interest rates that depository institutions charge each other for overnight loans to meet reserve requirements when one has a shortfall and another has an excess at the end of day (EOD). Though we say the Fed "sets" the fed funds rate, it is really using other tools, such as open-market operations, to make borrowing more expensive. When inflation is really high, the Fed wants people to chill out and stop spending money. So it nudges the fed funds rate upward, and banks then pass the cost along to consumers in the form of higher interest rates on everything from car loans to credit card payments. Everyone says, "Okay," and stops taking out financing, which slows the economy down, which eventually slows inflation.

When the economy isn't doing so hot, it's the opposite: The Fed wants people to spend money. So the people at the Fed push the funds rate downward—or slash it to zero, as they did in December 2008 and March 2020—making it cheaper to finance cars, homes, anything that you have to get a loan for. Everyone says, "Okay!" and starts taking out financing, speeding the economy up, which eventually speeds inflation up.

BEING A CENTRAL BANK IS ABOUT BELIEF

When the financial system started melting down during the 2008 Great Financial Crisis (GFC), the Fed had to implement new tools, as its existing playbook was no longer working. That was when quantitative easing (QE) came on the scene, similar to open-market operations, except that central banks buy long-term bonds and securities, such as mortgage securities, rather than just short-term Treasury bills, with the goal of impacting various interest rates and getting specific parts of the economy rolling again.

The Fed slashed rates in 2008 and did three rounds of QE (2008–2010, 2010–2011, and 2012–2014) as well as Operation Twist, selling short-term Treasury securities and buying an equivalent long-term to try to lower long-term rates without increasing the balance sheet. They also developed the Term Auction Facility and several other facilities to try to provide money to markets.

After letting the balance sheet grow substantially after 2008, in 2018 the Fed began to reduce the size of the balance sheet (an unprecedented move at the time!) in response to rising interest rates. It imposed a $10 billion cap on monthly runoff, increasing it to $50 billion over the course of a year.

Recent Balance-Sheet Trends

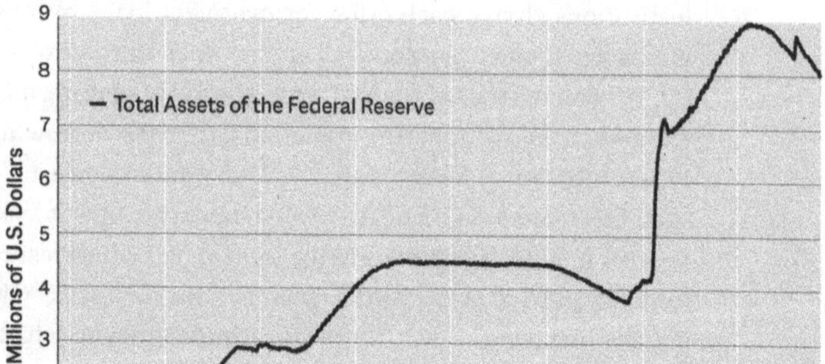

Source: Board of Governors of the Federal Reserve System

As the Fed began to increase the use of reverse repos to reduce its balance sheet, the demand for these transactions surged. Banks were stoked to lend money to the Fed, because what could be a safer and more reliable borrower than the Federal Reserve? But because the demand spiked, the interest rate on reverse repo transactions fell. At one point, it went negative, with banks paying to transact with the Fed.

Soon enough, there was a shortage of cash in the financial system. In September 2019, the U.S. overnight money market (financial markets in which short-term, low-risk debt securities are traded) experienced some wild volatility. There were two main causes: first, corporate tax payments were due September 16, so money left money market mutual fund accounts and banks and was sent to the Treasury, and second, $54 billion of Treasury debt was due. So a bunch of cash was drained.

Like $120 billion worth.

The rate movements were huge, and the Fed had to reverse its QT process in order to stabilize the financial system. Of course, that was a statistically wild event, but it was underscored by the ridiculousness of financial systems. It was a nightmarish mess and one that spooked people about monetary policy yet again.

Zero interest rates are a lot easier to deal with than "normal" interest rates are. This is known as zero interest rate policy, or ZIRP, and it brought a lot of excess in the years following the GFC. It indirectly led to many speculative bubbles, including meme mania.

There was a particularly grand spree of QE in 2020 after the covid-19 pandemic hit.

MONETARY POLICY IN 2020

The Fed wanted people to SPEND—to go buy homes, cars, and groceries to fill their fridge (and maybe even the fancy kind of pickles!). So it dropped the reserve requirement in the hope that banks would lend more, credit markets would get their groove back, and borrowing would be cheaper across the board for businesses and households.

It went on a shopping spree! It purchased a ton of Treasury securities and mortgage-backed securities (MBS), bundles of home loans and other real estate debt obligations that can be passed from the bank that issued them to other parties in large quantities to inject some cash into the financial system.

It implemented lending facilities. Think of these as being like support systems for credit markets, helping out businesses and even local governments. It was like giving them a helping hand to access the funding they needed during those tough times. Things like the Primary Dealer Credit Facility provided short-term loans to dealers (firms that trade directly with the Federal Reserve and U.S. Treasury), and the Commercial Paper Funding Facility facilitated the issuance of commercial paper to companies to help support credit flow to households—basically, they got money to people.

It also made sure that money market funds didn't freeze up, by providing them some liquidity injections.

It created the Main Street Lending Program, which was all about supporting small and midsized businesses. It wanted to make sure that mom-and-pop shops and growing companies got the help they needed to survive the economic downturn.

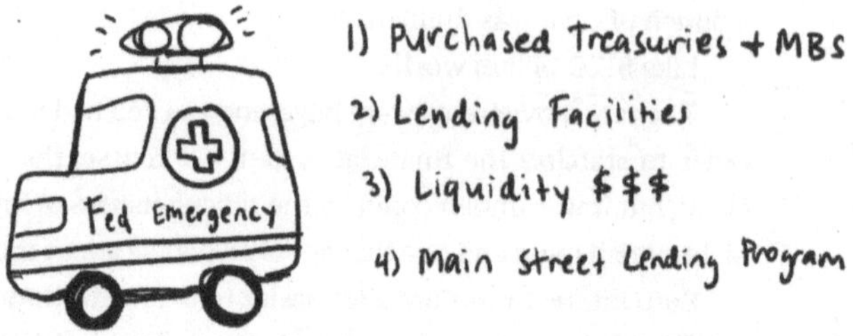

Those moves did much to stabilize the markets and probably helped us avoid another Great Depression. As Nick Timiraos of *The Wall Street Journal* wrote in *Trillion Dollar Triage*, a chronicle of the Fed's action during the pandemic: "The central bank can help boost demand when the economy slumps; there was no precedent for what policymakers would soon face—the equivalent of an economy placed into a medically induced coma. And rash action risked panicking the markets further. As he disembarked from the plane, Powell already knew one thing: doing nothing was not an option."

There has been a lot of criticism of what the Fed did during the pandemic, with some saying that it overstepped its authority and did too much, but it's also true that they (and everyone) were dealing with impossible circumstances.

Oil prices had suddenly gone negative, meaning that traders were paying buyers to take barrels off their hands—a historic quirk in the market that should never have happened. We're talking about our most traded commodity here! The head of oil markets at Rystad Energy, Bjørnar Tonhaugen, described it as an oil Everest but in reverse: "Oil prices not only hit rock bottom, but they also broke the rock." That goes against all the economic laws of the known universe.

Meanwhile, high-yield debt (high-risk, potentially high-reward bonds, also known as junk bonds) was blowing out, meaning that yields were skyrocketing, because no one wanted to own anything risky. And people were losing their jobs. Central banks around the world did what they thought was best—and doing too much was probably better than doing too little. If the central banks hadn't intervened, the world likely would have experienced a worldwide depression, as it did in 1929. The world was shutting down. It was a once-in-a-lifetime event, and it needed once-in-a-lifetime support. The following factors had to be taken into consideration.

1. People are the economy.
2. Monetary policy exists to stabilize the economy.
3. Monetary policy is meant to help people.
4. Does it *always*? No, of course not.

People really like policy only when the car is driving forward (cutting rates and quantitative easing) versus driving in reverse (raising rates and quantitative tightening). QT policies aim to shrink the Fed's balance sheet, reduce their bond holdings, or raise interest rates. The Fed begins QT with a process known as runoff, which allows bonds to mature without reinvesting the proceeds.

These contractionary policy tools are a bit slippery to pin down, as are most aspects of monetary policy, because, as much confidence as the Fed may project, *no one really knows* how they work. No one really knows what the best interest rate is or how shrinking the Fed's bond holdings will impact the economy. It's a guess.

For example, the 2022–2023 balance sheet runoff: its pace was much faster than in 2018. The Fed let $95 billion in securities mature every month, $60 billion in Treasuries, and $35 billion in mortgage-backed securities (a financial product in which banks sell debt obligations—in this case, home and real estate loans—to investors who take their place in waiting to collect repayment). This is a huge number, compounded by the Fed raising rates quickly.

But there was a Repo Crisis 2.0—kind of!

Silicon Valley Bank (SVB) failed in 2023 because it had no hedges and no protection on the bonds that it owned. It owned a lot of Treasury securities, and when the Fed started raising interest rates, those securities lost a lot of value. When the rates went up, the prices of the securities went down.

Silicon Valley Bank was caught in the crossfire of the fast and furious Federal Reserve moves. State regulators in California and at the Federal Reserve Bank of San Francisco had been aware of excessive risk-taking and poor internal management at SVB in the years leading up to its demise. Eyebrows had gone up, and reports had been issued, but oversight teams didn't apply enough pressure for the bank to get back onto the straight and narrow.

SVB was just one casualty of monetary policy. What the Fed did in 2023 also contributed to the downfall of Credit Suisse, a 167-year-old organization, causing distress in regional banks and showing the power of social media to create a bank run (the relationship between social media and bank runs could be a book in itself). The Swiss investment bank UBS acquired the remains of Credit Suisse and will likely downsize some parts of it and sell off others.

FED CRED

Being a central bank is hard. The Fed, for instance, has to rely on a few things that are technically outside its control to achieve the goal of slowing the economy down:

1. **People have to believe it can do it.** A lot of what the Fed does hinges on its credibility—which it arguably still has. But if all of a sudden, the market is like, "Ha-ha, Fed is lame and can't do anything," it makes its policy actions more difficult. If people expect inflation to rise, they are going to hurry up and buy things before they get more expensive. Employees also might be more aggressive about negotiating higher pay, and companies may preemptively raise prices to make up the difference (or just because everyone else is doing it and they can get away with it!). The central bank cares about

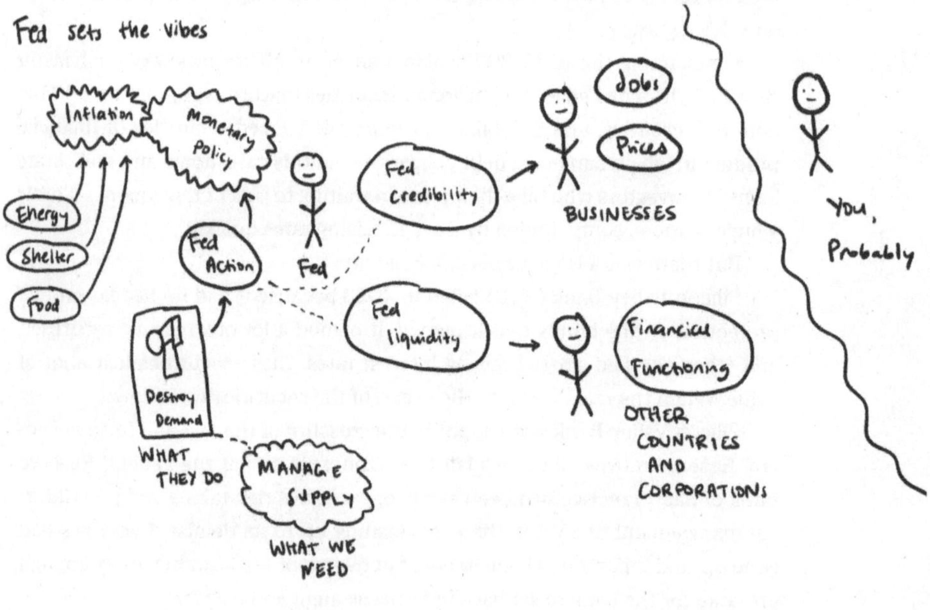

what people think is going to happen—because that's usually what ends up happening. That's why Fed cred—or the lack thereof—can be the downfall of monetary policy.

2. **The tool kit has to work.** The Fed bankers can push their levers of open-market operations, reverse repo, the discount rate, and attempts to project gravitas and credibility, but ultimately, all of these instruments are somewhat indirect. They don't have a 100 percent success rate. In the 2010s, for instance, the Fed wasn't able to boost inflation (and with it, economic growth) the way it wanted to.

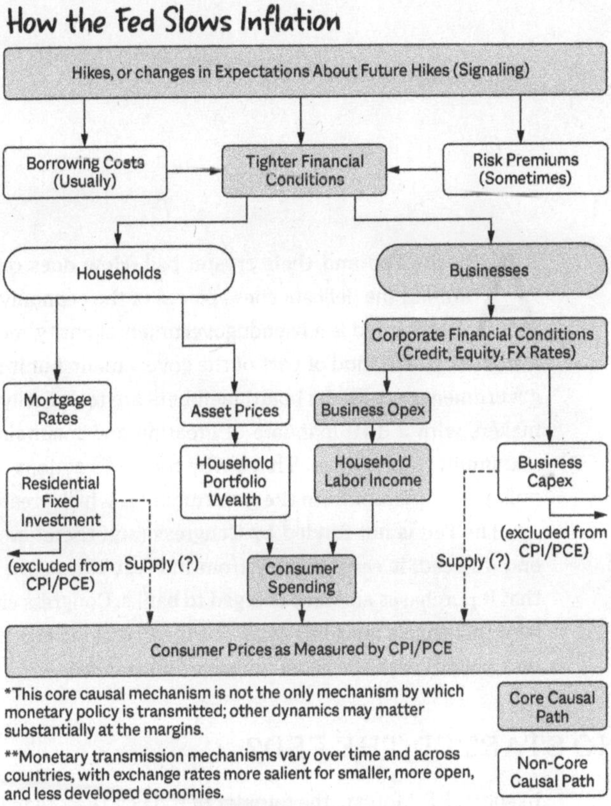

It's impossible to predict the future accurately, yet that is what we ask central bankers all over the world to do. So how do they do it?

CHAPTER 17

The Federal Reserve

Ah, the Fed and their crystal ball. How does one even begin to move around the delicate chess pieces of the economy?

The Fed is a pseudogovernmental entity, meaning that it reports to Congress, so it is kind of part of the government, but it isn't *really* a part of the government because its board members are technically independent decision-makers with a dual mandate of creating and maintaining price stability and maximum employment. That's why the Fed's actions, which create monetary policy, are different from the government's, which create fiscal policy.

The Fed is not funded by Congress (and therefore not funded by taxpayers). Instead, it earns money from interest earned on government securities that it purchases and fees charged to banks. Congress checks in with it to make sure that things are going okay, but the Fed alone has to make sure that monetary policy keeps the economy alive and stable.

WHO STARTED THE FED?

In short, J. P. Morgan, the founder of today's JPMorgan Chase bank.

In 1907, there were a lot of bank runs, when lots of customers rushed to pull their money out at the same time. The banking business model doesn't allow for everyone to say, "Give me my money right now please," because the banks have loaned out the money elsewhere and can't summon it back instantaneously. So people would rush to try to get their money, and the banks would have no money to give them. Because the planet wasn't as globalized as it is now, there weren't international bank runs—but that has clearly changed in recent years.

J. P. Morgan was getting really sick of it. As the owner of the most successful bank in the United States at the time, he had issued emergency loans to other banks that weren't managing their money as well. Finally, he put his powerful foot down and said, "Enough. I am too rich to exist in a society such as this." Speaking for all of us who have done work that was not ours to do, he threw his hands up in frustration and said, "This is *not* my job." Everything he'd done to keep the markets afloat gave him the leverage to push through the legislation needed to create a central bank.

The Fed was established and signed into law by President Woodrow Wilson in 1913. (His wife, Edith Wilson, who was also the first woman to hold a driver's license in Washington, D.C., probably played an outsized role. When Woodrow collapsed from a stroke in 1919, Edith Wilson took the helm of the ship, making decisions on behalf of the president and serving as his filter and access control point. She reviewed documents, worked with advisers, and went to meetings, acting as a pseudopresident in the day-to-day operations of the country. So it might seem as though it was just another group of dudes deciding the fate of the future, but perhaps the story is more complicated than that.)

The Fed was meant to be the solution to the plague of volatility and uncertainty that had haunted the 1800s, making sustained economic growth impossible. It would be a central bank that would be responsible for setting monetary policy to get the economy on track to grow sustainably, plus regulating banks, watching over financial institutions, managing the money supply, and reinforcing citizens' collective trust in that money, thereby exerting a massive influence on the stock market, bond market, and housing market.

The Fed was—and is—an economic vibe setter.

HOW DOES THE FEDERAL RESERVE WORK?

The Federal Reserve operates in twelve different districts. There is a central authority, the board of governors, located in Washington, D.C., along with a decentralized network of twelve Federal Reserve banks located throughout the United States, each with its own president.

The idea is that the power shouldn't be concentrated just in Washington, D.C., because the Fed serves the whole country. Each president rotates onto the Federal Open Market Committee (FOMC), which sets interest rates and manages government securities. The Fed has three main components:

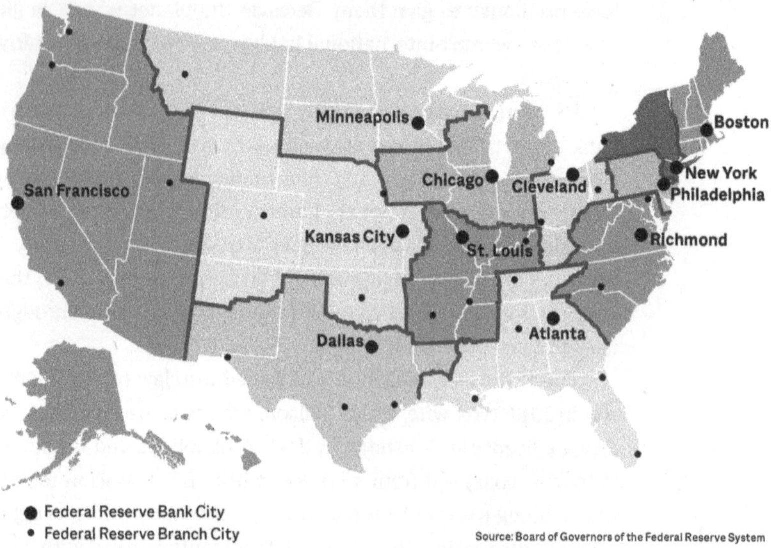

Source: Board of Governors of the Federal Reserve System

BOARD OF GOVERNORS

The board is made up of seven members, nominated by the president and confirmed by the Senate, which oversees the twelve Reserve Banks. The members serve staggered fourteen-year terms that expire in even-numbered years, so the whole board isn't up for renomination at the same time, preventing any sort of political influence resulting from one president stacking the board with his favorites.

FEDERAL OPEN MARKET COMMITTEE (FOMC)

The monetary policy unit of the Federal Reserve, the FOMC is composed of twelve members: the seven members who make up the board of governors and five of the twelve Reserve Bank presidents. The Federal Reserve chairperson heads up the committee, which meets eight times per year—every six weeks—to figure out how to steer the economic ship.

FEDERAL RESERVE BANKS

These are the operational arms of the Federal Reserve System that carry out the Fed's activities. The twelve districts are headquartered in Boston, New York, Philadelphia, Cleveland, Richmond, Atlanta, Chicago, St. Louis, Minneapolis, Kansas City, Dallas, and San Francisco.

Each bank has a board of directors divided into three "classes": A, B, and C. Class A directors are appointed by member banks and represent the banking industry. Class B directors are also appointed by member banks but represent the public interest. Class C directors are appointed by the Board of Governors and also represent the public interest. The board is responsible for overseeing the bank's operations and appointing the bank's president.

THE CHAIR OF THE BOARD

The president nominates the chairman of the Board of Governors, who then has to be approved by a majority vote in the U.S. Senate. It's an unspoken rule that a newly elected president should keep the chair that the previous president nominated. That's because the Fed is meant to be an independent organization. But its independence has been somewhat compromised by recent political moves.

A great example was during the Trump administration, when its not-so-well-kept secret and subsequent independence were breached when President Donald Trump replaced Janet Yellen with Jerome Powell. The next president, Joe Biden, kept Powell on board. That said, there was a question whether Powell would get to keep his seat when it came time for him to be renominated in 2022. At the time, the economy was a bit bonkers. Moderates wanted Powell to be appointed because they were concerned about inflation and wanted continuity during that ongoing crisis. Progressives, on the other hand, wanted a change and to nominate Lael Brainard, the Fed's vice chair, as she was seen as more aligned with President Biden's economic agenda, with a focus on climate change and a leading voice on tighter oversight for Wall Street.

The Fed chair appointment process has become increasingly political, like everything else, with people being nominated based on their views on climate change and other social issues rather than their takes on monetary policy. To be clear, it is important that the Fed consider these factors as main nudgers of the economy, but it has limited direct influence on these issues due to its congressional mandate. The Fed can only incentivize different initiatives to support climate change initiatives and other important legislation.

Of course, climate change poses a very clear systemic risk, and regulators will need to take it into consideration. But the continuous entanglement of the Fed into political issues is not the reason that the Fed exists. We need our elected government policymakers to do their jobs.

THE FED'S NARRATIVE

Constituents have to be told the right story. The Federal Reserve promotes the narrative that it is indispensable to the broader narrative of "stock market going up." Alan Greenspan, the chairman of the Federal Reserve from 1987 to 2006, began the era of the Fed and the markets being intimately intertwined. Not only does the Fed manage things quantitatively, but it also manages them qualitatively, which ends up being the driving force of its narrative creation process.

Greenspan's tenure as Fed chairman saw periods of strong economic growth and stability, but the Fed also faced a lot of challenges, such as the 1987 stock market crash, the bursting of the dot-com bubble in the early 2000s, and the aftermath of the 9/11 attacks. Throughout those events, he was often credited with effectively managing monetary policy to support economic growth while keeping inflation in check, awarding him the nickname "the Maestro."

On October 19, 1987, when the stock market experienced a sharp and sudden decline, the Fed, under Greenspan's leadership, took swift action to inject liquidity and stabilize the financial system. The Fed engaged in intraday rate cuts, meaning that it reduced the target federal funds rate and discount rate during the trading day, providing support to markets and tying it closely to the narrative of "stock market going up."

NARRATIVE CREATION

Most of what drives the Fed's narrative has to do with maintaining price stability and maximum employment:

- If inflation is raging, the Fed has to use its tool kit to manage it.
- If unemployment is skyrocketing, the Fed has to manage that, too.
- The Fed controls many aspects of its dual mandate through straight-up chatter.

A lot of the Federal Reserve's actions have become a political hot potato. It has to answer to Congress semiannually, but it also has to answer to the yells of politicians around the clock. Yes, its members can make decisions autonomously without the federal government's approval, but they're subject to some oversight by Congress and are charged with working to further the government's high-level economic objectives.

As talked about in the monetary policy chapter, the Fed has to remain credible. People need to believe in the Fed with all their might. That is the only way that the narrative creation process will work. Sometimes that means conducting monetary policy in a fast and furious way so everyone knows that the Fed isn't messing around.

RESISTANCE TO THE NARRATIVE

The biggest question about a lot of Federal Reserve actions is whether they will work or not. Monetary policy is nudge-nudge, wink-wink, and the underlying worry is that things won't work the way they are expected to. In fact, they often don't work the way they are expected to. A global pandemic, supply chain stressors, consumer credit overextension, the amount of oil stockpiles, and an unrecovered manufacturing sector have all created a lot of stress on the Fed's narrative. We can't forget at the end of the day that we exist with our feet on the ground. This may seem a bit dark, but if you die in the metaverse, you die in real life, as Mark Zuckerberg, the founder of Facebook, said.

The biggest nuance of all is the politicalization of markets. The Federal Reserve and other central banks have become primarily inflation firefighters. They have to deal with whatever is right in front of them. But the market is kind of like the one person who keeps calling the fire department because they can't open a jar. It's dramatic. It's loud. And the Fed still has to respond when they call.

There are a lot of examples of central banks losing their independence, as political interference begins to influence monetary policy. "In Turkey, central bank independence is now an endangered species," political scientists writing in *Foreign Policy* warned in 2022. As of the time of writing of this book, Turkish president Recep Tayyip Erdoğan has fired three bank governors who disagreed with his economic agenda, packing the bench with loyalists who enable his meddling. Despite surging inflation peaking at 85.5 percent in October 2022, Erdoğan pushed to lower interest rates dramatically, a puzzling move that defied economic orthodoxy. Naturally, this has raised concerns about the central bank's ability to maintain price stability independently and do its job well.

The United States has come under fire, too. Former president Trump was critical of the Federal Reserve's interest rate policy, urging the central bank to lower rates. A lot of the Fed's job—and this narrative maintenance—is actually quite similar to climbing a mountain.

THE FED'S MOUNTAIN

If you hike or climb, you know that many mountain trails are a series of switchbacks. Zigzagging up the sides of the mountain makes the path less steep and takes a certain amount of effort out of the hike.

THE 1970S

But sometimes the Fed climbs the mountain directly—no switchbacks, no trekking poles, just pure love of the grind. The 1970s were a good example of when the Fed was in grind mode. At the time, the United States faced a severe inflation crisis, with double-digit inflation rates and a stagnant economy. The crisis was sparked by the oil price shock of 1973, when OPEC put a squeeze on the world's oil supply. And of course, oil is in everything, so as oil skyrocketed in price, so did everything else. There were supply chain issues and eventually a wage-price spiral. Prices were rising quickly, wages were rising quickly, and everything was out of control.

Paul Volcker was appointed as the chairman of the Federal Reserve in 1979 and caused something called the Volcker Shock. (Sounds cool but was not.) He implemented tight monetary policy, which involved raising interest rates to unprecedented levels. The rate set by the Fed was 11% in 1979, but by 1980, it hit 20%, the highest level in U.S. history.

Volcker's aim was to reduce the money supply to slow economic activity and make inflation chill out. He increased the reserve requirement, let the dollar fall in value against other currencies, and collaborated with other central banks on anti-inflationary efforts. This aggressive move triggered a severe recession, marked by high unemployment and economic contraction. While it effectively reduced inflation to around 4 percent by 1987, the strategy had substantial short-term repercussions, including widespread unemployment and sluggish economic growth. That was, unsurprisingly, *very* unpopular. After making everyone mad, Volcker's Fed then implemented a gradual reduction in interest rates to stimulate growth and bring the economy out of recession. By the mid-1980s, inflation had fallen to more manageable levels. But the economy had paid a terrible price, hitting double-digit unemployment during a two-year-long recession.

Here's the thing: The Volcker Shock was one way to fight inflation, and it did get the job done eventually. But some economists argue that it wasn't the only way out. They say that other tools in the economic toolbox could have been used. For example, some suggest that the government could have focused on fiscal policies, such as controlling government spending or tweaking taxes, to address the inflation. Others argue that Volcker could have taken a more gradual approach to raising interest rates, giving businesses and people more time to adjust. That might have softened the blow to the economy and reduced the pain of the high interest rates. Before 1979, the Fed was subject to a lot of political pressure from Congress. But Volcker came in with a baseball bat and raised rates aggressively, setting a precedent for the Fed to focus on what was best for the economy in the long term, not just what was popular with members of Congress and the public in the short term. Of course, to stay with the theme of this book that "everything is weird," in a 2022 paper published by the Federal Reserve, the economists David Ratner and Jae Sim challenged the idea that central banks, particularly Paul Volcker's actions, were solely responsible for controlling inflation in the 1970s and 1980s. They wrote: "Conventional wisdom has it that the sound monetary policy since the 1980s not only conquered the Great Inflation, but also buried the Phillips curve itself. This paper provides an alternative explanation: labor market policies that have eroded worker bargaining power might have been the source of the demise of the Phillips curve."

This theory suggests that inflation was curbed not just through monetary policy but also through changes in labor dynamics, particularly the weakening of labor unions and reduced worker ability to negotiate higher wages.

This is a class-based theory of inflation, where the loss of bargaining power among workers contributed to lower inflation, not mega-high interest rates. Inflation subsided because workers lacked the power to sustain it. Not because monetary policy worked.

VOLCKER IN 2022

The Fed's 2021–2023 inflation fight was a bit of a Volcker-style takedown of the economy. During this period, there were rising prices and energy conflicts similar to those of the 1970s. However, the underlying inflationary dynamics were quite different. This raises questions about whether using the same tool (raising rates) was the best way to combat a different type of inflation. And remember, the Fed has a dual mandate. Its policies are meant to optimize both price stability and the labor market—and those two mandates were in conflict for most of the early 2020s.

In the 2021–2023 inflation fight, Fed officials often talked about how strong the labor market was and how they needed it to calm down. The dynamic between jobs and higher prices is a strange one, and it can feel disconcerting to hear things such as "Job growth remained stubbornly robust" or "The consumer is too strong for comfort," as the Fed once put it.

But the Fed had a job to do. So it raised interest rates à la Volcker, and somehow the labor market was still incredibly strong into 2023. But the dynamics of the labor market are shifting and evolving—to something that will likely require a whole new policy tool kit to deal with.

2 PERCENT TARGET

The Fed is going relentlessly after a target of 2 percent inflation. In order for it to summit and complete its hike, the economy needs to hit that 2 percent target. But what's supercool about the mountain is that no one knows where the summit is. There's no map, no GPS coordinates, no guides from people who have been there before. Being able to achieve 2 percent inflation and end our decades-long era of hikes is something we just kind of manifest into existence.

That's because the 2 percent figure is sort of random. The idea originally came from Arthur Grimes, the Labour Party finance minster of New Zealand in the 1980s. He went on TV and said, "Two percent should be our inflation target," and now everybody goes after that magic number.

Here's the secret, though: Inflation doesn't need to be 2 percent all the time. It's simply the general direction in which things are meant to be headed. And to be clear, we don't know what it takes to get down to 2 percent and we don't know if 2 percent is the right target in the first place. As are other things in this book: it's uncertain.

If the inflation target changed, it wouldn't be the end of the world; it might actually be good! Goldman Sachs found that a 3 percent target would be "positive for risk assets, as the tailwind from stronger economic growth would more than offset the headwind from higher nominal bond yields across the curve."

What that basically means is "good for stocks because the economy will grow faster even if bond yields are higher." Basically, the economy will normalize; 2 percent is not the be-all and end-all.

The Fed informs everyone where rates are and where it thinks they need to be in order to move toward the 2 percent inflation "summit" by releasing its Summary of Economic Projections, its projections of key economic indicators such as inflation, GDP growth, the unemployment rate, and the individual forecasts of each Federal Open Market Committee (FOMC) participant for the federal funds rate over the next few years.

The Summary of Economic Projections also includes the final resting point for rates, known as the terminal rate; this is the point at which they stop their upward journey (peak inflation). But of course, staying at the top of the mountain is a form of monetary policy, too—because the only way any hike really ends is if the rate comes back down.

HOW THE FED DEALS WITH MARKETS

To complete the analogy, the Fed also has to be mindful of unruly and unpredictable "snow" coming from the stock and bond markets, which could potentially lead to an avalanche and bury us all. Like a companion who signs up to hike a mountain with you, the Fed needs to make sure that its friends in the market understand that even if it rolls up to a yield or stop sign on the mountain, that doesn't mean it will be changing its course. A lot of the time the market interprets little signs by the Fed as signals that it is going in a certain direction—and freaks out in response. The Fed can't really control the "snow," but it can plow routes around it!

If you are a hiker, you know that choosing a companion can be tricky. Sometimes, you'll have a ride-or-die friend who is willing to grind with you. Other times, you'll have people with you who complain the whole way even if you take the easiest switchbacks possible.

The Fed is the same way. There are often questions as to whether the Fed is becoming too focused on the market response versus the economic response (because the two can be and often are different). I asked San Francisco Fed president Mary Daly about this in October

2023, specifically about how the Fed balances managing markets (making sure markets don't flip whenever the Fed says something) and telling people what they need to hear. Her response:

> *So when I look at the markets, I'm asking several questions. Are they understanding the reaction function that the Federal Reserve has, that the FOMC has? Do they see the data the way I'm seeing it? And if not, let me learn from what they're seeing and see if it builds my understanding.... So I use the financial markets as data and as opposed to managing them, I'm trying to communicate to them just like I am to all of you, so that they clearly understand what we're trying to achieve.*

Jerome Powell has addressed the market directly in some press conferences—for example, in 2021, stating that "what's been driving asset prices isn't monetary policy." But as the Fed itself said in 2022, "An unwarranted easing in financial conditions, especially if driven by a misperception by the public of the committee's reaction function, would complicate the committee's effort to restore price stability."

Translation? "F*ck off, markets. We have a job to do. And we are going to get it done."

Jerome Powell tends to follow the markets in terms of tone. When he was erroneously told in a November 2022 press conference that stocks had reacted positively to the Fed raising rates, he immediately began listing all the reasons why investors should *not* be happy that the Fed was raising rates. Managing expectations is a large part of the Fed's battle, and they did not need a happy market in this inflation battle. Neel Kashkari, the president of the Federal Reserve Bank of Minneapolis, said in 2022, "I certainly was not excited to see the stock market rallying after our last Federal Open Market Committee meeting.... Because I know how committed we all are to getting inflation down."

The Fed needs to balance ego and effect. Its members have to make sure that they don't become too focused on earning back Fed cred on the mountain hike and harming everybody else in the process.

THE FED AND THE LABOR MARKET

The whole point of hiking the mountain is to slow the economy down. The Fed has a dual mandate of creating and maintaining price stability and maximum employment. Price stability is achieved by raising or lowering rates, but this often comes at the expense of the labor market. We can think of the labor market as a mountain goat on the mountain, something that the Fed needs to work with but is sort of in the way.

Ultimately, the Fed wants to quietly lame the labor market goat off the mountain (nonviolently) because that will make the economy chill out. It's an unfortunate reality: When the labor market is strong, when the goat is hanging on to the mountain in an inflationary environment, the Fed doesn't love it. It makes the hike that much harder!

The labor market goat can be kicked off the mountain in one of two ways:

1. More people find jobs (labor force participation rate increases).
2. More people lose their jobs (unemployment rate increases).

The more harmful one (people losing their jobs) is usually easier to make happen. Increasing the labor force participation rate would tighten the labor market, put downward pressure on wage growth, and make it so there isn't so much slack for employers. An increase in the unemployment rate would do those three things as well, but in a more painful way.

You might be asking, "Why does the Fed need to sacrifice the labor market to get inflation down?" The main reason that the Fed freaks out so deeply about the labor market is that nominal wage growth is tied to an inflation measure that it paid a lot of attention to in 2022 called "core services ex shelter" (basically services that we need—or want, in some instances—including such things as transportation, healthcare, and haircuts), so it was worried that if wage growth—particularly in the services sector—didn't soften, inflation wouldn't soften. Unfortunately, the general idea behind battling inflation is that if the Fed raises interest rates, people will lose their jobs, and if they don't have jobs, they have no money to spend, so inflation will chill out. This makes sense in theory, but it creates problems such as wage growth imbalances and wealth inequality.

There's a short memoir called *The Crane Wife* by C. J. Hauser. Hauser had recently broken off an engagement and headed to Texas to study whooping cranes for a novel. This is what she says:

> *Here is what I learned once I began studying whooping cranes: only a small part of studying them has anything to do with the birds. Instead we counted berries. Counted crabs. Measured water salinity. Stood in the mud. Measured the speed of the wind.*
>
> *It turns out, if you want to save a species, you don't spend your time staring at the bird you want to save.* You look at the things it relies on to live instead. *You ask if there is enough to eat and drink. You ask if there is a safe place to sleep. Is there enough here to survive? (Author's emphasis.)*

When you want to save something, you increase the things it relies on to live. When you want to destroy something, you reduce the things it relies on to live. That's how monetary policy works, right? The Fed makes a move to slow wage rises in an attempt to slow the labor market in an attempt to slow hiring in an attempt to slow the economy in an attempt to slow inflation. Wages are the things we rely on to live. And they are often a tool in the fight against inflation.

The tool kit is limited.

NAVIGATING THE FOG

Its primary goal is to reach the summit of 2 percent inflation, even if it's foggy and confusing. But Jeremy Rudd, a senior Federal Reserve economist, published a paper in 2022 that talked about how inflation expectations don't really matter anymore. This is basically like saying the summit doesn't exist (and maybe never did). He wrote, "Economists and economic policymakers believe that households' and firms' expectations of future inflation are a key determinant of actual inflation. A review of the relevant theoretical and empirical literature suggests that this belief rests on *extremely shaky foundations*." (Author's emphasis.)

Rather than saying, "Oh, yes, we know exactly what is happening," Rudd was essentially saying, "Actually, we don't know what is happening, and using expectations as a policy tool is extremely concerning." Because when you zoom out and look at the overall situation, the Fed is wrong most of the time (as we all are).

It's not so much the level of the rates (rates can be low and things can be fine; rates can be high and things can be less fine but still okay) but rather the big moves in rates. Low rates aren't dangerous, but if they rise quickly, it's financially destabilizing.

So the whole economic situation is energy prices, it's a clearly higher cost of living, it's higher wages but not really, but price increases anyway, and it's supply chains and goods pressure—it's how fast the Fed moves, how well monetary policy works—it's a lot of little questions bubbling up to one big question: How can we fix it? It's a tightrope, right? Companies have to pay people more to get them to work to make the things that people want because people have to spend money so GDP will go up because then the economy will grow, but it can't grow too fast because then inflation will occur, but it can't grow too slowly because then a recession will occur.

But the economic data points and subsequent interpretation are all relative. In the long run, inflation expectations are important, and almost every market to some degree is driven by this behavior based on expectations.

How well people expect stocks and cryptocurrencies to perform has a role in how they do perform in the long run. So reality is really about expectations. The economy is made up of people, right? So it checks out that what people think is going to happen (expectations) will drive their behavior (reality) and thus the Fed's response (policy).

I mean technically, we are all the Federal Reserve.

PART V

Theories, Problems, and Opportunities

CHAPTER 18

Old Guy and New Theories

The amount of energy needed to refute bullshit is an order of magnitude bigger than to produce it.

—ALBERTO BRANDOLINI

The field of economics is riddled with theories.

And though they can seem dull, these schools of thought affect countless real-world outcomes, because when our politicians and leaders are zealous disciples of a particular doctrine, it shows up in their policy decisions and can have repercussions for generations.

Take, for instance, President Ronald Reagan and trickle-down economics (Reaganomics)—the absurd idea that tax cuts for the wealthy would somehow benefit everyone. When Reagan took office in 1981, the economy was experiencing severe stagnation and high inflation—stagflation. The whole idea of supply side economics is that if a government lowers taxes and decreases regulation, businesses and entrepreneurs will produce more things. So Reagan looked at the economic situation—which desperately needed production of more things—and enacted the Economic Recovery Tax Act (ERTA), as well as the Tax Reform Act.

The idea was that these tax cuts would help everyone—but nothing really flowed down from those who got the tax cuts. Similar story with the Tax Cuts and Jobs Act of 2017—the money basically went right into the stock market, bolstering buybacks and dividends, rather than helping the broader economy.

Economics and politics are very intertwined. There are many ways in which economic events have influenced politics, including the 2008 financial crisis, the Eurozone crisis, Brexit, and the U.S.-China trade war.

- **The Great Financial Crisis of 2008** was the beginning (or perhaps the catalyst) for a rise in populism, as people felt that government leaders didn't respond properly to the catastrophe.
- **The buckling of Greece, Spain, and Italy** raised questions about the financial sustainability of the EU and the constraints of the eurozone.
- **Brexit** was a function of the cost of EU membership and regulations, and has resulted in the stagnation of the United Kingdom.
- **The U.S.-China trade war** was a function of trade imbalance and the desire to bring manufacturing jobs back to the United States, with profound political implications.

In this chapter, I'll walk you through the economic theories most relevant to your daily life and provide light on the more controversial theories and their integration into the political landscape.

CLASSICAL ECONOMICS

Classical economics is a school of thought that emerged during the late eighteenth and early nineteenth centuries. This theory asserts that markets have a natural ability to self-regulate and that government intervention is generally unnecessary. The core assumption of classical economics is the belief in market efficiency, the theory that free markets, driven by supply and demand, will allocate resources efficiently.

It's a great concept, right? "Just leave it to the markets!" But as you and I are painfully aware, markets are not moral compasses; they are simply moneymaking machines. And that's fine! But markets end up operating out of the self-interest of those who play a big role in them. This can easily lead to a monopoly, where one firm gains a lot of power and market share over all other firms, which isn't very free or even a market past a certain point as there are no competitors anymore.

Free markets, or markets where people can conduct business based on their own self-interest and the pursuit of profit, are also fuzzy in the real world. There is a need for societal welfare and stability! The United States is probably one of the freest markets in the world, but we are now seeing some of the consequences of that.

Free markets can exacerbate income and wealth inequality. They can also create externalities like pollution, because making money sometimes matters more than the environment. That gets into short-term focus, profits over sustainability. Public goods, such as education and health, similarly may be deemed "unprofitable" for businesses but are crucial for societal well-being. Additionally, issues like monopolies, anti-competitive behaviors, and the risks associated with excessive corporate power can translate economic influence into political power. Striking a balance between individual pursuits and societal welfare becomes essential.

So is the free market doing what it was supposed to do? A lot of conversations and research papers have been dealing with this for centuries. The eighteenth-century Scottish economist Adam Smith's "invisible hand," the idea of laissez-faire, let-it-all-go-with-the-wind ideology, is a guiding force of many classical economics conversations. Producers specialize in what they are good at, making what and how much is needed, creating a beautiful web of interdependence and goodness.

Thomas Malthus, with his rather gloomy predictions about population growth outpacing food supply, instilled a sense of urgency in studying demographic impacts on economies. David Ricardo's theories on comparative advantage became a cornerstone of international trade principles, suggesting that nations should specialize in producing goods where they hold efficiency over their trading partners. Meanwhile, John Stuart Mill's work extended economic discussions to include the broader social impacts, and his considerations of equity and justice in the distribution of wealth provided an early bridge between economics and ethics. Together, these thinkers provided the pillars that would support much of economic thought and policy for centuries to come.

It's very much a chicken-and-egg sort of problem that highlights how complex these conversations can get. If the market is so good at doing its job, it shouldn't need government support, right? And maybe the government support is somehow politically motivated, because nobody wants a melting stock market on their hands when they're in office, right? And if the government keeps sticking its nose into stuff, bad firms may remain afloat, creating distorted market signals, and the free market can't do what it's meant to do.

KEYNESIAN ECONOMICS

The early-twentieth-century English economist John Maynard Keynes and the field of *Keynesian economics* love the government. Government intervention is everything; it's perfect and beautiful and lovely. To Keynes, government spending is the way out of recession, a way to get the economy moving and grooving again, a way to reduce unemployment. This theory arose in the 1930s during the Great Depression, when people were devastated by economic collapse. The New Deal, led by President Franklin D. Roosevelt, which pushed for increased government spending on infrastructure development, job creation, and social welfare, is a classic example of Keynesian policy.

Keynes theorized that when consumer confidence needs a boost, money from the government is the boost that people need. It will get them to spend again. The more people spend, the more money is a-flowin' in the Economic Kingdom. Mandating tax cuts, government spending, and unemployment benefits via expansionary fiscal policy is the solution to saving the sinking ship.

Of course, nothing is ever that simple, and a lot of Keynes's work highlights that complexity. Excessive government spending can be inflationary, and there is a vibes-based approach to how much government spending is the right amount of government spending. But for Keynes, as long as the government gets things moving again, the economy will recover.

MONETARISM

In contrast, *monetarism*, developed by Milton Friedman and Anna Schwartz, emphasizes the control of money supply to manage the economy. This has caused a number of M2 (a measure of money supply) charts to be posted to Twitter with the "pointing guys" meme. The idea is that if the money supply gets big, so does inflation. "Inflation is always and everywhere a monetary phenomenon," Friedman said.

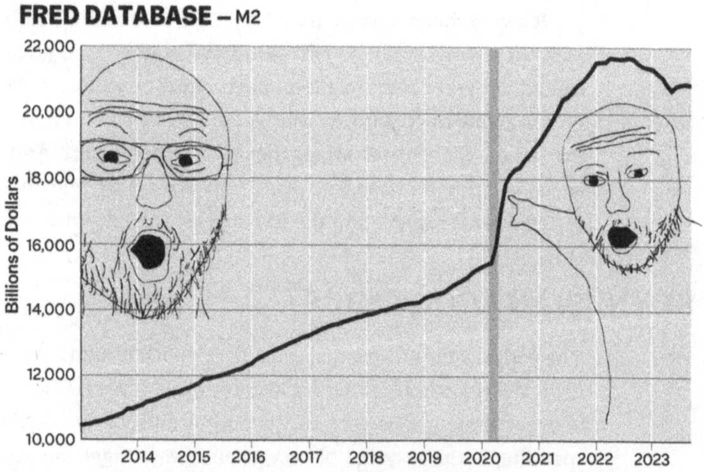

However, this is wrong; 1 percent money growth leads to only about 0.3 percent average higher inflation—it's not one for one, according to the Bank for International Settlements article "Does Money Growth Help Explain the Recent Inflation Surge?" Inflation is *not* always and everywhere a monetary phenomenon.

Monetarism falls prey to the same issues that Keynesian economics does: It's really hard to figure out how much of something is good and how much is bad, and the answer is usually a balance between them!

NEW GROWTH THEORY

New growth theory (NGT) is a newer economic concept that points out a lot of the human aspects of what people have to deal with. It highlights the role of human desires and unlimited wants in driving economic productivity. People's constant pursuit of profit creates growth. Human aspirations create economic progress. It challenges the idea that growth is influenced by factors outside our locus of control, such as government policy and technological advances. It recognizes that our capitalistic hamster brains can move the economy forward. NGT says that because we are little money garbage raccoons, we will always be throwing elbows to try to do things better or make new things in order to make a profit. Knowledge is an asset! Innovation should be nurtured!

Of course, this works in theory. But there are lots of questions. Eventually growth has diminishing returns! Growth hacks don't work forever! Both endogenous (growth driven from within the economy without the need for external forces—innovation, education, and research are key) and exogenous (growth outside the economic system—technological advancements and government policies are key) neoclassical models can't really explain growth in the long run because they often do not fully account for factors like technological advancements, changes in consumer preferences, geopolitical shifts, or environmental constraints.

OTHER THEORIES

There are also theories such as Modern Monetary Theory and Marxism, two very different schools of thought that both revolve around the idea of doing things differently.

Modern Monetary Theory (MMT) focuses on government spending. It says "Let governments spend" under the assumption that governments should be allowed to spend as much as they want, since they can create new money and use various mechanisms, such as raising taxes, to control inflation. The key is that a government, with its own sovereign currency, can't run out of money the same way people or businesses do because it can just create more. MMT says that the government can embark on a massive spending campaign to correct the economy, funding things such as job creation and public projects, all without immediate concern about creating a deficit. This is a good idea in theory, but in practice, it hasn't worked out.

Marxism focuses on social classes and the struggles that exist between them. In capitalist societies, the owning class (those who control the means of production, including factories, land, and money) exploit the working class (those who sell their labor for wages). The owning class takes the surplus generated by the workers and uses it to become richer. Members of the working class, who are unable to save any of the surplus for themselves, experience economic inequality and a lack of control over their labor and lives.

To explain this further, imagine the sweet town of Cookieville, where the MegaBite Bakery owns a factory where the bakers Chip and Crumb bake $100 worth of cookies every day. However, they are paid only $20 a day each. The owners of the MegaBite Bakery, even though they don't bake, take the remaining $60 surplus for themselves just because they control the factory. Though the bakery enjoys its surplus output, Chip and Crumb are economically disadvantaged and unable to increase their small wage because they do not own any of the factory resources. Marxism argues that we should stop this inequality by moving toward a classless society where resources and surplus are distributed equally or according to need. Chip and Crumb must seize the means of production!

A passage in Karl Marx's *Economic and Philosophic Manuscripts of 1844* expands on the above idea—that as we talk about the economy, it's good to reflect on human well-being:

> *The less you eat, drink and read books; the less you go to the theatre, the dance hall, the public house; the less you think, love, theorize, sing, paint, fence, etc., the more you save—the greater becomes your treasure which neither moths nor dust will devour—your capital. The less you are, the more you have; the less you express your own life, the greater is your alienated life—the greater is the store of your estranged being.*

What Marx was talking about is what we give up for want of "having": When all this ends, you can't take your money with you. It's really easy to get lost in these theories, to think, number one, that the theory is all that matters and that, number two, one must agree with all of it to agree with any of it. But it doesn't. And you don't. The world is a series of puzzle pieces, and you are the builder.

Existence is hard, and a lot of economic theory doesn't capture that because, well, why would it? The book *Dancing After Hours* by Andre Dubus is an exploration of normalcy—how people exist in the world. There is one section that talks about the shopping cart theory:

> *"There's something about taking the cart back instead of leaving it in the parking lot," she said. "I don't know when this came to me; it was a few years ago. There's a difference between leaving it where you empty it and taking it back to the front of the store. It's significant."*
>
> *"Because somebody has to take them in."*
>
> *"Yes. And if you know that, and you do it for that one guy, you do something else. You join the world....* You move out of your isolation and become universal." *(Author's emphasis.)*

We are increasingly forgetting about our commonalities. Many people have explored the disintegration of communities that has come with suburbanization and social media-ization, but it's becoming increasingly stark. The complexity scientist Peter Turchin explored this in his 2013 piece "The Strange Disappearance of Cooperation in America," and so many parts of it still ring true: "What we have then, is a 'strange disappearance' of cooperation at all levels within the American society: from the neighborhood bowling leagues to the national-level economic and political institutes."

We are breaking away from one another. This is not a novel phenomenon—as the piece outlines, the same thing happened in ancient and medieval empires. However, polarization is bad; it leads to less progress and eventual stagnation.

To avoid this, we need a world where participation is incentivized and encouraged versus the zero-sum individualistic culture and focused on innovation that truly makes the world better. There is an element of figuring out how to tap into what people are passionate about and giving them the space to explore it. As George Saunders wrote in *Congratulations, by the Way: Some Thoughts on Kindness*, "Find out what makes you kinder, what opens you up and brings out the most loving, generous, and unafraid version of you—and go after those things as if nothing else matters. Because, actually, nothing else does."

We are living in a world of increasing differentials, where our best case is becoming less probable and we are having to develop new models of thinking. We might be all experiencing the "same thing" as our economic world changes around us, but it shows up for all of us differently. And that is important to remember.

Many more economic concepts influence today's economic analysis, but most of them boil down to "Well, hmm, maybe, actually." Human behavior is not always predictable and is influenced by various factors, including emotions, social pressures, and individual circumstances. Though economic theory provides a framework for understanding behavior, it may not fully capture the complexity and nuances of real-world human decisions. There is no precise way to analyze phenomena driven by something as goofy as people's actions.

History has shown us instances where adhering strictly to economic orthodoxy or an established set of economic beliefs that set the precedent for managing economic issues, without room for nuances or flexibility, has led to disastrous outcomes.

For example:

1. **The Gold Standard and the Great Depression**

   Orthodoxy: The gold standard was championed as a mechanism to ensure fiscal discipline and monetary stability because everything would be tied to the value of gold, but during the Great Depression it magnified the crisis by preventing monetary expansion. Countries that left the gold standard earlier recovered faster.

   Weakness Highlighted: The belief that fixed exchange regimes (like the gold standard) provide superior economic stability. Even today, debates about fixed versus floating exchange rates get into this idea, with some still advocating for fixed regimes despite the clear lack of flexibility.

2. **Austerity Measures in the Eurozone Crisis**

   Orthodoxy: High public debt leads to economic instability, so austerity (reduced public spending and increased taxes) is necessary for economic recovery and to regain market confidence. But in countries like Greece, austerity (the government not being able to spend to save the economy) led to deep recessions, high unemployment, and social upheaval.

   Weakness Highlighted: The assumption that markets always favor austerity in times of crisis, or that the government having discipline with money is always preferable to growth-focused policies. This debate remains relevant as nations grapple with high public debts today.

3. **Washington Consensus and Latin America**

   Orthodoxy: Free-market reforms, privatization, and deregulation are the keys to rapid economic development. While some countries benefited, many saw increased inequality, social unrest, and inconsistent economic growth.

   Weakness Highlighted: The idea that there's a one-size-fits-all blueprint for economic development. Many of the Washington Consensus policies are still advocated for in various forms today, especially by international financial institutions.

4. 1997 Asian Financial Crisis

Orthodoxy: Capital account liberalization, or the idea that allowing capital to flow freely across borders is essential for economic growth. Rapid capital inflow followed by sudden outflow contributed to the crisis. Countries with capital controls, like India and China, were less affected.

Weakness Highlighted: The unquestioned belief in the virtues of completely open financial markets. While today there's broader acknowledgment of the risks, many still argue for free flow of money without sufficient safeguards.

5. Efficient Market Hypothesis and the 2008 Financial Crisis

Orthodoxy: Financial markets are efficient and always reflect all available information. This assumption was the core theory of many financial models and risk assessment tools. The 2008 crisis revealed how markets can be shortsighted, driven by herd behavior, and how financial "innovations" can hide risks.

Weakness Highlighted: Blind faith in market efficiency and the dangers of relying too heavily on models that don't account for extreme events or irrational behavior. The debate about market efficiency and the role of regulation remains alive today.

In piecing together the valuable aspects of these theories, one common thread emerges: balance. Economic theories can offer essential insights, but they often need to be tempered with a dose of real-world pragmatism. The key for policymakers and economists alike is to blend the wisdom from various theories, apply them judiciously, and remain adaptive to the ever-changing dynamics of the global economy. This adaptability, coupled with a thorough understanding of past lessons, can provide a more comprehensive tool kit for addressing future economic challenges.

Humans are complex, and the world we live in is complex, too. Remember that the next time someone is screaming at you on TV about this *being the one problem wreaking havoc on everything*. It never is just one thing! A lot of factors end up causing problems—and a lot of factors can be solutions.

CHAPTER 19

Problems

HOW TO GIVE UP

This chapter was very hard to write. It's hard to write about things that need to be fixed. It's hard to fix things that need to be fixed. I've tried my best to outline some of the issues that we are facing as a society, but I've missed many things.

By this point in the book, we've covered the basics of how the economy works.

But it's crucial to know how the economy fails.

THE STATE OF THE AMERICAN DREAM

I grew up in Kentucky, in the public school system, and my college was paid for via a very generous scholarship that was partially funded by the state lottery. I left Kentucky five days after I graduated school and headed out to Los Angeles for a wonderful job at Capital Group, an early career rotational program that would give me significant exposure to the industry.

But Los Angeles was huge. And I was small. The city changed me, in many ways, and then six months later, the pandemic hit. I was cooped up in a 350-square-foot studio (about the size of a very small bedroom) all alone. I was sitting on a cardboard box as my "chair" and my only interface with the outside world was through financial markets.

During those twelve months, we all watched policy decisions shape our reality.

The pandemic was a whirlwind lesson on how systems work—and how they can fail us. Essential workers were treated like heroes, but only at first. A few months in, their capes were ragged from carrying the immense burden of being both healers and morticians.

The pandemic highlighted the increasing bifurcation in our world. It didn't just reveal a wealth gap; it exposed an economy built around unreasonable expectations. Some would risk their lives so another could get a cheeseburger delivered to their door, while healthcare workers wore trash bags because, welp, we just didn't have enough personal protective equipment—or enough of anything, really.

So much of this book was shaped by that push and pull of abundance and scarcity.

We have a surplus of things we don't need and a shortage of things we do need. We need more workers. We need more homes. We need more public transit. We need more green energy.

We need, we need, we need. This endless cycle of "need" can be exhausting to hear because a lot of this is not things that the average person can really go out and fix. If someone could flip a switch that helps enact policy around immigration reform and nuclear power plants, that would be amazing! But it takes collective action to achieve anything substantial.

The main theme of this book is that "people are the economy." Countless poor policy choices have turned living in this economy into a tough gig. Many of us have witnessed the American Dream rot before our eyes. Higher education has become a luxury good, the housing crisis has exacerbated the cost of living, all backdropped by political stagnation and rapid (perhaps too rapid) technological advancement with things like AI.

One thing that was very striking to me about the last few years was the constant anger that bubbled underneath the surface. Nothing was working the way that it was supposed to. We were still dealing with the lingering effects of the pandemic, shipping constraints, rising energy costs, and natural disasters like droughts, floods, and fires. Wars unfolded. A crude list doesn't even begin to cover it—big pharma; student loans; mass shootings; wealth inequality; the aftershocks of ZIRP; credit card debt; the debt ceiling is as dumb as possible; commercial real estate is terrifying; so on and so forth.

It's scary. We are entering into the very, very vast unknown and it's increasingly easy to trend toward negativity, especially if it *feels* like life is punching you in the face repeatedly.

We all want to be informed, but a gap exists between knowledge and action. We are all overwhelmed with information, but we're alienated from any concrete sense of reality. We are pixels away from disaster, yet a vision for a safer world remains elusive.

ECONOMY AND MENTAL HEALTH

This book has heavily focused on the importance of emotions—and the communication of emotions—in shaping our perception of the economy. The writer and director Paul Auster touched on the complex nature of understanding others, underscoring the necessity of communication in his book *The Invention of Solitude*:

> *Impossible, I realize, to enter another's solitude. If it is true that we can ever come to know another human being, even to a small degree, it is only to the extent that he is willing to make himself known. A man will say: I am cold. Or else he will say nothing, and we will see him shivering. Either way, we will know that he is cold. But what of the man who says nothing and does not shiver? Where all is intractable, here all is hermetic and evasive, one can do no more than observe. But whether one can make sense of what he observes is another matter entirely. I do not want to presume anything.*

Auster notes that while it's impossible to totally understand another person, we can glean insight from their actions and expressions. For example, a person might shiver, indicating they are cold. That's helpful! But what about people who don't do anything? They might be freezing, they might not be freezing, but they don't *say* anything.

This scenario can be seen in the economy, too: There are moments when the economy visibly "shivers," indicating issues with GDP, inflation, or the labor market. But there are also times when the economy doesn't visibly shiver but still carries an undercurrent of distress.

Just because the economy isn't visibly shivering doesn't mean that things are great, and just because the economy is shivering doesn't mean it will be cold forever. There is a human side to this. The vibes, the data, all of it, influence how we feel about the economy and our place in it, of course. But there is something deeper going on here.

The current global mental health crisis profoundly affects the economy. This impact is reflected in both absenteeism and presenteeism at work, where individuals are less effective in their jobs due to mental health issues. *The Lancet Global Health* published a paper analyzing the economic impacts of mental health that stated:

> *From addiction to dementia to schizophrenia, almost 1 billion people worldwide suffer from a mental disorder. Lost productivity as a result of two of the most common mental disorders, anxiety and depression, costs the global economy U.S. $1 trillion each year. In total, poor mental health was estimated to cost the world economy approximately $2.5 trillion per year in poor health and reduced productivity in 2010, a cost projected to rise to $6 trillion by 2030.*

So sure, mental health challenges can influence workforce productivity, contribute to absenteeism, and lead to reduced job performance—which matter, but not more than how people are doing in the day-to-day. Some things supersede efficiency metrics, such as the well-being of humans. We have a mental health crisis that impacts vibes sometimes more than economic output does.

So, Auster's reflections on personal understanding resonate deeply with the economic landscape. Just as we struggle to comprehend another's internal world fully, trying to figure out how to care for one another, interpreting the economic "vibes" requires looking beyond surface data to understand the underlying human factors driving the economy.

THE SHIFTING NATURE OF WORK

There's a lot to say about the state of mental health and the labor market in the context of the early 2020s. I graduated right into the pandemic; I spent six months in the office, then—boom! It really changed my relationship with work and did the same for many of my peers. A lot of people my age (early to late twenties, even beyond) seem to have a new sort of relationship with work, haunted by their early adulthood not going as they expected it to.

For instance, Gen Z has experienced three major economic downturns even though some of them are barely in their mid-twenties. These crises occurred during their formative years, which has shaped their worldview, their relationships with others, and how they interact with themselves.

Erik Baker wrote an incredible piece, "The Age of the Crisis of Work," in which he explored the mismatch that workers were experiencing en masse in the 2020s:

> *[Within work there is] an inchoate sense of disillusionment. Tendrils of dissatisfaction are solidifying. Talk of a crisis of work suggests that many people today understand work itself, I think accurately, as a governing institution in its own right, analogous in some ways to the state.... work functions as a nation within a nation—an imagined community, in Benedict Anderson's famous definition. Its moral health is of obscure but paramount significance.*

Baker likened work to a benign tumor; it exists, but it is not a crisis in and of itself. Work has evolved around unnecessary provisions (like meetings that could have been an email, excessive middle-management approval layers, and an overemphasis on accreditation) and the age of surplus created the jobs of excess. The only way to stay ahead is to produce, produce, produce, but that's been increasingly strange because... what are we producing?

When people sat back after the pandemic, too many truths began to break the pattern of the story we had told ourselves in this age of industrial maturity about the work we do. Baker wrote, "Once the mascot of American entrepreneurship, *the entire tech industry is now in disgrace.* The outright frauds (Theranos, Juicero, etc.) occasionally seem preferable to the many companies that are actually disrupting things." (Author's emphasis.)

The stories of the industries that we used to revere are breaking apart. Things we thought were good can be kind of evil in reality (Facebook, other social media platforms, and so on). Heroes have become villains. And in that process, many came to the realization (especially in the rather work-obsessed United States) that work might not be the key to self-actualization.

For some people it is—but for the vast majority of people, it might not be. And that's okay! But it's also where our work story gets messed up: Work isn't what we thought it would be.

DEMOGRAPHICS

With the rise of individualism, especially in Western cultures, there's been a notable increase in feelings of loneliness and isolation. Asking for help is foundational to existence, as are the feelings of belonging and purpose that can only be found by allowing ourselves to become enmeshed in interdependent communities.

But we ignore this. And we try to solve the problems that require community support with our own personal resources and solutions, or reach for some numbing mechanism, and then get frustrated when we can't do the stuff and things that require the support of others.

Gen Z and Millennials are the first generations to truly be nihilistic. The loss of religion, extreme political polarization, the constant news flow, blah, blah—we are all very familiar. It creates a sense of "lmao okay, what is going on" that translates widely to massive disillusionment with a system and the suffering that takes place within that system.

WHEN SYSTEMS FAIL

There is frustration with the nine-to-five, with work not fulfilling the promise that it did for the boomers. There is no beginner mode anymore, a starter salary is not what it used to be, and the way we work and live has had to evolve in relation to that.

There have been a lot of blowups in recent years. Whether it is tulip bulbs or internet companies, the same sort of energy persists: people want in, they want money, and they want it now. The unprofitable internet companies that raised millions of dollars defined a time of superfluity that would only be amplified in the coming years—as a much bigger financial crisis shortly followed.

The year 2008 was very impactful for everyone. A lot of kids (myself included) saw their caregivers battle against uncontrollable economic forces. There were job losses, home foreclosures, a decimation of household wealth; almost no one was left unscathed (except the bankers who had caused the crisis).

The younger generations were furious as they witnessed a system fail in a way they couldn't comprehend. Economic stability, job stability, financial stability—all of those were big question marks. An image of parents holding their heads in their hands at the dining room table as they tried to figure out how to pay the mortgage is seared into the minds of many.

It was a systemic failure that resulted in economic inequality and social disparities, and it didn't seem as though the consequences were there for those who had caused it. The Golden Age of Grift had begun, and the first rug had been pulled. It was a world of fraud and deceit.

Around this same time, social media started to pop up. For the first time ever, everything was broadcasted to the world, and feelings became assets that could be traded for likes and retweets.

We don't have many physical third spaces—places to go that aren't work or home or school. The online world became the gathering space, a way to find and build community in a seemingly desolate landscape of individualism. So people started posting.

But that era was also defined by the rising power of corporations. Several laws that passed in the 2010s ended up turning the United States into three corporations in a trench suit—a monopoly. That gave corporations a lot of freedom, but it also gave advertisers a lot of power. Advertising became the economic model of the 2010s!

Our nervous systems became profit machines for anyone who could produce a fast-paced pleasure-producing candy dream. Eyeballs became monetization tools, creating a strange layer of interaction between consumers and advertisers. To advertisers, you are really nothing but clicks in the grand scheme of Making Money, and they are going to make you click! Somehow!

Of course, the buildup from the dot-com bubble to the 2008 crisis was exacerbated by the pandemic of 2020. For the Zoomers who were still in school, online learning replaced in-person lectures and shifted socialization. For the Zoomers who had just begun their careers (including myself), working from home became the only option. And death was the only constant. That shifted how a lot of people thought about work and life. People we titled "essential workers"—those in service, medical, transportation, agriculture, and some other fields—still had to go to work during the pandemic. Everything that had been bad before the pandemic only got worse.

For the past forty years, productivity has increased but wages have remained relatively stagnant. The minimum wage hasn't increased. The cost of living has skyrocketed, especially during the recent inflation crisis. And we all watched the horrific treatment of "essential workers," the people who kept food on our table, worked in meatpacking plants, staffed hospitals, and treated those who were sick. We all bore witness to the degradation caused by that treatment: The nurses didn't have enough PPE and had to wear trash bags, factories were overrun with covid cases, yet some workers were still forced to go to work, teachers tried to keep kids safe in a world that seemed increasingly intent on killing them, and countless more examples.

All of that shaped the way people think about work.

When we started getting to the other side of the pandemic, the narrative quickly became about bringing people back into the office—addressing the labor shortage, and the immediate demand for more workers. We never stopped to grieve. Instead, the important thing was getting the economy booming again.

Getting the economy booming again begins with education, but that's something we repeatedly seem to ignore. For trade school graduates, there is a reluctance by employers to train employees because of cost (along with a myriad of other problems with getting new people into trade positions). For university graduates, there is no guarantee that they will find a job, especially one related to the major they studied. In the United States, healthcare and benefits are tied to employment, which is kind of bonkers.

There is no real safety net; if you stumble, you can fall pretty hard.

Traditional work hasn't really worked over the past decade or so. Hence the rise of the gig economy and other income streams to try to plug the economic gap. People are trying to put together puzzle pieces that never really fit quite right.

People ask what the "revolution" will look like, and I don't know the answer to that (or else this would be a very different book). But I think the way we think about work is evolving—whether that be working from home, using tactics such as quiet quitting, working side jobs, or giving ourselves space to discover what we really care about. People need to be supported. The labor market should shift to become about ownership; support; safety nets. There are so many things that can be done for the people who make this economy work.

YOUR EYEBALLS ARE DOLLAR SIGNS

Given the sheer volume of information bombarding us all the time, it's simple to see how we have entered a world where our attention has become the ultimate commodity. When we log on to the internet, we are immediately exposed to thirty different things—from gut-wrenching to wondrous—in the span of one minute.

This can lead to cognitive dissonance, especially when we define ourselves through the lens of the content we consume—be it TikTok videos or Instagram Reels—which places artificial limits on our self-conception.

This media, whether it be images, videos, newsletters, or podcasts, distances us from reality. This all leads us to blur the line between feeling and action. As Susan Sontag wrote, "Thinking about images of suffering is not the same as doing anything about suffering. To treat the images of suffering as equivalent to the suffering itself is to participate in a cult of nostalgia."

The idea that "because I saw this image of war, I contributed to stopping the war" fosters a false sense of agency, of personal familiarity with far-off events and people. We live in a media ecosystem that's designed to outrage us. And we can see this clearly in the composition of pieces—the words and narratives published even by mainstream outlets. For example:

- In October 2022, Bloomberg published a piece titled "Forecast for US Recession Within Year Hits 100% in Blow to Biden." That did not happen. But it certainly scared people.
- *The New York Times* is known for publishing pretty terrible headlines (something something clickbait). During late 2023 with the Israel-Gaza war, they published the headline "Israeli Strike Kills Hundreds in Hospital, Palestinians Say" which has several problems, including inflammatory language and grouping Palestinians with the terrorist group Hamas. The article also included a photo of a bombed-out building that wasn't even associated with the hospital in question.

SOCIAL MEDIA MAKES IT WORSE

Social media only amplifies all of this. A place built to air grievances, where virality is a function of saying wrong things loudly, and incentives are totally misaligned. Eyeballs are monetization tools, and the only way that you are going to attract them is if you give them something to stare at.

There's also the symbolism involved with social media.

1. Showing anxiety is the way to prove that you care.
2. People will attach themselves to opinion because there is safety in certainty, even if the certainty is misplaced. Emotional regulation via based takes.

But the problem with this is that it creates grandstanding, where someone's personality and self-worth becomes completely tied into the suffering of others. The takes become completely detached from those that some claim to be advocating for because it's all signaling to others that they *get* it. Social desirability bias, the idea of making yourself into something that you aren't, in order to be good enough for others.

This creates a commodification of our feelings.

Social media platforms in particular have evolved into a kind of "sociological marketplace" where experiences are traded, liked, and shared based on their perceived value. Whether it's a scenic vacation, a gourmet meal, or even personal grief, everything is at risk of being transformed into a consumable asset.

For example, the compulsion to capture the "perfect" Instagram photo can distract from the genuine enjoyment of a moment. Instead of immersing ourselves in the beauty of a sunset or the joy of hanging out with buds, we may find ourselves analyzing angles, lighting, and potential captions—creating an asset out of the experience. Which is annoying to call out, because there is an element of just letting people live their lives, but still—what happens when everything becomes consumable? We try to assetify everything we experience to give it a sense of value on the sociological marketplace. We prevent ourselves from fully experiencing the world when we hyper-analyze what we *think*, what we are feeling, and what it "means" according to various psychological theories, as opposed to simply *feeling the feeling*.

"Therapycoded invalidation," a term coined by Visa Veerasamy, is the idea that our ability to understand and express ourselves has become limited by the growing influence of therapeutic language. While therapy and self-awareness are undeniably beneficial, there's a risk when every emotion or experience is filtered through this predetermined diagnostic lens. Instead of simply feeling sadness, joy, or anger, we might jump to self-analyze, label, and even pathologize our emotions. It's as though we're constantly trying to fit our feelings into neat boxes defined by a broader societal or psychological framework, which can prevent us from experiencing them in their raw, unfiltered form.

And to be fair, there is a balance between living life and allowing ourselves to assetify our feelings and whatnot, as well as being mindful of how experiences can get commodified. But when we get so deep into attaching some sort of value to what we feel like we should feel, when we develop entire complexes around it, that's where it can get really dicey. Susan Sontag would say we do this to give a sense of superiority over our experiences, constantly analyzing and therefore alienating ourselves from what we are doing.

This all happens because we feel like we are running out of time, running out of money, running out of space to think. There have been many efforts to make the internet into a third place, and it is, in a way. But you still log off eventually. You put down the phone or close out the tab on the computer, and it's still you, rattling around, somatically (soulfully?) alone.

MEDIA LITERACY CRISIS

There is a definite media literacy crisis in the United States. The limitations of the words we choose end up shaping the narratives we tell ourselves. Andy Clark, a philosopher and cognitive scientist, warned in his book *The Experience Machine*:

> *Human minds are not elusive, ghostly inner things. They are seething, swirling oceans of prediction, continuously orchestrated by brain, body,*

and world. We should be careful what kinds of material, digital, and social worlds we build, because in building those worlds we are building our own minds too.

And that's where we are at right now. It's about eyeballs. At any cost. A part of this is the unfortunate business model of media—to drive clicks, you have to freak people out. But there are consequences to clickability!

There is empirical evidence for this, as pointed out by David Rozado, Ruth Hughes, and Jamin Halberstadt in their 2022 paper "Longitudinal Analysis of Sentiment and Emotion in News Media Headlines Using Automated Labelling with Transformer Language Models."

Average yearly sentiment of news articles headlines in 47* popular news media outlets (n=23 million)

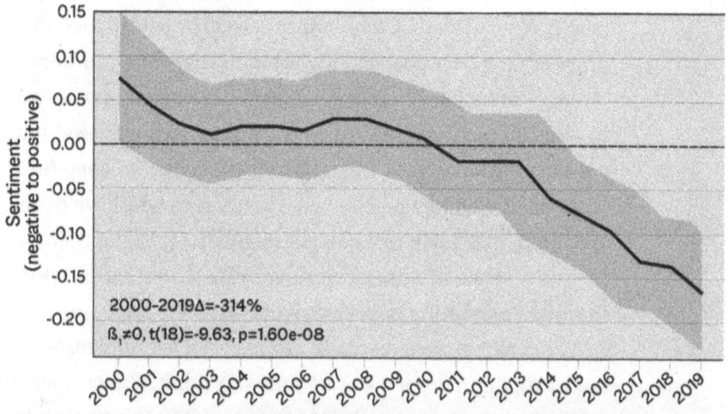

*Alternet. Democracy Now, Daily Beast, Huffington Post, The Intercept, Jacobin, Mother Jones, The New Yorker, The Nation, Slate, Vox, CNN, New York Times, ABC News, The Atlantic, Buzzfeed, CBS News, The Economist, The Guardian, NBC News, POLITICO, TIME, Washington Post, NPR, Associated Press, BBC, Bloomberg, Christian Science Monitor, REUTERS, The Hill, USA Today, Wall Street Journal, Reason, Washington Examiner, Washington Times, Fox News, American Spectator, Breitbart, The Blaze, Christian Broadcasting Network, The Daily Caller, The Daily Mail, The Daily Wire, The Federalist, National Review, New York Post, Newsmax

We are constantly getting riled up. The worst part is that the things we get riled up about are often figments of our imagination. They are real, of course, but there is whipped cream on top, fluff and froth to exacerbate each and every issue, so we become reactive, frustrated, and *mad*.

As Krista Tippett, the host of the podcast *On Being*, put it, "I don't actually think we are equipped . . . to be delivered catastrophic and confusing news and pictures, 24/7. We are analog creatures in a digital world."

This has created a very deep and prevalent sense of nihilism in the younger generations because they are constantly marketed the idea of Realness—but in the throes of the sociologist Jean Baudrillard's simulacra and simulation: "We live in a world where there is more and more information, and less and less meaning.... What every society looks for in continuing to produce, and to overproduce, is to restore the real that escapes it."

The same pundits that imply their wisdom can save the world from ending, hypothetically, are also the people sowing seeds of distrust in the discourse, postulating on Twitter about recessions, and often proclaiming that things are Much Worse Than They Actually Are. The marginal cost of plausible bullshit is effectively zero.

As Anne Applebaum, a reporter at *The Atlantic*, wrote:

> *The constant provision of absurd, conflicting explanations and ridiculous lies—the famous "firehouse of falsehoods"—encourages many people to believe that there is no truth at all. The result is widespread cynicism. If you don't know what's true, after all, then there isn't anything you can do about it. Protest is pointless. Engagement is useless.*

Because of this cynicism, we engage with nostalgia.

MEDIA, NOSTALGIA, AND CONSUMERISM

Commemorating the past feels easier than critically engaging with the present. We like to stay in pristine museum walls versus building new things! Especially because we tend to remember the past as being better than it actually was, and we often treat the present moment as far worse than it actually is.

Reminiscing about the good old days can be a dangerous form of reactivity. Nostalgia isn't merely a passive act of remembering the past, it's a reaction to circumstances. In times of political upheaval, technological advancement, and societal changes, people tend to turn toward a past that seems simpler, stable, and familiar. And it's a process:

- **We reinvent the past:** The idea of the past being more unpredictable than the future is a nod to the reinvention of time that we often do in our own heads.
- **And then we *remake* it:** We tend to look back fondly on moments that might not warrant such warmth—but then we go on and remake those feelings with our technology and our movies and our music. As cultural theo-

rist and artist Svetlana Boym wrote in her book *The Future of Nostalgia*, "technological advances and special effects are frequently used to recreate visions of the past, from the sinking *Titanic* to dying gladiators and extinct dinosaurs."

And it's mostly because we are scared: It's a form of escapism that protects us from thinking about the overwhelming speed at which we're hurtling toward some eventual inevitability. Boym again: "Nostalgia inevitably reappears as a defense mechanism in a time of accelerated rhythms of life and upheavals."

There are three important things to think about when it comes to the psychology of nostalgia, including hope, imagination, stagnation, and nihilism:

1. Hope requires imagination—and imagination requires work.
2. Nostalgia encourages stagnancy, and we are in a cultural moment that reinforces this.
3. As nostalgia deepens, innovative thought becomes rare, and hope for the future shrivels up, consumer sentiment dips. We've seen spending habits get weird, with people throwing all their cash into Dogecoin. Nihilism becomes the forcing function for companies and investments because people give up hope, so they just sort of gamble it all away.

To be fair, I do think there is a place for nostalgia! It's nice to share the past with people, and memories are the foundation of our personhood.

But nostalgia can be a means of abdicating ourselves from the responsibility to imagine and create a better world. It's a form of forgetting but also of escapism. "The problem with prefabricated nostalgia," Boym wrote, "is that it does not help us to deal with the future."

How do you dream about the future when you're always looking backward? The stories we tell on a broad scale are becoming less inspiring. So we reach for new iterations of the past—the way it "could have been"—hoping that this past will become our future. But we just get stuck in a loop.

THINGS ARE ALL THE SAME NOW

But from an economic perspective, it can get a bit skewed. As Derek Thompson points out: "It's crazy how many different forces in Hollywood are pushing toward infinitely recurring IP loops. Original stories need to shoot the moon with reviews and buzz to have a chance at $100m, while middlingly reviewed renditions of familiar IP throw up $200 million without breaking a sweat."

It's cheaper to be nostalgic! There's less risk, both for the consumer and the movie producer. Think of *The Super Mario Bros. Movie*, the Marvel Cinematic Universe, the *Barbie* movie, and the constant franchise reboots as the monetization of familiarity. They exist within a risk minimization bubble fueled by economic uncertainty.

Save money. Make more movies. Don't innovate.

This also results in the **commodification of self**, a way for us to align with stories and narratives (increasingly told by brands). We begin to define ourselves by what we end up consuming, by brands. Just look at any gym influencer or some of the conversations on various subreddits like r/streetwear startup and r/DidntKnowIWantedThat about new merch product drops or must-haves.

As we now know, consumer spending is 70% of GDP growth, so think about all the powerful entities who monetarily benefit when we feel loyal to the brands we follow and the products we buy, to the point where they become part of our identities. As technologist and writer Toby Shorin framed it, we have "an economy where culture is made in service of brands. To be even more literal: cultural production has become a service industry for the supply chain."

It's almost as if the economic machinery thinks, "Why reinvent the wheel when you can just repolish the old one?" Take the resurgence of 1990s and early 2000s fashion trends: bucket hats, platform shoes, and baggy jeans.

Brands aren't delving into new territories; they're digging into their old catalogs and simply re-releasing classic designs. Even the return of vinyl records in a digital age echoes this sentiment. It's the economics of familiarity. Why chance innovation when the past offers a seemingly guaranteed ROI? In essence, the consumer world is caught in an economically driven nostalgia loop: Recycle, resell, repeat.

WHAT GME REALLY MEANT

In a similar way to nostalgia and consumerism and media literacy, the fate of AMC and GameStop are actually signs of a broader shift, reflecting the ways investing has evolved alongside changes in people's lives. These instances symbolize more than mere market anomalies; they are indicative of a new era where retail investors and online communities have a significant impact on the stock market's dynamics.

There is a huge amount of resentment bubbling underneath the surface from people who are frustrated and angry at a system that has abandoned them.

Memefication was also a big part of that time. Memes create a narrative, which ultimately drives value. It doesn't have to be a narrative about how a company is going to produce a certain amount of revenue; it can just be the power of everyone deciding what is going to happen.

At one point, meme stonks—shares of companies that gain popularity through social media and online forums—accounted for more than 25 percent of all volume traded on the stock market. AMC's market cap grew to a healthy $33 billion and somehow it became larger than half the other companies in the S&P 500.

The first couple years of the 2020s were haunted by loneliness. We were deep in the throes of the pandemic, and people were desperate for connection. They used the stock market as a way to find community, a tool to connect with other people. Social investing apps became all the rage.

Community drove AMC and GameStop. The power of Reddit gave people a platform to drive the collective belief behind the value of an asset. One way to destroy a system that you don't believe in is to bet against it.

So the meme stonk era was driven by narratives, by the collective belief behind the value of an asset, which was driven by a craving for community. SPACs, GameStop, and so many money-making methods that arose during that time were the results of people testing the limits, memefying things all in an effort to reimagine wealth generation.

The idea of the financial industry as the gatekeeper of the ivory tower of money is still accurate, but it isn't as accurate as it used to be. In contrast, memefication is a function of information access, and the market was fueled by that. This weird era demonstrated the growing power of the retail investor, as well as the structural cracks in the markets.

The market was no longer driven by fundamentals, it was driven by memes. It was no longer a metaphor, but a living structure—the stonk market, characterized by a lot of get-rich-quick ideology, loneliness, irrational behavior, and pervasive fear as humans were haunted by those animal spirits.

ECONOMIC INEQUALITY AND COOPERATION

In 2013, Peter Turchin published a paper titled "The Strange Disappearance of Cooperation in America" that explored the idea of inequality driving coopera-

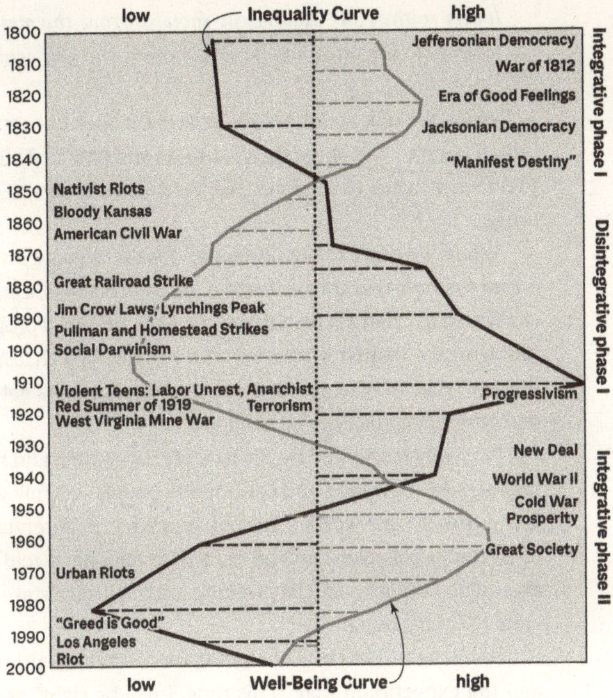

tion. It's the idea that if people are feeling good, they are generally going to work well together.

As we all know, economic inequality has increased, as shown by the increase in the income share of the top 1 percent. Political polarization has increased based on the number of filibusters in the Senate.

A few things Turchin highlights in the piece are really important:

> *You may think that political polarization is not so bad. What's wrong with different political parties holding strong opinions about how this country should be governed? The problem is, the clash of ideas inevitably leads to the clash of personalities. As political positions become separated by a deep ideological gulf the capacity for compromise disappears and political leaders become increasingly intransigent. The end result is political gridlock, something that became abundantly clear in the last few years, but has been developing over the last few decades.... What we have then, is a "strange disappearance" of cooperation at all*

levels within the American society: from the neighborhood bowling leagues to the national-level economic and political institutes.

When we talk about setting policy, the idea of cooperation is really important. If people can't agree on what to do and how to do it, it becomes impossible to do what needs to be done. We need to find ways to cooperate with one another.

When we don't really understand what is going on but pretend we do, we create systems that trap us further. As Tom Nichols, a staff writer at *The Atlantic*, tweeted, "There is no bill you can pass, no social program, that will solve the problem of a dentist or realtor who has decided that life is just too goddamn dull and that they're gonna spice up their week by getting some tactical gear and cosplaying the Second Civil War."

I'm really fascinated by the lack of cooperation and the polarization and the doomerism—how loud and confidently people will talk about what presumably is the end of their world. I am not sure why there tends to be an undercurrent of "If things collapse, I will be okay because I have gold bars" because if things do end up falling apart, they tend to exist within a state of rubble rather than a state of utility, but alas.

And I get it! The thrill of rooting for downfall, waiting for stocks to go down, and the expectation that "This time, I will be right" or whatever is inherently exciting. But it isn't useful.

I think it's okay to say, "Banks *are* failing, inflation *is* high, we have existed in a state of excess for years," because all of these things are true, but to simply bemoan these facts without developing a tangible plan to improve things (even on a micro level) is a passive course of action that yields no process, and, therefore, no results.

Lack of cooperation and doomerism are heavy on the spirit—and they can drown us in ineptitude if we aren't careful.

So how do we fix it?

CHAPTER 20

Opportunities

In a 2022 article published by *The Atlantic,* Derek Thompson highlighted what he called an "abundance agenda" that covers healthcare, housing, college, transportation, and energy. It's excellent, so I am going to include a modified version of it through the lens of healthcare, immigration, housing, education, and clean energy.

The real challenge lies in persuading people to believe and understand all of this.

We all like things to be a certain way, to have creature comforts and familiarity. We can have all of that and we don't have to sacrifice what we already like. In fact, this sort of abundance agenda is one of the only ways that we will be able to maintain the path that we are on.

We have to do these things. There is often a zero-sum mindset when it comes to new policy, which shows up in arguments against the abundance agenda and things like it.

For example:

HEALTHCARE

Here in the United States, we have a dismal life expectancy rate. This is due to a lot of factors outside of healthcare—like guns and motor vehicles—that are killing us, but a healthcare system that doesn't bankrupt people is probably a good goal to pursue. Living on the brink of financial distress due to a medical bill is a stressor for many. Americans should prioritize mental and physical health without fearing financial ruin. The decision to have children shouldn't be solely influenced by the cost of childcare. In 2021, three-quarters of Americans said the nation's healthcare system needs either "major" changes or needs to be "completely reformed."

"But I don't want to pay for other people's healthcare!" Okay! This is a fundamental principle of insurance. Insurance pools together what you and a bunch of other people pay monthly, and that's what people get paid out of—pooling premiums from many participants to pay for the expenses for a few. Everyone contributes to the pool with the understanding that if they need help, the pool will cover them, even though many will pay in more than they take out.

We need to rethink how private insurance functions. Instead of focusing on profits and exclusions, we need to aim for a system that prioritizes the well-being of the population. This requires more pricing transparency, increased accessible coverage, and fairer premiums based on collective risk-sharing. Companies like Ethos, Lemonade, and Oscar Health are focused on using technology through providing telemedicine services, simplifying what it takes to apply for a policy, as well as advocating for transparency.

There also need to be options for having coverage that is not employer-based. An expansion of government options like Medicare is clearly one option, but Medicare already faces funding issues. That's why there are two things here that are incredibly important to focus on:

- **State-level buy-in health insurance plans:** Public option plans (versus traditional private insurance) that operate with the goal of increasing affordable healthcare access, especially for lower-income individuals who don't qualify for Medicaid.
- **Mutual aid societies:** These are member-owned and operated funds that provide support to freelancers and others in the community that they serve.

Having more doctors can also make a difference. Expanding medical education programs and providing incentives for doctors to practice in underserved areas can aid in addressing the physician shortage. When more healthcare professionals are available, people can get the care they need without excessively long waits or unaffordable expenses.

Embracing preventative care can save lives and money in the long run. By investing in regular checkups, screenings, and education on healthy lifestyles, we can catch health issues earlier and reduce the need for costly treatments down the line. This is foundational—the earlier we catch stuff, the better. As Juan Enriquez wrote in *Scientific American* in 2022:

> *The U.S. uses a fee-for-service model, in which patients pay for the procedures that doctors perform, not for the outcomes they achieve. This financing structure has led to a health-care system that has advanced, technological interventions for the very sick, but poor public-health infrastructure. Fee-for-service has distorted health-care priorities in favor of expensive treatments for people who are sick, rather than measures to keep them from getting sick in the first place. It has encouraged health-care spending on rare diseases; special-interest groups lobby Congress and the National Institutes of Health on behalf of small groups of people, sometimes at the expense of focusing on preventive measures that could improve the lives of more people.*

Keeping people from getting sick in the first place is one of the biggest things we can do to reduce costs. In addition to that, across the board, price transparency is key to reining in healthcare costs, as well as pushing back on industry consolidation. More flexibility with insurance plans across the board, as well as encouraging use of programs such as health savings accounts and high-deductible plans, can help as well.

IMMIGRATION

"Immigrants will take our jobs!"

No! They won't! This is a beautiful example of how supply can enhance our world. We need to implement guardrails that protect against the mechanics of oversupply—too many people and not enough support for them in terms of jobs or housing is a recipe for disaster. If we can reform our working conditions, that will be beneficial to almost everyone.

By providing a streamlined pathway to citizenship for immigrants, we can tap in to a diverse pool of talent and skills, enriching our society and economy.

Ohio is a key example of how powerful immigration can be—and how it's not about taking jobs but creating opportunity. Ohio has struggled with population decline over the past many years. However, immigrants make up 4.2 percent of the state's population, but constitute 11.8 percent of its STEM (science, technology, engineering, mathematics) workforce.

During 2010 to 2015, Ohio saw a 120,000 increase in immigrant entrepreneurs, while business foundings by native-born Americans declined. Many have suggested a "state-sponsored immigrant program" allowing states like Ohio to benefit from bringing in people to build up their local communities.

When parents have access to affordable childcare, paid family leave, and flexible work arrangements, they can balance their work and family responsibilities more effectively. The United States has a horrendous maternal leave policy (with no federal paid maternity leave that covers all workers) and no paternal leave.

The current length of maternity leave in the United States is twelve weeks of unpaid leave under the Family Medical Leave Act (FMLA) but there is no federal mandate for paid parental leave. Some states have policies that provide paid leave, like California and New York, but the state of affairs is pretty abysmal. There probably isn't an ideal length for maternal and paternal leave, but the World Health Organization recommends breastfeeding for six months, which is probably an argument for at least six months of maternity leave. Allowing people to spend more time with their families is a long-term investment in the future of the country. This not only benefits families, but also boosts productivity and helps businesses retain talented employees, maintaining a more stable labor force participation rate.

We also need to address childcare—offering access to public education to pre-K students, ensuring after-school alternatives, as well as raising the pay of childcare workers to incentivize more people into the space. Children are the foundation of our future. The least we can do is take care of them.

As of May 2022, childcare workers are paid a mean annual wage of $29,750, which is incredibly low, especially considering the importance of this job. Ideal pay is always difficult, but perhaps we can at least compensate them similarly to elementary school teachers (who also deserve a raise).

Claire Suddath, a journalist in Brooklyn, has done a lot of work examining the cost of childcare and why it's so expensive—both for a provider (regulations such as fire-safety codes, CPR requirements, and square footage requirements make it expensive to run a facility) and for parents (because childcare facilities are expensive to run, and they only operate with a 1% profit margin, so it's *truly* expensive). Suddath explained on NPR's *Fresh Air* how childcare is not workable in the free-market sectors, and we need some sort of solution.

> *When you talk to economists, they say this is a perfect example of what they call a "classic market failure," which is when the price point for a good or a service—in this particular instance it's child care—is too ex-*

pensive for the consumers, by which I mean families, and too expensive or unaffordable for the providers, the people providing that service, in [this] case, child care owners and workers. And there's no way to fix that in a private market setting. And we have other examples of this in our society. We recognize that we want everyone, regardless of income, to have access to a fire department. If your house catches on fire, we don't ask, "Well, can you afford to put it out?" It's better for us collectively if we put the fire out, we collectively pay for a fire department, we put the fire out so that it doesn't spread to another person's home because they happen to live next to someone who can't afford the fire department. We have police, we have libraries, we have public schools, but child care has never been thought of in that way, even though I think, very obviously, it should have been a long time ago.

Our children are the future—they are the thing that arguably matters most in the world. It will take treating childcare as a sort of public good—similar to a fire station or a library—to ensure that our future (and those who are raising the future) are well taken care of.

Finally, creating accessible workplaces is key. By removing barriers and providing reasonable accommodations in the workplace, we can unlock the potential of many individuals who want to contribute to society—and deserve to be able to. Things like ramps, elevators, screen readers, voice recognition software, and flexible working arrangements can go a long way in bringing people into the workforce.

Giving people the opportunities that they want with jobs that they want is the key to economic growth. Reforming immigration, providing working parent support, and creating more accessible workplaces helps get more people to their dreams—and grows the economy along the way.

HOUSING

"More housing will make my own home value go down!"

We talked about how Americans make a lot of money from their homes in the chapter on labor markets. But here's the thing: Many people who scrimp and save to buy a piece of property never reap the highly touted financial benefits or reach the promised land of economic security. The sociologist John Dean's warning in his 1945 book *Homeownership: Is It Sound?* still holds true today: "For *some* families *some* houses represent wise buys, but a culture and real estate industry that give blanket endorsement to ownership fail to indicate *which* families and *which* houses." If we can find ways for people to own the businesses that they are affiliated with, or give them more access to informed investing opportunities, there will be less pressure on housing being a major source of wealth generation. Homes shouldn't be speculative assets! Homes should be homes!

It's essential to rethink the role of homes in our society. Instead of viewing them solely as speculative assets, let's prioritize their primary purpose—to be homes. A home is a place where families grow, memories are made, and communities thrive. It's about providing safe and stable living conditions for everyone, not just using housing as an investment vehicle for a few.

Now, I know it might sound wild—after all, who doesn't like making money from real estate?—and there's still room for that opportunity, but it's also essential to create an environment where everyone can have access to safe and stable housing. When we strike this balance, we can build a more equitable society where housing is not just a means of accumulating wealth but a fundamental right for all.

In 2022, Jerusalem Demsas wrote the piece "The Homeownership Society Was a Mistake," which addressed these points, specifically about the difference between seeing homes as an asset versus a place to live and be safe:

> *Wealth building through homeownership requires selling at the right time, and research indicates that longer tenures in a home translate to lower returns. But the right time to sell may not line up with the right time for you to move. "Buying low and selling high" when the asset we are talking about is where you live is pretty absurd advice. People want to live near family, near good schools, near parks, or in neighborhoods with the types of amenities they desire, not trade their location like penny stocks.*

The piece continues with a deep dive into the expectation of home price increases driving wealth—and how that isn't always a sustainable (nor reasonable) path for true wealth generation.

> *Paying off a mortgage is a form of "forced savings," in which people save by paying for shelter rather than consciously putting money aside. According to a report by an economist at the National Association of Realtors looking at the housing market from 2011 to 2021, however, price appreciation accounts for roughly 86 percent of the wealth associated with owning a home. That means almost all of the gains come not from*

paying down a mortgage (money that you literally put into the home) but from rising price tags outside of any individual homeowner's control. This is a key, uncomfortable point: Home values, which purportedly built the middle class, are predicated not on sweat equity or hard work but on luck.

A lot of wealth generated through home ownership is luck. And we need to create the conditions for more luck.

Rezoning is key for creating accessible housing supply. We have a housing crisis—rising home prices have crushed the American Dream. A lot of this is an imbalance of supply and demand—we have a 3.8 million home shortage, a number that has doubled over the past decade.

The housing crisis creates a bifurcation of wealth in two ways. The older generation that has house wealth will pass that off to their children. And those who got into the housing market when rates were 3% are locked in—for better and for worse. Two groups that create the haves and the have-nots.

A lot of fixing this will be amending restrictive zoning rules, especially in cities like Washington, D.C., Boston, and San Francisco. We need to reform single-family ordinances (*The New York Times* reported that 75 percent of residential land in American cities is limited to single-family homes) so developers will build more multifamily complexes or smaller, more affordable homes.

The solution here is to reform single-family zoning ordinances and behavior, making it legal (or incentivizing through tax credits, percentage of affordable unit mandates, or some other behavior-shaping mechanism) for developers to build multifamily housing units and for homeowners to build accessory dwelling units (ADUs) on their property, which would allow more people to inhabit the same plot of land.

It's not just a federal issue—twenty-two states currently limit or prohibit inclusionary zoning at the local level, which needs to be cleaned up. The government can provide financial incentives such as grants for inclusive zoning or block funding for exclusionary zoning.

Also, the concerns of the NIMBYs (Not in My Backyard) need to be addressed. Because housing is a speculative asset, they want their house to go up in value and really worry (naturally) when that's threatened by the expansion of other housing. There are two things here:

1. Homes should not be the only source of wealth. We need to encourage more stock ownership, as well as rethink ownership of businesses and companies that you work for.

2. Building new homes doesn't necessarily decrease the value of the homes around it. A state Supreme Court ruling in New Jersey, *Southern Burlington County NAACP v. Mount Laurel Township*, prohibits exclusionary zoning and requires that all municipalities provide a "fair share" of affordable residences. The mandate has forced more than 340 New Jersey towns to develop affordable housing units, and this did not lower property values or result in higher crime and higher taxes. And if residents really want to fight it, they can pay extra taxes for affordable units to be developed elsewhere. It's about accountability.

Owning a home is a big part of feeling connected to a community. It's also the economy (as Edward Leamer discussed in his ever-poignant paper "Housing IS the Business Cycle"). People deserve a place to live. And there are ways to provide that.

EDUCATION

"I don't want to pay for other people's college!"

Guess what, you don't have to! Endowments at many postsecondary institutions are essential for funding education. For instance, Harvard is practically a hedge fund with an academic logo. We can make education more accessible and affordable by controlling administrative bloat, educating students on the loans they are taking out (and yes, forgiving them), and exploring new forms of financing for school, such as the expansion of work-study programs.

But education is more than just college. We need to give workers more chances for better careers and pay. Companies should train their employees more, and community colleges play a big role but need improvement. There needs to be an expansion of post-high-school options, with realistic paths toward what students can achieve throughout their entire life (fostering ambition), versus just focusing on expanding wages.

Upskilling programs are key. A 2021 study of Walmart's Live Better U (where Walmart pays tuition and expenses for employees pursuing higher education) found that workers who completed the program were almost twice as likely to be promoted and were more satisfied with their work life.

As another example, a study of healthcare provider Cigna's 2012–2014 tuition reimbursement program found that participants were more likely to stay with the company. As a result, for every dollar the company invested in the program, it saved $1.29 in costs associated with hiring and management. It's not only a cost savings tool, but it also helps to create better informed economic citizens—a win for everyone.

An expansion of trade apprenticeship programs, especially in work for plumbers and electricians, is incredibly important. We are going to have a massive shortage of those who are able to do work that needs to happen (the real-world maintenance, if you will), which is concerning. Reforming community colleges, providing more resources such as transportation assistance, on-the-job training, and clear and accessible routes for students will go a long way in filling the gaps we have in the workforce.

CLEAN ENERGY

"Green energy is abandoning Big Oil!"

No, not really! We cannot implement green energy policy without green energy investment. We still need to keep fossil fuels up and running as we transition to a more sustainable world. Transitioning to clean energy systems isn't possible without constructing more power plants—which we'd need regardless to meet rising energy demand—and fossil fuels are required to build them. Very few existing industrial plants, mining operations, manufacturing facilities, and construction machines are powered by electricity. Batteries—including the ones needed to power electric vehicles—require enormous amounts of lithium, a commodity known as "white gold." Demand for lithium is surging across the planet. Extracting and processing it and other raw materials at the scale we need isn't possible without burning fossil fuels. Plus, we'll still rely on fossil fuel plants as backup for years due to the lack of scalable battery backup technology, as a full transition to nuclear, wind, and solar power is decades away.

Similarly, while many proclaim, "I would never take the train and want to keep my car," fast and reliable public transit is an incredible equalizer. If people can get to where they need to go safely and effectively, that is an economic boon!

In many cities, the areas with the worst access to public transit tend to be the most impoverished. And access to just about everything associated with economic opportunity—jobs, good-quality foods (escaping food deserts) and goods (at reasonable prices), healthcare, and schooling—relies on the ability to get around in an efficient way, and for an affordable price. In a widely cited 2013 study on economic mobility, economists led by Harvard's Raj Chetty found areas with shorter commutes have "significantly higher rates of upward mobility."

A 2015 study by the University of Minnesota titled "Access Across America" found that cities with better transit systems demonstrated a higher number of accessible job opportunities. Multiple studies, including one from the National Association of Realtors in the United States, have found that properties located closer to public transit lines tend to have higher values, suggesting that there's an economic premium on good transit accessibility. A 2013 report by APTA titled "The Role of Transit in Support of High Growth Business Clusters in the U.S." found that cities with robust public transit systems demonstrated better economic resilience during economic downturns.

This matters for everyone because if the city's transportation infrastructure—be it buses, trains, or walking paths—becomes more navigable, producing even a marginal improvement in the economy, this benefits everyone.

THE ABUNDANCE MINDSET

Finally, we need to embrace a new mindset.

In addition to the abundance agenda I've outlined, we should also embrace what Martin Gurri coined "an adventure mindset," valuing high risk and innovation more than fear-mongering and political impotence.

In order to fully embrace this mindset and agenda, we need systems and institutions in place that allow us to do so. Changing the economy and our collective financial health is truly about policy and demanding more from our policymakers.

In the coming years, the likelihood of seeing progress on all of this largely hinges on a confluence of political will, public demand, technological advancements, and global collaboration (which is kind of annoying). Substantive progress demands international cooperation on some level and domestic cooperation always. Things like:

- **Climate change:** International summits like the Paris Agreement, the World Economic Forum, and other big, flashy hangouts often end with world leaders making promising announcements about ambitious interventions and new targets, but they have a spotty record when it comes to follow-through. Pledging to reduce carbon emissions is one thing; navigating the logistics of modernizing outdated power grids, building renewable energy infrastructure, figuring out how to store renewable energy, getting approval from Congress to pass necessary bills (in the United States' case), etc., is another thing—and the United States and China, among other leading industrialized nations, have consistently fallen short of fulfilling their promises on the agreed-upon timelines.

- **Healthcare:** In the United States especially, everyone knows that our healthcare system is abysmal. But steps to change it often get bogged down in political debate or lobbying pressures, and patient welfare is put to the side in favor of profits. Other countries have managed to figure it out, and the United States can, too.
- **Housing Crisis:** We don't have enough affordable homes, and bureaucratic funding, red tape, zoning restrictions, and lack of funding can stall all these projects. Policymakers need to collaborate with the private sector to build more homes. (The government can't do everything, but they can incentivize everything.)

Yet, significant headway (American individualism, lobbying resistance, all of that) requires the alignment of policies with financial mechanisms, such as green bonds or carbon pricing, to incentivize businesses to adopt sustainable practices. Grassroots movements, environmental advocacy, and an informed electorate will be paramount in pushing policymakers toward more assertive action—and it will happen.

This can seem like a long road, but it's one that we can walk. We know what to do, but we need to start walking and, along the way, convince others that it's the right path for everyone. Humans are so brilliant and innovative. The emergence of artificial intelligence and how fast technology is advancing shows us that. The key to our collective future is enabling everyone to create brilliant and innovative changes and improvements that foster a sustainable world.

In *The Artist's Way*, Julia Cameron talked about how many people end up in fields adjacent to their real dreams, just to feel close to what they truly want. Of course, we can't always get what we want; the world does not exist to fulfill our every desire. But carrying that truth—recognizing where our passions are—is really important.

The more we can say, "This is what I care about, this is what my community cares about," the better we can be! Of course, doing so isn't easy. We have to find one another again, but that might not be the answer, either. We are stories upon stories, and as the Japanese Nobel laureate Kazuo Ishiguro put it, "But in the end, stories are about one person saying to another: this is the way it feels to me. Can you understand what I'm saying? Does it feel this way to you?"

The way forward for the economy and society at large is some form of reconnection. As the Canadian comedian Norm Macdonald said, "We are not superior to the Universe but merely a fraction of it."

1. Policy is fundamentally broken. (We already knew that.) We know that we can fix it. We just have to engage with the capital-*S* System and each other.
2. But policy is broken because we have forgotten about the people underlying the economy. We have become so accustomed to the "consumption-on-demand" society we operate in that we have forgotten that this society is based on people. We have to tell better stories so we can learn to cooperate with one another again.

We have to find hope and avoid cynicism. As Maria Popova said in her 2016 commencement address at the University of Pennsylvania:

> *Today, the soul is in dire need of stewardship and protection from cynicism. The best defense against it is vigorous, intelligent, sincere hope—not blind optimism, because that too is a form of resignation, to believe that everything will work out just fine and we need not apply ourselves. I mean hope bolstered by critical thinking that is clear-headed in identifying what is lacking, in ourselves or the world, but then envisions ways to create it and endeavors to do that. In its passivity and resignation, cynicism is a hardening, a calcification of the soul. Hope is a stretching of its ligaments, a limber reach for something greater.*

There are things to be nervous (yet excited) about, like artificial intelligence. The Austrian priest and social critic Ivan Illich talked about how we "are degraded to the status of mere consumers" as the power of the machines around us increases. There is a world in which humans and machines grow together—AI can make humans smarter, for example—but there are trade-offs to that.

Not to get too woo-woo, but the energy we create determines the way we engage with the world around us, and in turn, shapes our collective future. The philosopher and psychiatrist Iain McGilchrist described our communion with reality this way:

> *The world we experience—which is the only one we can know—is affected by the kind of attention we pay to it... Attention is not just another "cognitive function": it is... the disposition adopted by one's consciousness towards the world. Absent, present, detached, engaged,*

alienated, empathic, broad or narrow, sustained or piecemeal, it therefore has the power to alter whatever it meets.

But we also have to learn to accept that suffering is intrinsic to the human condition—a tenet of many religions, and something the secular world could take more cues from. Mary Gaitskill, novelist and essayist, wrote:

Whatever the suffering is, it's not to be endured, for God's sake, not felt and never, ever accepted. It's to be triumphed over. And because some things cannot be triumphed over unless they are first accepted and endured, because, indeed, some things cannot be triumphed over at all, the "story" must be told again and again in endless pursuit of a happy ending. To be human is finally to be a loser, for we are all fated to lose our carefully constructed sense of self, our physical strength, our health, our precious dignity, and finally our lives. A refusal to tolerate this reality is a refusal to tolerate life, and art based on the empowering message and positive image is just such a refusal.

I know it's hard—for me, I struggle with all of it! Overthinking, anxiety, loneliness (being human mostly), and some other rocks in my shoe. And it's hard to maintain positivity with the toxicity of social media—a world built on takes, on monetized opinion, on who can yell the loudest.

Imagination, which Ursula K. Le Guin described as "an essential tool of the mind, a fundamental way of thinking, an indispensable means of becoming and remaining human" is important. But so is real-world data. We have to make sure people get paid enough to live. And we have to use our imagination to create a better world for all of us to live in.

People are the economy. So let's make the economy about people.

Acknowledgments

To everyone who has ever supported me, which would include far too many names to list—thank you. So many people have taken a chance on my ideas and my work and have helped get me to where I am today. I have had so many doors open through someone saying, "Hey, give it a try"—and thank you for pushing me to try.

Thank you to Morgan Housel, Nick Magguilli, Tracy Alloway, Kai Ryssdal, Joe Weisenthal, and so many more for giving me this opportunity.

To Matt Bebb, Zach Cowie, Regina Gerbeaux, Alex Good, Grant Gregory, Kristen Hemenez, Katie Hightchew, David Hoag, Cam Iadeluca, Doug McLaughlin, David Phelps, Andrew Rea, Ben Wheeler, and Fran Wilson, for always believing in me even when I didn't believe in myself.

To Anna Toderas and Ananya Kannan for doing so much incredible editing work and helping to keep me on track.

To everyone who tunes in to the TikToks and the Instagram Reels and the YouTubes and the shorts and the newsletter and the podcast—thank you. You're the reason that this book is possible, and you have all shaped me into who I am today. You are incredible.

To Dr. Chhachhi, Dr. Lebendinsky, and everyone else at Western Kentucky University—you also made me who I am today. Your unconditional support for whatever wild idea I wanted to run with gave me the creative freedom to test out a lot of things, to fail with grace, and stand back up again.

To the team at Penguin Random House, especially Leah Trouwborst for letting me get some of these ideas on paper.

Notes

9 **"What goes too long":** Ursula K. Le Guin, "Dragonfly," in Le Guin, *Tales from Earthsea: Dragonfly* (New York: Harcourt, 2001), 147.

13 ***animal spirits:*** John Maynard Keynes, *The General Theory of Employment, Interest, and Money* (New York: Harcourt, Brace, 1936), page 81.

14 ***reflexivity:*** Soros, *The Alchemy of Finance.*

16 **"Evidence is always partial":** Hilary Mantel, "Hilary Mantel: Why I Became a Historical Novelist," *The Guardian,* June 3, 2017, https://www.theguardian.com/books/2017/jun/03/hilary-mantel-why-i-became-a-historical-novelist.

17 **When there is a gap:** "Consumer Confidence Declined Moderately in July," The Conference Board, July 26, 2022, https://www.conference-board.org/topics/consumer-confidence/press/CCI-July-2022.

18 **"Expected inflation":** Josh Zumbrun, "The Strange Art of Asking People How Much Inflation They Expect," *The Wall Street Journal,* June 24, 2022, https://www.wsj.com/articles/the-strange-art-of-asking-people-how-much-inflation-they-expect-11656063003.

23 **"We do know":** Edward Chancellor, *The Price of Time: The Real Story of Interest* (New York: Grove Press, 2022), 1.

38 **"Netflix says":** Jack Farley, Twitter, October 18, 2022, https://twitter.com/JackFarley96/status/1582492334800850944.

38 **"The most important aspect":** Karthik Sankaran, Twitter, May 31, 2023, https://twitter.com/RajaKorman/status/1663948296476577794.

38 **"The only 'real' hedge":** Xiang Fang, Yang Liu, and Nikolai Roussanov, "Getting to the Core: Inflation Risks Within and Across Asset Classes," Working Paper 30169, National Bureau of Economic Research, June 2022, https://www.nber.org/papers/w30169.

40 **The IMF sees the shift:** Serkan Arslanalp, Barry J. Eichengreen, and Chima Simpson-Bell, "The Stealth Erosion of Dollar Dominance: Active Diversifiers and the Rise of Nontraditional Reserve Currencies," International Monetary Fund, March 24, 2022, https://www.imf.org/-/media/Files/Publications/WP/2022/English/wpiea2022058-print-pdf.ashx.

40 **This ties into:** Matthew C. Klein, "The Implications of Unrestricted Financial Warfare," The Overshoot, March 8, 2022, https://theovershoot.co/p/the-implications-of-unrestricted.

40 **Michael Pettis:** Michael Pettis, "The High Price of Dollar Dominance: The Dollar Is the Worst Reserve Currency—Except for All the Rest," *Foreign Affairs,* June 30, 2023, https://www.foreignaffairs.com/united-states/high-price-dollar-dominance.

41 **"Waiting for the day":** Brad Setser, Twitter, May 15, 2023, https://twitter.com/Brad_Setser/status/1658122177319772163.

42 **"If a bottle":** Samuel Hammond, Twitter, July 9, 2022, https://twitter.com/hamandcheese/status/1545636287255908353.

42 **"The logic of why":** Joe Weisenthal and Tracy Alloway, "Transcript: Zoltan Pozsar and Perry Mehrling Debate the Dollar," Bloomberg, September 13, 2022, https://www.bloomberg.com/news/articles/2022-09-13/transcript-zoltan-pozsar-and-perry-mehrling-debate-the-dollar#xj4y7vzkg.

42 **"Wine seems to just be":** Samuel Hammond, Twitter, July 9, 2022, https://twitter.com/hamandcheese/status/1545635186527846400.

47 **"Mankind must acquire":** Bertrand Russell, *The Collected Papers of Bertrand Russell, Volume 11: Last Philosophical Testament 1947-68* (Routledge, 1997), 81.

51 **This 2022 chart:** Derek Thompson, Twitter, June 28, 2022, https://twitter.com/DKThomp/status/1541759983536177153.

53 **a 40 percent jump:** "Wholesale Used-Vehicle Prices Increase in January," Cox Automotive, February 7, 2023, https://www.coxautoinc.com/market-insights/january-2023-muvvi/.

54 **Manufacturers' profits surged:** Matt Phillips, "Fewer Autos and Bigger Profits for Carmakers," Axios, January 6, 2023, https://www.axios.com/2023/01/06/fewer-autos-and-bigger-profits-for-carmakers.

54 **People who were used:** ettingermentum, Twitter, July 14, 2023, https://twitter.com/ettingermentum/status/1679944594694324225.

55 **"High consumer prices":** Mike Gauntner, "Customs Reports Eggs Being Smuggled from Mexico," WFMJ, January 23, 2023, https://www.wfmj.com/story/48208074/customs-reports-egg-being-smuggled-from-mexico.

56 **"Port truckers":** Josh Wingrove, Jill R. Shah, and Brendan Case, "U.S. Supply Chain: Biden Tackles Crisis with Few Tools, Clock Ticking," Bloomberg, October 21, 2021, https://www.bloomberg.com/news/articles/2021-10-21/biden-tackles-supply-chain-crisis-with-few-tools-clock-ticking#xj4y7vzkg.

57 **"As resources get cheaper":** Anthony Lee Zhang, Twitter, August 17, 2022, https://twitter.com/AnthonyLeeZhang/status/1559928401334616065.

67 **"As trend GDP growth slows":** Tyler Atkinson, Victor Wei, and Xiaoqing Zhou, "U.S. Likely Didn't Slip into Recession in Early 2022 Despite Negative GDP Growth," Federal Reserve Bank of Dallas, August 2, 2022, https://www.dallasfed.org/research/economics/2022/0802/.

67 **"If everyone is spending":** Matt Haig, *Notes on a Nervous Planet* (New York: Viking, 2018), 176.

68 **"Tomorrow the sun":** Terry Pratchett, *Night Watch* (New York: HarperTorch, 2002), 294.

69 **"The reasonable man":** George Bernard Shaw, *Man and Superman* (The University Press: Cambridge, 1903), 238.

72 **"Do Gasoline Prices":** Severin Borenstein, A. Colin Cameron, and Richard Gilbert, "Do Gasoline Prices Respond Asymmetrically to Crude Oil Price Changes?," *Quarterly Journal of Economics* 112, no. 1 (1997): 305-39, http://faculty.haas.berkeley.edu/borenste/download/QJE97GasAsym.pdf.

72 **As Bloomberg reported:** Faseeh Mangi and Elizabeth Low, "Pakistan Struggling to Buy Enough Diesel Due to Global Crunch," Bloomberg, March 15, 2022, https://www.bloomberg.com/news/articles/2022-03-15/pakistan-struggling-to-buy-enough-diesel-due-to-global-crunch#xj4y7vzkg.

77 **"Like a farmer":** Maria Popova, "Lichens and the Meaning of Life," The Marginalian, March 25, 2023, https://www.themarginalian.org/2023/03/25/lichens/.

78 **"Panics do not destroy":** On Credit Cycles, and the Origin of Commercial Panics. United Kingdom: n.p., 1868, 18.

78 **As Ryan Sweet at Moody's:** Jeanna Smialek, Twitter, February 10, 2022, https://twitter.com/jeannasmialek/status/1491838792109637633.

82 **Joseph Haubrich and Sara Millington:** Joseph G. Haubrich and Sara E. Millington, "PCE and CPI Inflation: What's the Difference?," Federal Reserve Bank of Cleveland, April 17, 2014, https://www.clevelandfed.org/en/publications/economic-trends/2014/et-20140417-pce-and-cpi-inflation-difference.

82 **They do the same thing:** "Inflation Charting," Federal Reserve Bank of Cleveland, accessed May 2023, https://www.clevelandfed.org/center-for-inflation-research/inflation-charting.

84 **Politico's "inflation cheeseburger":** Ximena Bustillo and Steven Overly, "This Cheeseburger Explains Why You're Paying So Much for Food These Days," Politico, April 13, 2022, https://www.politico.com/interactives/2022/food-prices-rising-inflation-2022/.

86 **There are various charts:** "The Markets & the Economy—What We're Watching," Rockland Trust, July 18, 2022, https://www.rocklandtrust.com/wealth—investments/the-markets—the-economy—what-were-watching—july-18-2022.

87 **Our work shows:** Julian di Giovanni, "How Much Did Supply Constraints Boost U.S. Inflation?," Federal Reserve Bank of New York, August 24, 2022, https://libertystreeteconomics.newyorkfed.org/2022/08/how-much-did-supply-constraints-boost-u-s-inflation/.

87 **The San Francisco Fed:** "Supply- and Demand-Driven PCE Inflation," Federal Reserve Bank of San Francisco, https://www.frbsf.org/economic-research/indicators-data/supply-and-demand-driven-pce-inflation/.

87 **"To consider excessive":** Glenn Hubbard, "Post-pandemic Fiscal Spending Bears Much of the Blame for US Inflation," Financial Times, November 14, 2022, https://www.ft.com/content/48d41445-544d-41e9-891f-3b50a2f1a3eb.

88 **"sticky prices":** Francesco Ferrante, Sebastian Graves, and Matteo Iacoviello, "The Inflationary Effects of Sectoral Reallocation," International Finance Discussion Papers 1369, Board of Governors of the Federal Reserve System, February 2023, https://doi.org/10.17016/IFDP.2023.1369.

89 **In 2023, Isabella Weber:** Isabella M. Weber and Evan Wasner, "Sellers' Inflation, Profits and Conflict: Why Can Large Firms Hike Prices in an Emergency?," Working Paper no. 2023-2, 2023, University of Massachusetts Amherst, https://scholarworks.umass.edu/econ_workingpaper/343/.

89 **Unfortunately, the Weber-Wasner:** Isabella M. Weber, Twitter, June 1, 2023, https://twitter.com/IsabellaMWeber/status/1664255216080896005.

89 **excuseflation:** Tracy Alloway and Joe Weisenthal, "How 'Excuseflation' Is Keeping Prices—and Corporate Profits—High," Bloomberg, March 9, 2023, https://www.bloomberg.com/news/articles/2023-03-09/how-excuseflation-is-keeping-prices-and-corporate-profits-high.

90 **We can look at:** Apple Inc., Form 10-K, 2022,

https://s2.q4cdn.com/470004039/files/doc_financials/2022/q4/_10-K-2022-(As-Filed).pdf.

90 **Procter & Gamble's Q1 2023:** "P&G Announces Fiscal Year 2023 First Quarter Results," https://s1.q4cdn.com/695946674/files/doc_news/2022/FY2223-Q1-JAS-8-K-Final.pdf.

92 **"Two forces have combined":** Paul Donovan, "Fed Should Make Clear That Rising Profit Margins Are Spurring Inflation," *Financial Times*, November 2, 2022, https://www.ft.com/content/837c3863-fc15-476c-841d-340c623565ae.

93 **"institutional changes also hint":** Frederic Boissay et al., "Are Major Advanced Economies on the Verge of a Wage-Price Spiral?," *BIS Bulletin*, no. 53, May 4, 2022, https://www.bis.org/publ/bisbull53.pdf.

94 **"Retail markups":** Lael Brainard, "Staying the Course to Bring Inflation Down," Board of Governors of the Federal Reserve System, January 19, 2023, https://www.federalreserve.gov/newsevents/speech/brainard20230119a.htm.

96 **"I think we now understand":** John Cassidy, "Jerome Powell and the Fed Are Still Struggling to Understand a Crazy Economy Hit by the Pandemic and War," *The New Yorker*, July 5, 2022, https://www.newyorker.com/news/our-columnists/jerome-powell-and-the-fed-are-still-struggling-to-understand-a-crazy-economy-hit-by-the-pandemic-and-war.

99 **"Satisfaction with family life":** Stefani Milovanska-Farrington and Stephen Farrington, "Happiness, Domains of Life Satisfaction, Perceptions, and Valuation Differences Across Genders," *Acta Psychologica* 230 (October 2022): 103720, https://doi.org/10.1016/j.actpsy.2022.103720.

101 **The unemployment rate:** "Unemployment Rate," Federal Reserve Bank of St. Louis, https://fred.stlouisfed.org/series/UNRATE.

102 **When the labor force:** "Labor Force Participation Rate," Federal Reserve Bank of St. Louis, https://fred.stlouisfed.org/series/CIVPART.

103 **both surveys are revised:** "Comparing Employment from the BLS Household and Payroll Surveys," U.S. Bureau of Labor Statistics, https://www.bls.gov/web/empsit/ces_cps_trends.htm.

104 **"Job openings":** Ibid.

104 **"We talk a lot":** Preston Mui, "Quits vs. Openings: The Fed Needs to Choose Wisely," Employ America, March 8, 2023, https://www.employamerica.org/blog/quits-vs-openings-the-fed-needs-to-choose-wisely/.

105 **A March 2023:** Te-Ping Chen, "Job Listings Abound, but Many Are Fake," *The Wall Street Journal*, March 20, 2023, https://www.wsj.com/articles/that-plum-job-listing-may-just-be-a-ghost-3aafc794.

106 **the main reason:** Aaron De Smet et al., "The Great Attrition Is Making Hiring Harder. Are You Searching the Right Talent Pools?," McKinsey & Company, July 13, 2022, https://www.mckinsey.com/capabilities/people-and-organizational-performance/our-insights/the-great-attrition-is-making-hiring-harder-are-you-searching-the-right-talent-pools.

106 **nobody wants to work for $7:** "Employment-Population Ratio—25-54 Yrs."

106 **provides insights into:** "Wages and Salaries and Benefits in Private Industry, 12-Month Percent Change," U.S. Bureau of Labor Statistics, https://www.bls.gov/charts/employment-cost-index/wages-and-salaries-and-benefits-in-private-industry-12-month-percent-change.htm.

107 **76.1 million Americans:** "Characteristics of Minimum Wage Workers, 2021," U.S. Bureau of Labor Statistics, April 2022, https://www.bls.gov/opub/reports/minimum-wage/2021/home.htm.

107 **As Carter Price and Kathryn Edwards:** Carter C. Price and Kathryn A. Edwards, "Trends in Income from 1975 to 2018," RAND, September 2020, https://www.rand.org/pubs/working_papers/WRA516-1.html.

108 **"[The unemployment rate] is important":** Whizy Kim, "There's No Money in Working Anymore," Refinery29, July 21, 2020, https:/www.refinery29.com/en-us/2020/07/9919819/low-wage-workers-in-america-statistics.

108 **"There is little evidence":** Dale Belman and Paul J. Wolfson, *What Does the Minimum Wage Do?* (Kalamazoo, MI: W. E. Upjohn Institute for Employment Research, 2014), https://doi.org/10.17848/9780880994583.

108 **If the minimum wage:** Dean Baker, "What the Minimum Wage Would Be if It Kept Pace with Productivity," CounterPunch, January 24, 2020, https://www.counterpunch.org/2020/01/24/what-the-minimum-wage-would-be-if-it-kept-pace-with-productivity/.

108 **To begin with:** "Out of Reach: The High Cost of Housing," National Low Income Housing Coalition, https://nlihc.org/oor.

109 **This feeling of being rich:** Sarah O'Connor, "The Gig Economy Is a Symptom of Bigger Problems," *Financial Times*, November 9, 2020, https://www.ft.com/content/a90d9ba8-4d2e-4ec4-b971-24ebebd5822d.

110 **"In the United States":** Kellen Browning, "$388 in Sushi. Just a $20 Tip: The Brutal Math of Uber Eats and DoorDash," *The New York Times*, April 9, 2023, https://www.nytimes.com/2023/04/09/business/uber-eats-door-dash-delivery-tips.html.

111 **"China will compete":** Michael Pettis, "Bad Trade," American Compass, October 7, 2022, https://americancompass.org/bad-trade/.

112 **"The purpose of international trade":** Ibid.

112 **In 2022 . . . Andrew Bailey:** Karen Gilchrist, "'Outrageous': Bank of England Chief Slammed for Asking Brits Not to Demand a Big Pay Raise," CNBC, February 8, 2022, https://www.cnbc.com/2022/02/08/bank-of-englands-bailey-faces-backlash-after-discouraging-pay-rises.html.

113 **"There is a way":** G. K. Chesterton, *The Autobiography of G. K. Chesterton* (London: Hutchinson & Co., 1936), 331.

113 **"These are all methods":** Ibid., 332.

114 **As Eric Basmajian:** EPB Research, "My Final Thoughts on the Coming Recession," YouTube, March 10, 2023, https://www.youtube.com/watch?v=roEljzOKk3I.

114 **The reservation wage:** Felix Aidala and Gizem Kosar, "SCE Labor Market Survey Shows Average Reservation Wage Continues Upward Trend—Liberty Street Economics," Liberty Street Economics, December 19, 2022, https://libertystreeteconomics.newyorkfed.org/2022/12/sce-labor-market-survey-shows-average-reservation-wage-continues-upward-trend/.

115 **"What did happen":** Bryce Covert, "An Unemployment System Frozen in Amber," *The American Prospect*, May 31, 2023, https://prospect.org/labor/2023-05-31-unemployment-system-frozen-in-amber/.

115 **We have to be mindful:** The Daily Shot, Twitter, November 4, 2022, https://twitter.com/SoberLook/status/1588478813058760705.

116 **"doubling the size":** Marta Prato, "The Global Race for Talent: Brain Drain, Knowledge Transfer, and Growth," Social Science Research Network, November 27, 2022, https://ssrn.com/abstract=4287268.

116 **A 2022 report by Oxfam:** "Ten Richest Men Double Their Fortunes in Pandemic While Incomes of 99 Percent of Humanity Fall," Oxfam International, January 17, 2022, https://www.oxfam.org/en/press-releases/ten-richest-men-double-their-fortunes-pandemic-while-incomes-99-percent-humanity.

116 **According to data:** "Distribution of Household Wealth in the U.S. Since 1989," Board of Governors of the Federal Reserve System, https://www.federalreserve.gov/releases/z1/dataviz/dfa/distribute/table/.

116 **add around 3.5 million:** Kathryn Anne Edwards, Twitter, October 18, 2022, https://twitter.com/keds_economist/status/1582435868497051649.

116 **Highly skilled Byzantine:** Andreas Link, "The Fall of Constantinople and the Rise of the West," February 28, 2023, https://ssrn.com/abstract=4372477.

116 **workers with disabilities:** Office of Disability Employment Policy, United States Department of Labor, "Analysis of Trends During the COVID-19 Pandemic," February 2022, https://www.dol.gov/sites/dolgov/files/ODEP/pdf/Employment_for_PWD-Analysis_of_Trends_during_COVID_2022.pdf.

117 **In 2023:** Talmon Joseph Smith, "The Greatest Wealth Transfer in History Is Here, with Familiar (Rich) Winners," *The New York Times*, May 23, 2023, https:/www.nytimes.com/2023/05/14/business/economy/wealth-generations.html.

117 **It has an employee stock:** "Publix Super Markets Inc. Employee Stock Ownership Plan, Amended and Restated as of January 1, 2007," https://www.sec.gov/Archives/edgar/data/81061/000119312508043806/dex103.htm.

118 **"Public perception":** Molly Smith, "Your Side Hustle Is Another Sign of a Tight US Job Market," Bloomberg, February 21, 2023, https://www.bloomberg.com/news/articles/2023-02-21/working-side-jobs-is-another-sign-of-the-tight-us-labor-market.

119 **The economist Adam Ozimek:** Adam Ozimek, "The Simple Mistake That Almost Triggered a Recession," *The Atlantic*, July 5, 2023, https://www.theatlantic.com/ideas/archive/2023/07/inflation-jobs-unemployment-recession/674593/.

120 **"the dream of a land":** James Truslow Adams, *The Epic of America* (Little, Brown, and Company: Cambridge, 1931), 238.

120 **How many brilliant:** tautologer, Twitter, November 29, 2022, https://twitter.com/tautologer/status/1597776450475941889.

120 **A house costs 4.5 times:** Noah Smith, Twitter, February 13, 2023, https://twitter.com/Noahpinion/status/1625289178803228673.

122 **Rates bottomed out:** "30-Year Fixed Rate Mortgage Average in the United States," Federal Reserve Bank of St. Louis, July 28, 2023, https://fred.stlouisfed.org/series/MORTGAGE30US.

124 **Over half of Airbnb's:** Jamie Lane, Twitter, October 18, 2022, https://twitter.com/Jamie_Lane/status/1582420915756757000.

126 **"By allowing":** Maia Mindel, "House Hoarders," Liberal Currents, April 10, 2023, https://www.liberalcurrents.com/house-hoarders/.

126 **"Westerners are fond":** Barbara Alice Mann, *Iroquoian Women: The Gantowisas* (Bristol, UK: Peter Lang, 2006).

126 **Using a home as an investment vehicle:** Aditya Aladangady, Elliot Anenberg, and Daniel Garcia, "House Price Growth and Inflation During COVID-19," Board of Governors of the Federal Reserve System, November 17, 2022, https://www.federalreserve.gov/econres/notes/feds-notes/house-price-growth-and-inflation-during-covid-19-20221117.html.

127 **An amortization schedule:** "Amortization Schedule Calculator," Bankrate, https://www.bankrate.com/mortgages/amortization-calculator/.

127 **South Bend, Indiana:** Michael Divita, Twitter, June 1, 2023, https://twitter.com/MichaelPDivita/status/1664429622371713025.

129 **"Markets can remain":** A. Gary Shilling, "Scoreboard," *Forbes*, vol. 151, issue 4, February 15, 1993, 236.

131 **"Compared to industrial giants":** Ethan Mollick, Twitter, October 31, 2022, https://twitter.com/emollick/status/1586953770956644352.

135 **In 2022, Vanguard:** Eric Balchunas, Twitter, September 30, 2022, https://twitter.com/EricBalchunas/status/1575845193156362240.

136 **"Investors' decisions":** Ibid.

136 **"Something else":** Tracy Alloway, Dani Burger, and Rachel Evans, "Index Providers Rule the World—for Now, at Least," Bloomberg, November 26, 2017, https://www.bloomberg.com/news/articles/2017-11-27/index-providers-rule-the-world-for-now-at-least.

137 **The efficient market hypothesis:** Eugene F. Fama, "Efficient Capital Markets: A Review of Theory and Empirical Work," *The Journal of Finance* 25, no. 2, Papers and Proceedings of the Twenty-Eighth Annual Meeting of the American Finance Association, New York, N.Y., December, 28–30, 1969 (May 1970): 383–417, https://doi.org/10.2307/2325486.

138 **"Are there any people":** Elizabeth Lopatto, "Robinhood Has Figured Out How to Monetize Financial Nihilism," The Verge, July 13, 2021, https://www.theverge.com/2021/7/13/22574133/robinhood-meme-trades-dogecoin-ipo.

140 **"I have written":** Jamie Dimon, "Chairman & CEO Letter to Shareholders," JPMorgan Chase & Co., April 4, 2023, https://reports.jpmorganchase.com/investor-relations/2022/ar-ceo-letters.htm.

141 **"Financial markets have grown":** Michael Pettis, Twitter, March 27, 2023, https://twitter.com/michaelxpettis/status/1640225947399106560.

148 **Treasury yields:** Kristina Zucchi, "10-Year Treasury Bond Yield: What It Is and Why It Matters," Investopedia, May 24, 2023, https://www.investopedia.com/articles/investing/100814/why-10-year-us-treasury-rates-matter.asp.

149 **"It is not valid":** Eric C. Engstrom and Steven A. Sharpe, "(Don't Fear) the Yield Curve, Reprise," Board of Governors of the Federal Reserve System, March 25, 2022, https://www.federalreserve.gov/econres/notes/feds-notes/dont-fear-the-yield-curve-reprise-20220325.html.

150 **"Nowhere does history":** Edwin Lefèvre, *Reminiscences of a Stock Operator* (New York: George H. Doran Co., 1923), 180.

150 **There's a list of investing rules:** Martin Zweig, "The Market Technician's Association Monthly Meeting Notes," Shearson Lehman, November 4, 1990 (New York: Grand Central Publishing, 1970), https://twitter.com/QCompounding/status/1630659100219416580.

151 **"It's fascinating":** Wasteland Capital, Twitter, November 15, 2022, https://twitter.com/ecommerceshares/status/1592441370664636416.

151 **"Price has driven":** Lisa Abramowicz, Twitter, March 6, 2023, https://twitter.com/lisaabramowicz1/status/1632701107456692230.

151 **"Yet these past 20 years":** Martin Sandbu, "The Investment Drought of the Past Two Decades Is Catching Up with Us," *Financial Times*, July 19, 2022, https://www.ft.com/content/3a8731bc-aad3-42ca-b99e-b3a553974ccf.

152 **"The pressure on these":** Lu Wang, "Corporate America Earnings Quality Is the Worst in Three Decades," Bloomberg, March 1, 2023, https://www.bloomberg.com/news/articles/2023-03-01/corporate-america-s-earnings-quality-is-worst-in-three-decades.

162 **"A global recession":** "Chartbook #152 The Anti-inflation Pivot of 2022—How Uncoordinated & Contractionary Monetary & Fiscal Policy Risk a Global Recession," September 18, 2022, adamtooze.substack.com/p/chartbook-152-the-anti-inflation.

164 **"The NBER's dates":** James D. Hamilton, "The Econbrowser Recession Indicator Index," Econbrowser, https://econbrowser.com/recession-index.

165 **For example, the inverted yield curve:** Evan F. Koenig and Keith R. Phillips, "Inverted Yield Curve (Nearly Always) Signals Tight Monetary Policy, Rising Unemployment," Federal Reserve Bank of Dallas, February 12, 2019, https://www.dallasfed.org/research/economics/2019/0212.

166 **"Mario games teach us":** Cheesemeister, Twitter, July 13, 2022, https://twitter.com/Cheesemeister3k/status/1547440825420099586.

168 **"The problem with the banks":** Eryn Brown, "A 'Subprime' Crisis in Housing? Think Again," *Knowable Magazine*, November 7, 2018, https://doi.org/10.1146/knowable-110718-39.

169 **The recession of 2020–2021:** "NBER Based Recession Indicators for the United States from the Period Following the Peak Through the Trough," Federal Reserve Bank of St. Louis, https://fred.stlouisfed.org/series/USREC.

170 **"unable to cover debt servicing":** Ryan Niladri Banerjee and Boris Hofmann, "The Rise of Zombie Firms: Causes and Consequences," *BIS Quarterly Review*, September 23, 2018, https://www.bis.org/publ/qtrpdf/r_qt1809g.htm.

171 **For example, the number of Americans:** "2022 General Social Survey," NORC, https://gssdataexplorer.norc.org/trends?category=Current%20Affairs&measure=natheal.

171 **We have three different definitions:** Matt Darling, Twitter, Jan 11, 2024 https://twitter.com/besttrousers/status/1745464553100792024?s=20.

173 **"There are known knowns":** Donald Rumsfeld, "Known and Unknown: Author's Note," The Rumsfeld Papers, https://papers.rumsfeld.com/about/page/authors-note.

174 **"Fascism talks ideology":** Toni Morrison, *The Source of Self-Regard* (New York: Alfred A. Knopf, 2019), 16.

174 **"I believe if there's":** *Before Sunrise*, directed by Richard Linklater, 1995.

183 **But taxpayers in the United Kingdom:** Nichola Rutherford, "Scottish Budget: How Will the Changes Affect You?," BBC News, December 15, 2022, https://www.bbc.com/news/uk-scotland-63635369.

183 **Similarly to the United States:** Kate Dore, "Inflation Boosted the 2023 Federal Income Tax Brackets. Here's How Your Taxes May Compare to 2022," CNBC, March 6, 2023, https://www.cnbc.com/2023/03/06/inflation-boosted-the-2023-federal-income-tax-brackets.html.

186 **it has moved the debt ceiling:** Olivier Blanchard, "Public Debt and Low Interest Rates," *American Economic Review* 109, no. 4 (April 2019): 1197-1229. https://doi.org/10.1257/aer.109.4.1197.

188 **In one example:** Christopher Whittall, "Update: LDI Selling Forces BoE to Intervene in Gilt Market," IFR, September 28, 2022, https://www.ifre.com/story/3533046/ldi-selling-forces-boe-to-intervene-in-gilt-market-vOjbjvpwvh.

189 **"There should be":** Dow, Twitter, July 31, 2023, https://twitter.com/mark_dow/status/1685997944858910720.

189 **"to the astonishment":** Peter Spiegel, "How the Euro Was Saved—FT Series." *Financial Times*, May 11, 2014, https://www.ft.com/content/f6f4d6b4-ca2e-11e3-ac05-00144feabdc0.

192 **"We are spinning":** William James, *Habit* (New York: H. Holt, 1890), 67.

200 **"Oil prices not only":** Harry Robertson, "The US Oil Price Turned Negative a Year Ago Today. Analysts Now Sees [*sic*] It Rising 20% to above $75 as Countries Plot a Return to Normality," *Business Insider*, April 21, 2021, https://markets.businessinsider.com/news/stocks/oil-prices-negative-year-ago-analysts-bullish-recovery-vaccine-opec-2021-4-1030324288.

203 **The tool kit has to:** "Rethinking the Fed's 2 Percent Inflation Target," Brookings Institution, https://www.brookings.edu/collection/rethinking-the-feds-2-percent-inflation-target/.

209 **"In Turkey, central bank independence":** Sandra Ahmadi and Aseem Prakash, "Autocrats Are Exploiting COVID-19 to Weaken Central Bank Independence," *Foreign Policy*, January 10, 2022, https://foreignpolicy.com/2022/01/10/covid-19-pandemic-economy-central-bank-independence-turkey-china-monetary-policy/.

209 **There are a lot:** Skanda Amarnath and Alex Williams, "What Are You Expecting? How the Fed Slows Down Inflation Through the Labor Market," Employ America, February 9, 2022, https://www.employamerica.org/researchreports/how-the-fed-affects-inflation/.

211 **"Conventional wisdom":** David Ratner and Jae Sim, "Who Killed the Phillips Curve? A Murder Mystery," Board of Governors of the Federal Reserve System, May 2022, https://www.federalreserve.gov/econres/feds/who-kill.

212 **"positive for risk assets":** James Ashley and Simona Gambarini, "Is 3% the New 2%? Sizing Up a Scenario of Higher Inflation Targets," Goldman Sachs Asset Management, November 10, 2022, https://www.gsam.com/content/gsam/us/en/institutions/market-insights/gsam-insights/2022/is-3-percent-the-new-2-percent.html#section-none.

212 **The dynamic between:** Nick Timiraos, "Cash-Rich Consumers Could Mean Higher Interest Rates for Longer," *The Wall Street Journal*, October 30, 2022, https://www.wsj.com/articles/cash-rich-consumers-could-mean-higher-interest-rates-for-longer-11667075614.

212 **He went on TV:** Robert Smith et al., "How 2% Became the Target for Inflation," NPR, December 22, 2022, https://www.npr.org/2022/12/22/1145096244/how-2-became-the-target-for-inflation.

213 **But of course:** "Federal Reserve Board and Federal Open Market Committee Release Economic Projections from the December 13-14 FOMC Meeting," Board of Governors of the Federal Reserve System, December 14, 2022, https://www.federalreserve.gov/newsevents/pressreleases/monetary20221214b.htm.

214 **"An unwarranted easing":** Courtenay Brown, "Fed Chair Says Low Interest Rates Aren't Driving Stock Market Prices," Axios, January 27, 2021, https://www.axios.com/2021/01/27/fed-jerome-powell-low-interest-rates-stock-market.

214 **"I certainly was not excited":** Joe Weisenthal, Tracy Alloway, and Jonnelle Marte, "Neel Kashkari 'Happy' to See the Stock Market's Reaction After Jackson Hole," Bloomberg, August 30, 2022, https://www.bloomberg.com/news/articles/2022-08-29/neel-kashkari-happy-to-see-the-stock-market-s-reaction-to-jackson-hole.

214 **When he was erroneously told:** Andy West, Twitter, November 2, 2022, https://twitter.com/andycwest/status/1587912245656551425.

216 **"Here is what I learned":** C. J. Hauser, "The Crane Wife," *The Paris Review*, July 16, 2019, https://www.theparisreview.org/blog/2019/07/16/the-crane-wife/.

217 **"Economists and economic policymakers":** Jeremy B. Rudd, "Why Do We Think That Inflation Expectations Matter for Inflation? (And Should We?)," Federal Reserve, Finance and Economics Discussion Series 2021-062, 2021, https://doi.org/10.17016/FEDS.2021.062.

217 **Low rates aren't dangerous:** J. W. Mason, "At Barron's: Are Low Rates to Blame for Bubbles?," April 21, 2023, https://jwmason.org/slackwire/at-barrons-are-low-rates-to-blame-for-bubbles/.

221 **"The amount of energy":** Alberto Brandolini, Twitter, January 11, 2013, https://twitter.com/ziobrando/status/289635060758507521?lang=en.

224 **"Inflation is always":** Milton Friedman, "The Counter-revolution in Monetary Theory," Wincott Memorial Lecture, Institute of Economic Affairs, Occasional Paper 33, 1970, https://miltonfriedman.hoover.org/internal/media/dispatcher/214480/full.

225 **"Does Money Growth":** Claudio Borio, Boris Hofmann, and Egon Zakrajšek, "Does Money Growth Help Explain the Recent Inflation Surge?," *BIS Bulletin*, no. 67, January 26, 2023, https://www.bis.org/publ/bisbull67.pdf.

226 **"The less you eat":** Karl Marx, "Human Requirement and Division of Labour Under the Rule of

Private Property" in *Economic and Philosophic Manuscripts of 1844* (Moscow: Progress Publishers, 1844), 112.

227 **"'There's something about'":** Andre Dubus, *Dancing After Hours* (New York: Vintage, 1996), 191.

227 **"Find out what makes":** George Saunders, *Congratulations, by the Way: Some Thoughts on Kindness* (New York: Random House, 2014), 50.

227 **"What we have then":** Peter Turchin, "The Strange Disappearance of Cooperation in America," June 21, 2023, https://peterturchin.com/strange-disappearance/.

231 **political stagnation:** Bryan Caplan, Twitter, February 10, 2021, https://twitter.com/bryan_caplan/status/1359547307503550467.

231 **higher education has become:** "Fast Facts: Tuition Costs of Colleges and Universities," National Center for Education Statistics, https://nces.ed.gov/fastfacts/display.asp?id=76.

232 **"Impossible, I realize":** Paul Auster, *The Invention of Solitude* (New York: SUNY Press, 1982), 17.

233 **"From addiction to dementia":** "Mental Health Matters," *The Lancet Global Health* 8, no. 11 (November 2020): e1352, https://doi.org/10.1016/S2214-109X(20)30432-0.

234 **"Once the mascot":** Ibid.

234 **"an inchoate sense":** Erik Baker, "The Age of the Crisis of Work," *Harper's Magazine*, June 2023, https://harpers.org/archive/2023/05/the-age-of-the-crisis-of-work-quiet-quitting-great-resignation/.

235 **The younger generations were furious:** "About," Occupy Wall Street, http://occupywallst.org/about/.

235 **Gen Z:** "List of Recessions in the United States," Wikipedia, https://en.wikipedia.org/wiki/List_of_recessions_in_the_United_States.

235 **physical third spaces:** Allie Conti, "Do Yourself a Favor and Go Find a 'Third Place,'" *The Atlantic*, April 4, 2022, https://www.theatlantic.com/family/archive/2022/04/third-places-meet-new-people-pandemic/629468/.

235 **The younger generations:** Sophie, "Hyper Individualization," Inevitability Research, July 8, 2023, https://www.inevitabilityresearch.com/p/hyper-individualization.

235 **whether it is tulip bulbs:** Lorraine Boissoneault, "There Never Was a Real Tulip Fever," *Smithsonian Magazine*, September 18, 2017, https://www.smithsonianmag.com/history/there-never-was-real-tulip-fever-180964915/.

235 **the Golden Age of Grift:** Jack Raines, "The Golden Age of Grift," *Young Money*, November 17, 2021, https://youngmoneyweekly.substack.com/p/the-golden-age-of-grift.

236 **But that era:** Zia Qureshi, "The Rise of Corporate Market Power," Brookings Institution, May 21, 2019, https://www.brookings.edu/articles/the-rise-of-corporate-market-power/.

236 **Advertising became:** T. J. Jackson Lears, "The Rise of American Advertising," *The Wilson Quarterly* 7, no. 5 (Winter 1983): 156–67, https://www.jstor.org/stable/40257575.

236 **Eyeballs became:** Thales X. Teixeira, "The Rising Cost of Consumer Attention: Why You Should Care, and What You Can Do About It," Working Paper, Harvard Business School, January 2014, https://www.hbs.edu/faculty/Pages/item.aspx?num=46132.

236 **the dot-com bubble:** Eli Ofek and Matthew Richardson, "DotCom Mania: The Rise and Fall of Internet Stock Prices," *Journal of Applied Corporate Finance* 15, no. 43 (June 2003): 1113–37, https://pages.stern.nyu.edu/~eofek/DotComMania_JF_Final.pdf.

236 **People we titled:** "COVID-19: Essential Workers in the States," National Conference of State Legislatures, January 11, 2021, https://www.ncsl.org/labor-and-employment/covid-19-essential-workers-in-the-states.

236 **For the past forty years:** Juhohn Lee, "Why American Wages Haven't Grown Despite Increases in Productivity," CNBC, July 19, 2022, https://www.cnbc.com/2022/07/19/heres-how-labor-dynamism-affects-wage-growth-in-america.html.

236 **When we started getting:** Chris Capossela, "To Get People Back in the Office, Make It Social," *Harvard Business Review*, September 22, 2022, https://hbr.org/2022/09/to-get-people-back-in-the-office-make-it-social.

236 **For trade school graduates:** Emily Pontecorvo, "To Ditch Fossil Fuels, We'll Need to Raise an Army of Electricians," *Mother Jones*, April 18, 2023, https://www.motherjones.com/environment/2023/04/electrician-shortage-training-inflation-reduction-act-fossil-fuels/.

237 **Hence, the rise:** "Gig Economy: Definition, Factors Behind It, Critique & Gig Work," Investopedia, October 2022, https://www.investopedia.com/terms/g/gig-economy.asp.

239 **The Experience Machine:** Andy Clark, *The Experience Machine* (New York: Pantheon, 2023), 103.

240 **"I don't actually think":** Amanda Ripley, "I Stopped Reading the News. Is the Problem Me—or the Product?," *The Washington Post*, July 8, 2022, https://www.washingtonpost.com/opinions/2022/07/08/how-to-fix-news-media/.

240 **their 2022 paper:** David Rozado, Ruth Hughes, and Jamin Halberstadt, "Longitudinal Analysis of Sentiment and Emotion in News Media Headlines Using Automated Labelling with Transformer Language Models," *PLOS ONE* 17, no. 10 (2022): e0276367, https://doi.org/10.1371/journal.pone.0276367.

241 **"We live in a world":** Jean Baudrillard, *Simulacra and Simulation (The Body, in Theory: Histories of Cultural Materialism)*, translated by Sheila Faria Glaser (Ann Arbor: University of Michigan Press, 1994), 79.

241 **As Anne Applebaum:** Anne Applebaum, "Putin Is

Caught in His Own Trap," *The Atlantic*, June 25, 2023.

242 **Boym again:** Boym, *The Future of Nostalgia*, 351.

242 **in her book:** Svetlana Boym, *The Future of Nostalgia* (New York: Basic Books, 2001), 103.

244 **In 2013, Peter Turchin:** Peter Turchin, "The Strange Disappearance of Cooperation in America," June 21, 2023, https://peterturchin.com/strange-disappearance/.

246 **"There is no bill":** Tom Nichols, Twitter, December 5, 2022, https://twitter.com/RadioFreeTom/status/1599977886613635075.

249 **As Juan Enriquez:** Juan Enriquez, "In the U.S. Healthcare Industry, a Slow Shift toward Prevention," *Scientific American*, December 2022, https://www.scientificamerican.com/custom-media/the-new-science-of-wellness/in-the-u-s-healthcare-industry-a-slow-shift-toward-prevention/.

250 **As of May 2022:** Bureau of Labor Statistics, U.S. Department of Labor. (2022). Occupational employment and wages, May 2022, 39-9011 Childcare Workers. Retrieved from https//www.bls.gov/oes/current/oes399011.htm.

251 **Suddath explained:** Terry Gross, "As Child Care Costs Soar, Providers Are Barely Getting by. Is There Any Fix?," *Fresh Air*, December 16, 2021, https://www.npr.org/2021/12/16/1064794349/child-care-costs-biden-plan.

252 **Wealth building through homeownership:** Jerusalem Demsas, "The Homeownership Society Was a Mistake," *The Atlantic*, December 20, 2022, https//www.theatlantic.com/newsletters/archive/2022/12/homeownership-real-estate-investment-renting/672511/.

254 **as Edward Leamer discussed:** Edward Leamer, "Housing IS the Business Cycle" (working paper, National Bureau of Economic Research, Cambridge, MA, September 2007, https://doi.org/10.3386/w13428.

256 **A 2013 report:** American Public Transportation Association (2013), "The Role of Transit in Support of High Growth Business Clusters in the U.S.," https://www.apta.com/research-technical-resources/economic-impact-of-public-transit/.

256 **A 2015 study:** Andrew Owen, Brendan Murphy, and David M. Levinson, "Access Across America: Transit 2015," University of Minnesota, Center for Transportation Studies.

256 **In a widely cited:** Raj Chetty and Nathaniel Hendren, "The Impacts of Neighborhoods on Intergenerational Mobility," *Quarterly Journal of Economics* 133, no. 3 (August 2018), 1107-1162, https://doi.org/10.1093/qje/qjy007.

256 **Multiple studies:** American Public Transportation Association: 2014 Update, "Economic Impact of Public Transportation Investment," May 2014, https://www.apta.com/research-technical-resources/economic-impact-of-public-transit/.

257 **But carrying that truth:** Julia Cameron, *The Artist's Way: A Spiritual Path to Higher Creativity, 30th Anniversary Edition* (New York: Tarcher-Perigee, 2016).

258 **"We are not superior":** Norm Macdonald, Twitter, April 10, 2019, https://twitter.com/normmacdonald/status/1116159872393867265.

258 **"But in the end":** Kazuo Ishiguro, "My Twentieth Century Evening and Other Small Breakthroughs: The Nobel Lecture," The Nobel Foundation, December 7, 2017, https://www.nobelprize.org/uploads/2018/06/ishiguro-lecture_en-1.pdf.

258 **"are degraded":** "Ivan Illich: Conviviality (1973)," Panarchy, https://www.panarchy.org/illich/conviviality.html.

258 **As Maria Popova:** Maria Popova, "On the Soul-Sustaining Necessity of Resisting Self-Comparison and Fighting Cynicism: A Commencement Address," 2016, https//www.themarginalian.org/2016/05/16/annenberg-commencement/.

258 **Iain McGilchrist:** Iain McGilchrist, *The Matter with Things: Our Brains, Our Delusions, and the Unmaking of the World* (Dagenham, U.K.: Perspectiva Press, 2021).

259 **Mary Gaitskill:** Mary Gaitskill, *Somebody with a Little Hammer: Essays* (New York: Vintage, 2017), 82.

259 **Ursula K. Le Guin:** Ursula K. Le Guin, *Words Are My Matter: Writings About Life and Books* (Easthampton, MA: Small Beer Press, 2016), page 30.

Index

abundance agenda, 247
accessibility, workplace, 116, 251
accounting equation, 32
Adams, James Truslow, 120
adventure mindset, 256
agricultural products, 70
Airbnb, 124
Alameda Research, 159-160
Alloway, Tracy, 89, 136
Amazon, 141, 172
AMC Entertainment Holdings, 137-139, 140, 243-244
American Dream, 120, 230-232
American Recovery and Reinvestment Act (ARRA), 169
Apple, 52, 90-91, 141
Applebaum, Anne, 241
Argentina, hyperinflation in, 98
Aristotle, 173
artificial intelligence (AI), 76-77, 119, 257, 258
Asian financial crisis (1997), 229
assets, 32
asymmetric price transmission, 73
Auster, Paul, 232, 233
austerity, 188, 189, 228
Australia, housing crisis in, 125
automotive market, 53-54

Bailey, Andrew, 112
Baker, Erik, 233-234
balance sheets, 32, 198-199
Baldwin, James, 18
Baltic Dry Index, 70
Banerjee, Ryan Niladri, 170
Bank of England, 161, 188, 192
Bank of Japan, 26, 161, 192
Bankman-Fried, Sam, 159-160
banks and banking. *see also* Federal Reserve
  bank runs, 35, 204-205
  business model, 29-30
  central, 26, 192
  deposits, 32
  discount rate, 197
  in early America, 25
  failure, 35-37, 201-202
  fractional reserve banking, 30-32
  hedging strategies, 34-35
  lending, 32
  money-spending process, 28
  repurchase (repo) agreements, 195-196, 199
  reserve requirements, 33-34, 35-37, 194
bartering, 23, 36
Basmajian, Eric, 114
Belman, Dale, 108-109
Bezos, Jeff, 106
Biden, Joe, 207
Biden administration, 190
Binance, 159
Bitcoin, 157
Black, Fischer, 15
BlackRock, 135
Blanchard, Olivier, 191
Blinder, Alan, xix
blockchain technology, 161
Bloomberg Economics, 174
blue-collar jobs, 113-114

bonds and bond markets
about, 143-146
corporate, 28-29, 129, 147-148, 184-185
credit spread, 146-147
effect of interest rates on prices, 146
Federal Reserve and, 213-214
high-yield, 146-147
municipal, 184
ratings, 146
role of, 129-130
treasury market, 148-149, 185
United Kingdom, 188
Boym, Svetlana, 242
Brainard, Lael, 95, 207
Brandolini, Alberto, 221
Brexit, 112-113, 222
Buffett, Warren, 142
Buffett Indicator, 172
Bundesbank, 26
Bureau of Economic Analysis (BEA), 83
Bureau of Labor Statistics (BLS), 80, 82, 103-104
Burger, Dani, 136
businesses, 11, 169-170

Cameron, Julia, 257
Canada
income taxes in, 183-184
mortgages in, 125
capital gains, 134
car prices, 53-54
central banks, 26, 161, 192, 198-203, 209. *see also* Federal Reserve
Chancellor, Edward, 23
Changpeng Zhao, 159
Chesterton, G. K., 113
Chetty, Raj, 256
childcare, 248, 250-251
China
central bank, 192
U.S.-China trade war, 112, 222
CHIPS Act (2022), 190
Cigna, 255
circular flow model, 11-12
Clark, Andy, 239-240
classical economics, 222-223
clean energy, 255-256
climate change, 67, 75-76, 184, 207, 256-257
Clinton, Bill, 111
Coca-Cola, 93
cognitive dissonance, 16, 237-238
coins, 23-24
collateralized debt obligation (CDO), 35-37
Commercial Paper Funding Facility, 200
commodification of self, 243
commodities
artificial intelligence (AI) and, 76-77
common, 70-71
defined, 7, 69
external factors and, 71-72
globalization and, 69-71
metals, 74
oil, 71, 72-74
Commodity Research Bureau (CRB) Index, 71
community, 234-237
Conference Board Global Consumer Confidence Index, 17
construction jobs, 114
Consumer Confidence Survey, 17
Consumer Price Index (CPI), 79-84
consumer sentiment, 15-16, 60
consumer spending, 13, 60-61, 227, 243
consumerism, 66-67, 236, 241-242
consumption, 60-61, 65-66
cooperation, disappearance of, 227, 244-246
Coronavirus Aid, Relief, and Economic Security (CARES) Act (2020), 87
corporate bonds, 28-29, 129, 147-148, 184-185
Covert, Bryce, 115
covid-19 pandemic
2020 recession caused by, 163-164, 169-170
effects of, 230-232, 236
monetary policy during, 199-202
post-pandemic labor market, 99
supply chain problems, 87, 95
credit markets, 28-29
Credit Suisse, 201-202
cryptocurrency
coins, 157-158
FTX, 158-160
memefication of, 140
narratives, 154-157
nonfungible tokens (NFTs), 157
resistance to, 161
tokens, 157
currency. *see also* cryptocurrency
creation, 28-29
defined, 23
digital, 161
fiat, 24, 26, 36
history of American, 24-27
nontraditional reserve, 39
reserve, 37-39, 41-42, 186
Current Employment Statistics (CES) survey, 103
Current Population Survey (CPS), 103

Daly, Mary, 100, 213-214
Dean, John, 252
debt
ceiling, 63, 185-187
debt-fueled growth, 63-64
government, 184-185
interest payments, 181
dedollarization, 40-42
defense and security spending, 181

deflation, 78, 96-97
degrowth, 66
democracy, 182
Demsas, Jerusalem, 252-253
Di Giovanni, Julian, 87
Dimon, Jamie, 140-141, 154
disability policies, 116, 251
discouraged workers, 101
disinflation, 78
dividends, 134
Dogecoin, 157-158
dollar. *see* U.S. dollar
Dollar General, 172
Dollar Tree, 172
Donovan, Paul, 92
Dow, Mark, 189
Dubus, Andre, 226-227

ecological economics, 66
economic activity, daily life as, xx-xxi
economic inequality, 244-246
Economic Recovery Tax Act (ERTA), 221
economic theory
  classical economics, 222-223
  emotions and, 13-14
  Keynesian economics, 223-224
  Marxism, 226
  Modern Monetary Theory (MMT), 225-226
  Monetarism, 224-225
  new growth theory (NGT), 225
  vibes and, 16
economics, defined, xx, 10
education, 236-237, 254-255
Edwards, Kathryn Anne, 107, 116
efficient market hypothesis, 137-139, 229
eggflation, 54-56
electric vehicles (EVs), 76
Ellison, Caroline, 159
employee stock ownership programs (ESOPs), 117-118
employment, maximum, 192, 208, 214
Employment Cost Index (ECI), 106
Employment Situation Summary, 103
energy markets, 95-96
energy resources, 70, 72-74, 255-256
Enriquez, Juan, 249
equity, 32
equity risk, 130
Erdoğan, Recep Tayyip, 209
Ethereum, 157
European Central Bank (ECB), 26, 189, 192, 197-198
European energy crisis (2022), 72, 75, 95-96
European Financial Stability Facility (EFSF), 189
European Stability Mechanism (ESM), 189
European Union (EU), 25
eurozone crisis, 25, 189, 222, 228
Evans, Rachel, 136
exchange rates, 37
exchange-traded funds (ETFs), 135
excuseflation, 89

Fama, Eugene, 137
Family Medical Leave Act (FMLA), 250
Fang, Xiang, 38
Farley, Jack, 38
Farrington, Stephen, 99
fed funds rate, 197-198
Federal Deposit Insurance Corporation (FDIC), 35
Federal Home Loan Mortgage Corporation (Freddie Mac), 124
Federal Open Market Committee (FOMC), 205, 206, 212
Federal Reserve
  1970s monetary policy, 210-211
  2020 monetary policy, 199-202
  balance-sheet trends, 198-199
  banks, 206-207
  Board of Governors, 206
  chair of the Board, 207
  discount rate, 197
  establishment of, 204-205
  fed funds rate, 197-198
  Federal Open Market Committee (FOMC), 205, 206, 212
  inflation slowing tactics, 79, 202-203
  inflation target, 212-213
  labor market and, 100, 214-216
  mandates of, 192-194, 212
  markets and, 208, 213-214
  monetary policy, 5-6, 86, 192
  mountain climber analogy, 209-217
  narrative of, 208-209
  open-market operations, 194-195
  as a pseudogovernmental entity, 204
  repurchase (repo) agreements, 195-196
  reserve requirements, 33-34, 35-37, 194
  Summary of Economic Projections, 212
  Survey of Consumer Expectations Labor Market Survey, 114
  tools of, 194-198, 203
  trust in, 202-203, 208-209
FedNow digital payment system, 161
Fedspeak, xix
fiat currency, 24, 26, 36
financial crisis (2008), 24-25, 112, 152, 167-169, 196, 198-199, 222, 229, 235
First Bank of the United States, 24-25
fiscal policy, 179-180, 188-191
Fisher, Gregg, 152
Fitch Ratings, 63-64
foreign aid spending, 181
fractional reserve banking, 30-32
Free Banking Era, 26
free markets, 222-223
free trade agreements, 112
friendshoring, 95

Frying Pan Chart, 190–191
FTSE Russell, 135
FTX, 158–160

Gaitskill, Mary, 259
gambling, 139
Gamestop, 137–139, 140, 170, 243–244
gasoline prices, 12–13, 72–74
Gauntner, Mike, 55
GDP. *see* gross domestic product (GDP)
General Mills, 172
GfK, 17
gig economy, 237
gilts, 188
global economy, 30–32
Global Supply Chain Pressure Index, 50
globalization, 69–71, 95, 111–113, 139–140
gold standard, 26, 228
Goldman Sachs, 212
government
  in the circular flow model, 11
  currency backed by, 24, 26, 36
  debt, 184–185
  debt ceiling, 185–187
  fiscal policy, 180, 190–191
  as money creator, 28–29
  purchase and GDP, 61
  spending, 181, 223–224, 225–226
  spending misconceptions, 179–180
  trust in, 181–182
Graeber, David, 23
Great Depression, 223, 228
greedflation, 89
green building practices, 128
green energy transition, 75–76
Greenspan, Alan, 208
Grimes, Arthur, 212
gross domestic product (GDP), 7, 13, 26, 59–68, 79
growth
  at any cost, 66–67
  debt-fueled, 63–64
  new growth theory (NGT), 225
  valuation models, 134–135
  wage, 105–107
Gurri, Martin, 256

Haig, Matt, 67
Halberstadt, Jamin, 240
Hamilton, Alexander, 24–25
Hamilton, James, 164
Hammond, Samuel, 42
Haubrich, Joseph, 82–83
Hauser, C. J., 216
healthcare, 183–184, 247–249, 257
hedge fund assets, 152
Hofmann, Boris, 170
Household Consumption Expenditure (HCE), 82
households, in the circular flow model, 11
housing market
  2008 financial crisis and, 167–169
  business cycle and, 121
  Edgehill neighborhood, Nashville, 8–9
  homeownership, 252–254
  housing crisis, 7, 8–9, 123–124, 253–254, 257
  mortgages, 121–123, 127
  solutions to housing crisis, 126–128
  South Bend, Indiana, 127
  and subprime mortgages, 35–37
Howey Test, 156
Hubbard, Glenn, 87
Hughes, Ruth, 240
Hunt, Jeremy, 183
hyperinflation, 38, 78–79, 97–98

Illich, Ivan, 258
illiquidity, 35
imagination, 259
immigration policy, 116, 249–251
income taxes, 181–182
India, Consumer Price Index (CPI), 80
indices
  commodity, 70–71
  market performance, 135–136
individualism, 234–235
Industrial Producer Price Index (IPPI), 84
inflation
  1970s, 210–211
  2020s, 211
  causes of, 87–96
  class-based theory of, 211
  components of, 87
  Consumer Price Index (CPI), 79–84
  core services ex shelter measure, 215
  defined, 5, 78
  deflation, 78, 96–97
  disinflation, 78
  dollar as hedge against, 38
  eggflation, 54–56
  energy markets and, 95–96
  expectations, 86–87
  globalization and, 95
  hyperinflation, 78–79, 97–98
  inflation pizza, 84–86
  interest rates and, 191
  labor market and, 93–94, 214–216
  metrics, 79
  Personal Consumption Expenditures (PCE), 82–83
  price hikes, 89–93
  Producer Price Index (PPI), 84
  slowing, 202–203
  stagflation, 79, 221
  2 percent target, 212–213, 216
  vibes and, 18
Inflation Reduction Act (2022), 190

infrastructure development spending, 181, 256
Infrastructure Investment and Jobs Act (2021), 190
insolvency, 35
interest rates
  bond prices and, 146
  discount rate, 197
  fed funds rate, 197-198
  and inflation, 191
  mortgages, 121-123, 127
  open-market operations and, 194-195
  quantitative easing (QE), 198-199
  risks in, 130
  swaps, 34-35
  terminal rate, 212
  Volcker Shock, 210-211
  zero-interest rate policy (ZIRP), 36, 199
Internal Revenue Service (IRS), 182
International Monetary Fund (IMF), 40, 189
internet bubble, 14
investment, 61, 136-137, 139. *see also* stocks and stock market
Ipsos, 17
Ishiguro, Kazuo, 258

Jackson, Andrew, 26
James, William, 192
Japan
  central bank, 26, 161, 192
  Consumer Price Index (CPI), 80
  fiscal policy, 190
Jefferson, Thomas, 24-25
Job Openings and Labor Turnover Survey (JOLTS), 104-105
JPMorgan Chase, 86, 204

Kashkari, Neel, 214
Keynes, John Maynard, 13, 179, 190, 223-224
Kimberly-Clark, 90
Krugman, Paul, 154
Kuwait Petroleum Corporation, 72

labor market
  blue-collar vs. white-collar jobs, 113-114
  Federal Reserve and, 5-6, 8, 100, 212, 214-216
  gig economy, 237
  importance of, 99
  improving, 115-116
  inflation and, 93-94
  labor force participation rate (LFPR), 102, 118-119
  mental health and, 232-234
  metrics, 100-105
  policies, 9
  post-pandemic, 99-100
  surveys, 103-105
  unemployment rate, 100-102, 118-119
  wages, 105-113
  worker power, 114-115

Lancet Global Health, 233
Le Guin, Ursula, 9, 259
Leamer, Edward, 120-121, 254
Lefèvre, Edwin, 150
lending, 24-25, 32
lending facilities, 199-200
liabilities, 32
liability-driven investment (LDI) funds, 188
Link, Andreas, 116
liquefied natural gas (LNG), 95-96
liquidity, 34
Liu, Yang, 38
Livermore, Jesse, 150
loans, 32, 34-35, 121-123, 127
London Metal Exchange (LME) Index, 71
loneliness, 234-235, 244
Lopatto, Elizabeth, 138-139
Lydia, 23-24
Lynch, Peter, 5

M2 charts, 224
Macdonald, Norm, 258
Main Street Lending Program, 200
Malthus, Thomas, 223
Manheim Used Vehicle Value Index, 50
Mann, Barbara Alice, 126
Mantel, Hilary, 16
marginal tax brackets, 182, 183
Margulis, Lynn, 77
market price, 48-50
markets. *see also specific markets*
  efficient market hypothesis, 137-138, 229
  Federal Reserve and, 213-214
  free, 222-223
  globalization of, 139-140
  index providers, 135-136
  memefication of, 140
  passive vs. active investing, 136-137
  politicization of, 209
  risks in, 130
  role of, 129-130
  speculation, 139
  as vibe reflectors, 150-153
Marx, Karl, 226
maternity/paternity leave, 116, 250
McDonald's, 172
McGilchrist, Ian, 258-259
media literacy crisis, 239-241
Medicare, 63, 248
Mehrling, Perry, 42
memefication, 140, 244
mental health, 232-234
Merkel, Angela, 189
Mesopotamia, 23
Meta, 141
metals, 71, 74
Microsoft, 132-133, 141, 172

Mill, John Stuart, 78, 223
Millington, Sara, 82-83
Milovanska-Farrington, Stefani, 99
Mindel, Maia, 126
minimum wage, 107-109
Modern Monetary Theory (MMT), 225-226
Mollick, Ethan, 131
Monetarism, 224-225
monetary policy, 5-9, 42, 86, 192-194, 199-202
monetary systems, 23-24
money, 21-24, 28-29, 32-34. *see also* coins; currency; U.S. dollar
money multiplier effect, 34
monopolies, 48, 222, 236
Moody's, 63, 146
Morgan, J. P., 204-205
Morgan Stanley, 151
Morrison, Toni, 174
mortgage-backed securities (MBSs), 35-37, 123, 168, 199
mortgages, 121-123, 127
MSCI, 135
Mui, Preston, 104
municipal bonds, 184
Musk, Elon, 136, 140
mutual aid societies, 248

National Banking Act (1863), 26
National Bureau of Economic Research (NBER), 163-164
National Health Service, 183
Nestlé, 90, 93
net worth, 32
Netflix, 38, 39, 172
New Deal, 223-224
new growth theory (NGT), 225
The New York Times, 238
Nichols, Tom, 246
Nielsen, 17
nihilism, 235, 240-241, 242
NIMBYism, 254
nonfungible tokens (NFTs), 157
North American Free Trade Agreement (NAFTA), 112
nostalgia, 241-242
Nvidia, 141

Obama, Barack, 189
O'Connor, Sarah, 109
oil markets, 13, 72-74, 169, 200, 210
Opendoor, 124
open-market operations, 194-195, 197-198
Operation Twist, 198
Organization of the Petroleum Exporting Countries (OPEC), 13, 72, 75, 210
ownership, as wealth generation, 116-118
Ozimek, Adam, 119

Pakistan State Oil Company, 72
Papandreou, George, 189
parental leave policies, 116, 250
pensions, 189-190
People's Bank of China, 192
PepsiCo, 90
Personal Consumption Expenditures (PCE), 79, 82-83
Pettis, Michael, 40, 111-112, 141-142
planned obsolescence, 65-66
Pokémon Company, 47-48
Politico, 84, 86
politics, economic influences on, 221-222
Pollack, Julia, 118
Popova, Maria, 258
postgrowth, 66
Powell, Jerome, 55, 96, 104, 120, 207, 214
Pratchett, Terry, 68
Prato, Maria, 116
presidential election (2016), 112
Price, Carter, 107
prices. *see also* inflation
  asymmetric price transmission, 73
  Consumer Price Index (CPI), 79-84
  gasoline, 12-13, 72-74
  hikes, 89-93
  market, 48-50
  vs. narrative, 151
  Producer Price Index (PPI), 84
  stability, 192, 208
  target, 134
  used cars, 53-54
  wage-price spiral, 93-94, 117, 210
Primary Dealer Credit Facility, 200
Proctor & Gamble, 90, 92-93, 173
Producer Price Index (PPI), 79, 84
productivity, 65
profits, 89-93
prosperity, GDP as measure of, 7
public services spending, 181
public transit, 256
Publix, 117

quantitative easing (QE), 198-199

rare earth metals, 74
rational expectations theory, 15
Ratner, David, 211
Ray, John J., III, 160
Reagan, Ronald, 221
recessions
  1980s, 210-211
  2008, 167-169
  2020-2021, 163-164, 169-170
  benefits of, 172-175
  determination of, 162-167
  effects of, 166-167
  government response to, 180
  vibecession, 170-172
reflexivity, 14-15, 139

renewable energy, 75-76
repurchase (repo) agreements, 195-196, 199
research and development spending, 181
reserve currency, 37-39, 41-42, 187
reserve requirements, 33-34, 35-37, 194
reshoring, 95
resources. *see* commodities
retained earnings, 134
Ricardo, David, 223
risk management, 34-35, 130, 147-148
Roosevelt, Franklin D., 223
Ross, Martha, 108
Ross Stores, 173
Roussanov, Nikolai, 38
Rozado, David, 240
Rudd, Jeremy, 216-217
Rumsfeld, Donald, 173
runoff, 201
Russell, Bertrand, 47

Sandbu, Martin, 151-152
Sankaran, Karthik, 38
Sarkozy, Nicholas, 189
Saunders, George, 227
Schoar, Antoinette, 168
Schrödinger coin, 157-158
Second Bank of the United States, 25-26
securities, 79, 194-195, 198
  cryptocurrency as, 156-157
  mortgage-backed (MBSs), 35-37, 123, 168, 199
Securities and Exchange Commission (SEC), 156
semiconductor crisis, 52-53
Setser, Brad, 41
shale oil production, 75
Shaw, George Bernard, 69
Shiba Inu (SHIB) coin, 157-158
Shilling, Gary, 129
shopping cart theory, 227
Shorin, Toby, 243
Silicon Valley Bank (SVB), 35, 201-202
Sim, Jae, 211
Smith, Adam, 223
Smith, Talmon Joseph, 117
social media, 235-236, 238-239
social programs spending, 181
Social Security, 63, 79, 189-190
Solow, Robert, 65, 111
Soros, George, 14
Southern Burlington County NAACP v. Mount Laurel Township, 254
speculation, 139, 155, 156, 157-158
spending, 179-181, 185-187, 223-226
stagflation, 79, 221
Standard & Poor's (S&P), 63, 146
  500, 136-137, 141
  Dow Jones, 135
  GSCI Index, 71
Standing Repo Facility (SRF), 196
Starbucks, 132-133, 146
stocks and stock market
  vs. economy, 131-132
  efficient market hypothesis, 137-139, 229
  employee stock ownership programs (ESOPs), 117-118
  exchange-traded funds (ETFs), 135
  Federal Reserve and, 208, 213-214
  making money in, 133-134
  market capitalization, 133
  memefication of, 140, 244
  role of, 129
  tech domination of, 140-142
  valuation, 132-135, 142
  zero days to expiration (ODTE) options activity, 138
subprime mortgages, 35-37
subsidies and grants spending, 181
Suddath, Claire, 250-251
suffering, 259
supply and demand
  banana bread example, 30-32, 49-50
  eggflation, 54-56
  equilibrium, 48-50
  housing market, 123-124
  and inflation, 87-89
  policy and, 56
  semiconductor crisis, 52-53
  theory of, 47-48
  used cars, 53-54
supply chains
  about, 50-51
  covid-19 pandemic effects on, 50, 87, 95, 124, 169
  improving, 56-58
sustainability, 128, 255-256
Sweet, Ryan, 78
Swift, Taylor, 47-48
systemic risk, 130
systems failures, 235-237

tax avoidance, 41
Tax Cuts and Jobs Act (2017), 221
Tax Reform Act, 221
taxes, 181-184, 221
Term Auction Facility, 198
terminal rate, 212
Tesla, 52-53, 136-137, 141
therapycoded invalidation, 239
Thompson, Derek, 242, 247
Ticketmaster, 48
Timiraos, Nick, 200
Tippett, Krista, 240
tipping culture, 109-111
TJX Companies, 173
Tonhaugen, Bjørnar, 200
Trans-Pacific Partnership (TPP), 112
Treasury Inflation-Protected Securities (TIPS), 79
treasury market, 148-149, 185

trickle-down economics, 221
Troubled Asset Relief Program (TARP), 169
Trump, Donald, 207, 209
Trump administration, 190, 207
Truss, Liz, 188
TSMC, 53
Turchin, Peter, 227, 244-245

UBS, 202
uncertainty, 10, 15-16, 18
underemployment, 101
unemployment rate, 100-102, 118-119
United Kingdom
 bank rate, 197-198
 central bank, 161, 188, 192
 Consumer Price Index (CPI), 80
 fiscal policy, 188-189
 income taxes in, 183-184
 mortgages in, 125
UPS, 90
U.S. Bureau of Engraving, 28-29
U.S. Congress, 185-187, 204, 207, 208
U.S. dollar, 37-42, 187
U.S. Mint, 28-29
U.S. Treasury, 28-29, 35, 186. *see also* treasury market
U.S.-China trade war, 112, 222

value added tax (VAT), 182
Vanguard, 135
Vasi, Alonso Segura, 136
Veerasamy, Visa, 239
venture capital (VC) market, 130
Verma, Sid, 21
vibes
 and consumer sentiment, 15-16, 18
 and economic theory, 16
 and the economy, 7-9, 14-15
 and inflation, 18, 86
 and markets, 150-153
 vibecession, 170-172
Viscelli, Steve, 57
Volcker, Paul, 210-211

wage-price spiral, 93-94, 117, 210
wages, 105-115
Walmart, 172, 255
Washington Consensus, 228-229
Wasner, Evan, 89
Wasteland Capital, 151
wealth generation, 116-118, 253
Weber, Isabella, 89
Weimar Republic, hyperinflation in, 97-98
WeWork, 170
white-collar jobs, 113-114
Wholesale Price Index (WPI), 79
Williams, Alex, 189
Wilson, Edith, 205
Wilson, Woodrow, 205
Wolfson, Paul, 108-109
worker power, 114-115
World Health Organization, 250

Yellen, Janet, 207
yield curve, 149, 165

zero-interest rate policy (ZIRP), 36, 199
Zhang, Anthony Lee, 57
Zillow, 124
Zimbabwe, hyperinflation in, 98
zombie companies, 170
zoning laws, 123, 126-127, 253-254
Zuckerberg, Mark, 209
Zumbrun, Josh, 18
Zweig, Martin, 150-151

About the Author

KYLA SCANLON is a writer and video creator focused on human-centric economic analysis that demystifies complexity and provides context behind the headlines. She is also the founder of the financial education company Bread. Previously, she was an associate at Capital Group, conducting macroeconomic analysis and modeling investment strategies.